A Note on the Authors

Stephen Fay has written extensively on finance, the theatre and cricket. His books include *Tom Graveney at Lord's*, and he is a former editor of *Wisden Cricket Monthly*.

David Kynaston has written twenty books, including *Austerity Britain*, *Family Britain* and *Modernity Britain*. His most recent cricket book is *WG's Birthday Party*, an account of the historic 1898 Gentlemen v Players match at Lord's.

ARLOTT, SWANTON AND THE SOUL OF ENGLISH CRICKET

Stephen Fay and
David Kynaston

BLOOMSBURY PUBLISHING
LONDON · OXFORD · NEW YORK · NEW DELHI · SYDNEY

BLOOMSBURY PUBLISHING
Bloomsbury Publishing Plc
50 Bedford Square, London, WC1B 3DP, UK

BLOOMSBURY, BLOOMSBURY PUBLISHING and the Diana logo are
trademarks of Bloomsbury Publishing Plc

First published in Great Britain 2018
This edition published 2019

ISBN: HB: 978-1-4088-9540-5; PB: 978-1-4088-9537-5; EBOOK: 978-1-4088-9539-9

2 4 6 8 10 9 7 5 3 1

Typeset by Newgen KnowledgeWorks Pvt. Ltd., Chennai, India
Printed and bound in Great Britain by CPI Group (UK) Ltd, Croydon CR0 4YY

To find out more about our authors and books visit
www.bloomsbury.com and sign up for our newsletters

Contents

Introduction

For more than a quarter of a century after the Second World War, two of the instantly recognisable English voices were commentators at games of cricket. As the BBC tightened its grip on the national consciousness, their voices revealed mannerisms and prejudices that transformed the broadcasting of the nation's summer game into a national institution. Each of them drew people into a sport whose complexity was and remains part of its charm. Together they stamped their imprint on a whole social as well as cricketing era.

Both were very capable newspaper journalists, but their fame was based on the way they sounded as broadcasters. John Arlott performed principally on the radio, where his Hampshire burr was the rare sound on the BBC of an English dialect. E. W. ('Jim') Swanton's commanding voice was associated with his crisp, authoritative summaries of a day's Test cricket, on television as well as the radio.

In those post-war years, England's class system had a slot for almost everyone. Men and women were identified by where they came from, what they read and how they sounded. Within a few minutes of the start of a conversation about cricket, it would be possible to identify the speaker as an Arlott Man or a Swanton Man, and to make a good guess at the speaker's education, occupation and politics. Because of their strong personalities and convictions, each had a loyal following.

Swanton was cricket correspondent of the *Daily Telegraph*. The paper would by the 1960s be known as the 'Torygraph'; its readers were mainly middle-class, and their politics were predictably right of centre. Many followed cricket, too, as players or spectators. A BBC producer specialising in poetry, Arlott became a cricket commentator by a fluke. His personality, and his books on the Test series on which he had commentated, propelled him towards journalism, and eventually he became the cricket correspondent of the *Guardian*. It had fewer readers than the *Telegraph*, but it spoke for the liberal centre-left, who admired the style and dash of its sports pages.

Both had a deep and thoughtful love of cricket and cricketers. Swanton, though, was more interested in the grandees of the Marylebone Cricket Club (MCC) at Lord's who ran the game, whereas Arlott preferred the company of professional cricketers and never warmed to the toffs at Lord's. Both men watched the England cricket team in its rare purple patches and in inglorious defeats; although both wanted to see England win, they cared most about the quality of the cricket and the spirit in which it was played. One more thing they had in common was a detestation of racism in cricket. Swanton once observed that this might surprise Arlott, but it was firmly based on a delight in the West Indies and its cricketers; Arlott loathed racism because of his contempt for apartheid in South Africa. But the most intriguing quality of this story is not so much about what they had in common as on where and how they differed. They were well-defined specimens of two varieties of English life.

Swanton was born into a relatively modest middle-class family, the son of a stockbroker who never quite became 'something in the City'. He boarded at a public school, which he left at the age of seventeen to become a journalist. Arlott was the son of a working-class council employee, educated at state schools until he quit suddenly at sixteen. Not going to university was all their backgrounds had in common. Swanton's further education was the job in Fleet Street; Arlott, an autodidact, taught himself very well. He was a published poet with a wide appreciation of literature (his favourite novel was Thomas Hardy's *Jude the Obscure*). He was a sentimental family man who married three times and grieved for the rest of his life after the early deaths of his eldest son and his second wife. Swanton was a bachelor until his early fifties, when he married a widow who was good at golf and whom he delighted in showing off.

Arlott, though he hid it well, suffered from the insecurity of a freelance journalist who never turned down an offer of work in case he might not be asked again. Swanton was utterly secure at the *Telegraph*, where he was a legendary negotiator of his own salary, generous expenses and secretarial assistance. Both earned a comfortable living. Swanton had an agreeable life-style and was a generous donor to charities. Arlott was a compulsive collector of books, glass, aquatints and wine, who required money to pay for his acquisitions. Arlott was a buyer; Swanton a willing seller when memorabilia came to hand.

The differences between them were deeply embedded. Swanton was a High Churchman, an Anglo-Catholic. Although he wrote a few hymns as a favour to a broadcasting colleague, Arlott had no allegiance to organised religion. Swanton was a Tory; Arlott a Liberal who ran for Parliament. He was for most of his life a strong supporter of the trade union movement, and was president of the professional cricketers' union. Swanton was a convivial drinker, and he would have a glass of whisky before his broadcast summary of a day's play. Arlott was a heavy drinker whose days almost invariably included at least a couple of bottles of red wine.

Swanton was a rugby football man, Arlott followed association football; each also wrote about their game for their newspapers. Swanton was a self-confessed snob; Arlott liked to think of himself as a man of the people. On the field of play, Swanton became an accomplished amateur cricketer who opened the batting for the club he formed. Arlott lived with the knowledge that his hand/eye coordination left much to be desired, and in his mid-twenties humbly retired from playing any serious cricket. Neither tired of the game, ever.

During the lives of these two cricket writers and broadcasters, England changed. In 1945 it was an old, class-based society, secure in the knowledge of its historic survival and recent victory against Fascism. After the war, it gradually became a more egalitarian society. A generation later, the class system had survived, but it was being defined differently – less in terms of social standing, and instead based more on income, wealth and celebrity. This process affected all facets of national life. Nothing was immune, and nothing stayed the same, including professional cricket.

Throughout their active lives, Arlott and Swanton remained loyal to the cricket they had grown up to love. As they approached retirement, they were united in their opposition to the drift, inspired by television, towards the commercialisation that drew cricket away from a summer sport towards the entertainment and leisure industry. Neither man ever grew to like the other; but each had a leading role in the battle for the soul of English cricket.

Jim Swanton:
Young Man in a Hurry

In 1999, shortly before he died, Jim Swanton wrote for the *Daily Telegraph* a cheerful account of his life. 'I was conceived in 1906, the year in which Kent became county champions for the first time, and just about when the left-handed Frank Woolley was starting his wonderful career', it began. By the start of the second paragraph, his childhood was finished. Undeniably, it was a consistent approach. Back in the early 1970s, in a first volume of autobiography entitled *Sort of a Cricket Person*, he had not mentioned his childhood at all; while later that decade, in *Follow On*, he had dismissed his childhood as being of no interest: 'I stick to my contention that in most cases the interval between cradle and adolescence is best taken as read unless it has been in any respect extraordinary.' In no respect were Swanton's childhood and adolescence extraordinary. Even so, those early years deserve better than just to be taken as read, revealing as they do a startling catalogue of disappointment and underachievement. At his public school, Cranleigh in Surrey, he was not selected to play in either the First XI or the First XV; in the classroom, he was not considered

Oxbridge material. His childhood and adolescence were a contradiction of his adult opinion of himself, and he spent the better part of his life determined to show that the early judgements of his worth were incorrect.

———

Ernest William Swanton was born on 11 February 1907 in the south-east London suburb of Forest Hill. His father, William Swanton, worked in the City for an obscure firm of stockbrokers, William Norton & Co., first as a clerk and eventually as a partner. His mother, Lillian, had a German father, a merchant who had changed his name from Wolters to Walters after he had married an Englishwoman and started a business in London. Lillian's son, whom she always knew as Jim, was thus one-quarter German.

The Swantons were a conventional and unremarkable English middle-class family. William Swanton's City job was secure, though not lucrative. Lillian remarked that her husband seemed to make money, 'but not for us'. Despite poor eyesight, he liked games, especially cricket, and proved a reliable treasurer of the Forest Hill Cricket Club; and he could see just well enough to captain the club's Third XI. This physical disability exempted him from army service in the First World War, and Swanton would be hurt by the memory of ugly scenes from his childhood when his father had been accused of dodging active service. There was no question about their loyalty to England's national sport: the whole family was involved with the cricket club. Lillian helped with the teas and recruited her two daughters, Ruth and Tina, who were also required to bowl at Jim in their back garden. The family told the story of Jim being taken in his pram to see W. G. Grace playing nearby, at Forest Hill in 1907, as though it had been a form of baptism. But the first sighting of Swanton at a first-class cricket match was at the age of twelve, when William took his son to The Oval. Father and son supported Kent, but Surrey were the local team, and his father arranged a junior membership of the county club in 1921. 'Cricket began to pull at my heart strings with undeniable persistence,' Swanton wrote in his autobiography. He saw his first Test match that year, with heavy rain in south London helping England, unusually, to avoid defeat against Warwick Armstrong's Australians. Sitting in the pavilion, and between stoppages, he watched two legendary fast bowlers, Ted McDonald and Jack Gregory, as Hampshire's Phil Mead patiently accumulated an undefeated 182.

Saturdays was cricket; Sundays church. The whole family attended morning service, though not necessarily at the same church. William and his daughters picked and mixed, attending the services of various denominations; Swanton and his mother stuck with the Church of England; and Swanton himself developed a taste for High Church Anglo-Catholicism. He preferred his family Sundays to school religion at Cranleigh which was, he recalled unfondly, much more about duty and behaviour than God and his Church: 'no whiff or tinkle of smells and bells for us'.

William Swanton's job in the City had not made the family wealthy, but he could just afford a private education for his only son. Swanton was a weekly boarder at a preparatory school for Dulwich College called Brightlands, but the budget did not stretch to Dulwich itself; instead, aged fourteen, Swanton went to Cranleigh, which had been established in 1865 on the edge of the Surrey hills to educate sons of the aspirational middle class. Swanton's pioneer biographer, David Rayvern Allen, lists the salient qualities – and perceived virtues – of a public school education: respect, responsibility, hierarchical privileges and the minutiae of regulation and prescription. For some adolescents, this agenda would have been challenging; but Swanton was a conventional boy. By the time he passed School Certificate in 1924, Cranleigh had produced a young man who was conscious of his class, not particularly intellectual, devoted to sport and religion, and keen to get on. He had no specific ambition, but had had a good English and Latin master of 'awesome dignity' named G. L. N. Antrobus. 'It was he who impressed in my lazy head the proper construction of a sentence,' remembered Swanton. 'He gave me a respect for good English and some sort of a critical standard.'

———

How to put this skill to good use? Swanton would recall that 'in my last year at Cranleigh it was decided, since I had no ambition to follow my father into the Stock Exchange, that my future might lie in journalism'. Enter, almost inevitably, the old pals act. William Swanton often travelled on the same morning train to the City with Tod Anderson, a director of Amalgamated Press, a conglomerate publishing everything from encyclopaedias to weekly magazines and comics. Father asked Anderson if there might be a place for his son; Anderson asked if the boy could write at all; William replied that he thought his son could write a decent essay; Anderson said he would be happy to meet him. Having made the right impression, Swanton became a journalist at the age of seventeen, making the tea, running errands and learning to type. His wage was twenty-five shillings a week.

He was learning a trade rather than joining a profession. Few journalists had degrees, but apprentice reporters were not yet expected to work for three years in the provinces before getting a job on Fleet Street. Experienced hands became editors of news, foreign affairs, or sport, and they freely commissioned work from freelance writers as well as the staff. There was no shortage of opportunity for ambitious and hard-working young men (women were exotic flowers on Fleet Street). Swanton targeted an Amalgamated Press magazine, *All Sports Illustrated Weekly*. The coverage of cricket came from J. A. H. Catton, once regarded as the greatest sports writer of his day, and possessor of a prodigious command of cliché. Jack Hobbs was the 'Oval idol' and the 'Surrey crack' who would 'dispatch the leather spheroid to the ropes'; Swanton, the 'priggish young subeditor' (his words), cut Catton heavily and rewrote extensively. When Catton did not complain, Swanton concluded that he never read a word in print. 'There's professionalism for you,' Swanton later reflected.

His first published piece appeared in *All Sports Illustrated Weekly* in July 1926, shortly after his nineteenth birthday. An interview with Frank Woolley, the great Kent all-rounder, was bylined 'By Ernest Swanton', the only appearance in print of his baptismal name. 'If you win his confidence,' he wrote, 'which is not easy, because he is inclined to be shy and retiring with strangers, and talks about anything or anybody rather than himself – you may learn something about his cricket before the day on which he first played for Kent.' It was a particularly fluent debut that may have received a lift from a more experienced subeditor, but Swanton would in later years be happy to include it in anthologies of his work.

Fleet Street itself was a market for news, open all hours. Journalists exchanged news and gossip walking down the Street, and at the bars of pubs in the dark alleys that led off it. Swanton consciously cultivated his elders, loyally listening to their memories, feeding off their experience and picking up work. He reported rugger matches (always rugger, not rugby) for *The Times*, delivering his copy to the Baynard Castle (now the Cos Bar) in Queen Victoria Street, where it was subedited over a glass of beer. Shrewdly, Swanton focused on sport in the public schools. There was an appetite for stories on the sports pages about their games, and a live audience at Lord's for their cricket: the annual Eton and Harrow match regularly drew 40,000 over two days. Swanton was hired by the *Evening Standard* to write a column on school sports, bylined 'Juventas'. Aged twenty, his prose was already authoritative. He confidently dispensed advice to batting coaches ('A boy's individuality must be given play'), and declared that he thought Harrow would be a stronger side than Eton that year.

The young Swanton was also displaying the dog-eat-dog quality that would enable him to move swiftly through the gears of a career in sports writing. School cricket had provided a regular income for an elderly hack called A. Podmore ('Poddy' to his pals). Swanton wrote that Poddy's complexion matched the cerise of his Old Haileyburian tie. 'I had the presumption to move in on the preserves of this, to me, rather formidable figure,' he qualmlessly recalled. Poor old Poddy; meanwhile, Swanton's freelance earnings were rising steadily. He was being paid around £10 a week from the *Evening Standard* alone, before in 1927, always conscious of money and status, he offered the paper a deal: for

£13 a week they could command his services full-time. A wage demand of £676 a year was a princely sum for a reporter in his early twenties, but the paper took Swanton seriously enough to make a counter-offer of £11 a week – still riches, especially as he was continuing to live at home. The first thing he did with the money was to spend £100 on a royal-blue AC Tourer.

The *Standard* was the evening paper of preference for London's middle classes. It had recently been acquired by Lord Beaverbrook, who sought to improve its profile by recruiting clever men-about-town, such as the former diplomat Harold Nicolson. He was not impressed, declaring of his new colleagues that it was 'very soiling to live among people so extremely empirical, quotidian, shallow and mean'. As for the sports department, it got no encouragement from its new Canadian proprietor. In a memorandum written in November 1930 to his general manager, Beaverbrook asserted: 'Many readers hate cricket. Most of them know nothing about it. The cricket public is dwindling every day.' No one seems to have taken any notice. The memo was written five months after Swanton's first international match as a cricket reporter, the Lord's Test against Australia. He had become that summer, at the age of twenty-three, the *Standard*'s No. 2 cricket writer, the junior to no less a man than Jimmy Catton, whose copy he had happily savaged at Amalgamated Press. The older man might have sensed that his time would soon be up.

When Swanton wrote at length about that Ashes encounter more than thirty-five years later, he asserted that he could remember it in clearer detail than any Test since. 'Who does not remember the Saturday of his first Lord's

Test? ... The crowd in baking heat, spilling out on to the grass, watching quietly while Woodfull and Ponsford laid their careful foundations ... The small, slight, bearded figure of King George [V] with grey bowler hat, button-hole, and rather high walking-stick, moving up and down the lines of the teams ...' That particular Test was hard to forget: the young prodigy Don Bradman scored 254 out of 729 for 6 declared, setting up an Australian win by seven wickets. Years later, the Don told Swanton it was his best innings of all.

By the summer of 1931, Swanton had indeed deposed Catton as the *Standard*'s cricket *and* rugby correspondent. He was a young man in a hurry, equipped with the latest tools of the trade. He claimed he was the first journalist to use a typewriter in the press box at Twickenham. But his ambition centred on cricket, and his work was liked well enough for the sports editor to contemplate sending Swanton to cover England's tour of Australia in 1932–3, which would have made him the first cricket writer to have been sent on an overseas tour by his paper. His luck, how-ever, finally deserted him at Leyton in mid-June, when Yorkshire's Percy Holmes and Herbert Sutcliffe put on against Essex a world-record stand of 555 for the first wicket. The Press Association and all three London evening papers were on hand to dictate a great story to the office, but there was only a single telephone box in the ground. One of journalism's dark arts in the pre-mobile age was to know how to get and keep a phone line, but Swanton seems not yet to have learned it well enough. When he missed his 4 p.m. *Standard* deadline, the paper decided instead to send to Australia its lawn tennis correspondent. (It was a decision that subsequently made no sense to Alex Bannister, who became the *Daily Mail*'s formidable cricket correspondent. Swanton was not the first to miss a deadline, he observed; the shortage of phone lines meant that it was a common occurrence; and Bannister wondered whether Swanton had not already made a vengeful enemy in the sports department.) The tour he missed was the infamous Bodyline series, when England's captain, Douglas Jardine, deployed intimidatory fast bowling in such a systematically calculating way as not only to check the Bradman phenomenon but to cause a near-fatal rift between the two countries; and Rayvern Allen reports that in conversation in later years, Swanton wondered if a quiet word from him into Jardine's ear might not have persuaded him to call a halt to Bodyline. Had Jardine done so, it would have been the first and only time that he had taken advice from a journalist, let alone one who was only twenty-five years old.

If the *Standard* was not going to oblige with sufficient work, Swanton decided it was time to become a broadcaster. The BBC had initially thought that cricket was not lively enough for large chunks of running commentary. They proposed to concentrate instead on football, boxing and racing – and changed their mind only once they found the right man for cricket commentary. Howard Marshall was, reckoned Swanton, 'the first of the great cricket voices'. The technology was in its infancy, too: the Bodyline series in Australia was reported via a studio in Paris by a former cricketer who created a running story from sheaves of incoming cables.

Accordingly, Swanton embarked on a campaign to ingratiate himself with the formidable Seymour de Lotbinière, who was soon to become Head of Outside Broadcasts. De Lotbinière passed Swanton on to the Talks Department, saying he had the Howard Marshall manner and might prove useful if a topical talk was required. 'His is not a very attractive personality,' he added, 'but I think he might do the job reasonably well.' Fortunately, the Talks Department was more sympathetic, and Swanton was judged to have a good voice and a strong personality, irrespective of whether it was attractive or not. They had recently been asked to start supplying talks to the new BBC Empire Service (forerunner of the World Service), and Swanton was asked to contribute a weekly summary about rugby – his second string. The advice he got was 'speak slowly, and with plenty of emphasis'. Swanton's first broadcast was heard as early as February 1934, but the learning curve rose only slowly. In the next five years, he received letters and memoranda saying that he talked too fast, and punctuated sentences with 'ers'; that his delivery was too hesitant or jerky; that his script was too long or illegible; and that he must not be late.

His biographer, an experienced BBC producer himself, read the internal correspondence between Swanton and his colleagues. 'One is left with an overriding impression that Jim's youthful arrogance and imperious manner had not helped his cause,' judged Rayvern Allen. 'He was still constantly striving to achieve more. It left little time or inclination to nurture the goodwill of those who were the cogs that made the wheels go round – those, he perhaps felt, who were less important.' Swanton's legendary short temper eventually caught up with him in December 1937, when a subeditor working on the journalist's script was so deeply offended that he made an official complaint. Soon afterwards, Swanton was informed that, since the format of the programme was changing, his contract would not be renewed.

But in any case, Swanton's restless energy in the 1930s was not to be tamed by writing and broadcasting – he always made time to play the game itself. After leaving school, he had set out to turn himself into a good club cricketer, mainly as an orthodox right-handed batsman. Now, he talked his way on to a tour of North America in 1933 organised by the wealthy Midland industrialist Sir Julien Cahn, scoring half-centuries in Ottawa, Chicago and New York. He joined MCC as a playing member in 1936 in a summer in which he scored 2,000 runs representing eight different clubs, including the one he had founded the previous year: called the Arabs, its one absolute club rule was that Swanton should open the batting. Arabs' teams were decent players drawn mainly from public schools and Oxbridge, with a sprinkling of first-class cricketers; while being the son of a viscount seemed to ensure automatic selection.

Walter Robins, the England player who then captained Middlesex, endeared himself to Swanton by selecting him for the county's Second XI in the 1936 Minor Counties Championship. He made 49 against Kent, and 46 against Surrey, averaging 27.71 in seven matches. In 1937 he played for Middlesex twice against the university teams – which allowed him to say that he had been a first-class cricketer, however briefly – and again once in 1938. An aggregate of 67 runs in five completed innings (highest score: 26 against Cambridge) was the full extent of his life at the top; but getting that far was testament to his capacity for self-improvement.

As a sports writer, meanwhile, he always accepted work and was seldom knowingly underpaid. James Wentworth Day, his editor at the *Illustrated Sporting and Dramatic News*, described him as a 'pillar of the Old School Tie', a posture he never vacated. However, the sports editor of the *Evening Standard* interrupted this apparently effortless rise and rise by terminating his contract as cricket correspondent in 1938. 'A certain incompatibility,' recalled Swanton in explanation, 'grew up between the Sports Editor and the brash young man who had too many irons in the fire for his liking.'

One of those irons was the *Cricketer* magazine, for which he wrote his first long piece, damning with faint praise Len Hutton's record 364 in the Ashes Test at The Oval in August 1938. The pitch, he argued, had not resembled the ordinary good English wicket: 'It was infinitely easier because there was so little pace left in it ... By ceaseless watering, and rolling when the turf is saturated, you get a surface that acts like a thick hearth-rug, or a huge piece of felt.' That same year, a second iron hit the fire. Playing club cricket in the early 1930s at the lovely Saffrons ground in Eastbourne, he had become acquainted with the Winchester schoolmaster Harry Altham – author of *A History of Cricket*, acclaimed by Sir Pelham ('Plum') Warner, former England captain and manager, as 'the greatest book ever written on Cricket'. The history had moved on since it had first appeared in 1926, and Altham's publishers asked him for an updated edition. Out of the blue, Altham wrote to Swanton wondering if he would 'entertain the proposal' that they might collaborate on a new edition. There was one condition: 'I should like to have the last say in any general verdict on major issues, e.g. Bodyline and the policy of MCC.' The younger man, never short at this stage of self-belief or an instinct for self-promotion, accepted the offer unhesitatingly. Warner would describe Swanton as Altham's chief of staff; and Altham himself credited to his new colleague the greater part of the work of the revised edition. Remarkably, only eighteen weeks separated commission and publication. The new edition of the *History* was a critical success, and a bestseller, reprinted five times in the next eleven years. Swanton's name on the spine, at the age of thirty-one, was his key to the cricket establishment's door.

Swanton still longed to broadcast an overseas tour, and he had started a campaign of self-advertisement to persuade the BBC to commission him to cover England's tour of South Africa that winter. He waited impatiently until late in the 1938 season, when Surrey were playing Lancashire at The Oval, for a chance to give ball-by-ball commentary – in effect, his audition. The chosen day coincided with the marriage in Dulwich of his flatmate Henry Longhurst, the golf writer; and having performed his duties as an usher, Swanton returned to The Oval 'full of bonhomie' to be told that he would shortly be on air. His performance, joking about a last-wicket stand and then talking extemporaneously during the ten-minute break between innings, might have been a disaster; but the combination of adrenalin and alcohol transformed the broadcast into a tour de force. De Lotbinière passed an appreciative comment via the BBC technician right away.

His work at The Oval expunged doubts about his temper and temperament. He was told that he would be sent to South Africa during the winter of 1938–9 to do twenty hours of commentary for a fee of £120. On Christmas Eve, during the first Test at Johannesburg's Old Wanderers ground, he made the first live cricket commentary to England from abroad – and did it well enough to persuade South African broadcasters that they should use him, too. By the time the tour was over, Swanton had become an experienced ball-by-ball cricket commentator; the tour itself included the finale at Durban, etched in the history of cricket. It had been scheduled as a timeless Test, and would not end until there was a winner. By the end of the tenth day of play there was still no result, at which point the English team had to catch a train to take them to their liner in Cape Town. It was the longest Test ever played, a record that presumably will never be broken, and the BBC paid Swanton twenty-five guineas for five extra days' work. 'I showed a small profit on the enterprise,' he claimed.

The Great Depression of the 1930s appears to have had no impact on Swanton's life, or that of his parents. He always had work, sometimes too much, perhaps, and he earned enough to live comfortably. He shared a flat in the Temple, off Fleet Street, with Ian Peebles, who had had a short career (1927–31) as a spin bowler for England, and played on for Middlesex. They had met when Swanton was helping Peebles with a piece for the *Standard*, and became friends when they travelled together on Cahn's North American tour. Later they were joined in the Temple by Longhurst (pre-marriage), with the trio enjoying the services of a 'treasure' who cleaned and cooked for them. Peebles described the young Swanton in his 1977 autobiography *Spinner's Yarn*: 'His great size and his resonant bass voice ... occasionally overawed the uninitiated'; and, added Peebles about Swanton old as well as young, 'it might be said that he does not deliberately seek the company of fools in order to suffer them gladly'. Peebles admired Swanton's cricket writing, which, he said, was 'lucidly expressed with force and decision'. 'I do not necessarily agree with all his views but admire the sincerity of his judgements and the courage with which they are presented, even when unpopular.' A strong social and professional taste for Swanton was not at this stage easily acquired, but Peebles and Longhurst shared it.

In the summer of 1939, Swanton applied to the *Daily Telegraph* for the cricket correspondent's job. He did not get it; but soon after he was asked to take over from the legendary Neville Cardus as the *Field*'s cricket writer from 1940. That at least was the intention, but of course no one knew what might be happening by that time. Indeed, during the return voyage from South Africa in March 1939, he and Peebles had become acquainted with Colonel Stanley Harris of the Bedfordshire Yeomanry, who had declared that since the war would begin at the end of the summer they might like to join his regiment. In the event, they joined the Territorial Army together a week before war was declared on 3 September; and when they were posted to a Royal Artillery battery in Uxbridge, Swanton suddenly remembered a string he had not yet pulled. He sent a telegram to Harris, c/o the Cavalry Club, to tell him that he and Peebles had joined up. Soon after their arrival in Uxbridge, Harris arranged for their transfer to his regiment in Dunstable, as commanding officers could do, and saw to it that they were commissioned as officers in the 148th Field Regiment of the RA, formerly the Bedfordshire Yeomanry.

This informal, privileged means of access to the officer class that Swanton enjoyed did not ingratiate him with colleagues who had worked hard to get where he was. But he was an enthusiastic new member of the regiment. He liked, for instance, to be able to order his batman to draw a bath – though the batman thought Swanton could manage that for himself and quit the post in high dudgeon. He was a committed disciplinarian with a reputation for active leadership. Soldiers got to know their officers well enough not just to approve or disapprove; in a cloistered environment, secrets were difficult to maintain. David Rayvern Allen interviewed soldiers from the other ranks while researching his biography, and perhaps the most startling revelation was that Swanton was believed to have had a homosexual liaison with a lance-bombardier.

Swanton's London life in the 1930s had been spent mostly with other chaps, especially on the cricket field where he appeared to enjoy being surrounded by good-looking youthful contemporaries, but there was no suggestion that he was gay. Rayvern Allen quotes only one source for the allegation, adding a second-hand reference. As evidence, it seemed at the time of publication (2004) a bit thin; but when some of Swanton's close friends hotly denied the story, he asserted that it had been confirmed to him by other men from the ranks. Formally, homosexuality in the army was a court-martial offence, but peacetime morality frequently collapsed among men faced by the thought of imminent death. Commenting on the relevance of the soldiers' allegation, Rayvern Allen plausibly wondered whether – in what was still a largely homophobic society – Swanton's sexual yearnings caused inner tension that expressed itself in prickly behaviour.

Looking back on his part in the war, Swanton could be forgiven for regretting that he had not stuck with the RA in Uxbridge, because the Bedfordshires turned out to be victims of a great military disaster in Singapore. The defence of that strategically significant British colony was based on the conviction that the city could be defended from a Japanese invasion by ranging powerful batteries of guns pointing out to sea, capable of sinking any invasion force. The Bedfordshires' arrival in Singapore Harbour on 29 January 1942 was signalled by a flight of large bombers overhead. The trouble was that they were not British bombers. The awful truth was that Singapore was no less vulnerable to a land invasion from Malaya than from the sea, and Swanton's troops were deployed to try to resist the waves of Japanese soldiers crossing the short strait that divided Singapore from the Malay Peninsula. Barely a fortnight after his regiment had arrived, it was forced to surrender. The day before, he had been nicked by a bullet in the right arm, just below the funny bone. The wound was dressed in hospital, and he was returned to his unit the following morning, to discover that he was now Acting Captain Swanton.

Cricket did not – as he would recall in his classic 1946 *Wisden Cricketers' Almanack* article, 'Cricket under the Japs' – stop with imprisonment. Five improvised Tests were played between British and Australian troops in Changi Jail before the autumn of 1942, when the Allied prisoners of war were transferred to camps. There, they were used as slave labour to build the Thailand–Burma Railway (often called the Death Railway). Each prisoner was permitted to take two books, and one of Swanton's was the 1939 *Wisden*, which the Japanese stamped as 'Not subversive'. When it joined the camp's library, it was borrowed so regularly that it needed to be rebound in remnants of gas cape (a cape worn to provide protection against poison gas) and glued with rice paste.

The preoccupation among prisoners was survival. The Japanese controlling the camps – known to prisoners as 'Nips' – behaved with well-documented barbaric cruelty. Like many others, Swanton was brutally beaten; but his accounts of his time in captivity focus on his work in the primitive libraries in the camps, and as the entertainments officer. He built a makeshift theatre in which he produced a weekly show of talks, complete with sound effects, called a Radio Newsreel. His copy of *Wisden* provided his script for simulated commentaries on Ashes Tests. One memorable programme was devoted to 'The Life of Donald Bradman', given, said the announcer, by 'the well-known sporting personality, E. W. Swanton (Jim)'. The subject and the enthusiastic performance by Swanton seemed to allow the audience of prisoners to forget their dreadful situation. On leaving the scene with an Australian colleague, Swanton wrote: 'Our minds were strangely at peace and we knew we had just experienced something we would always remember.' The New Year in 1945 was celebrated by a version of the real thing, a match between England and Australia played on a small area measuring 60 by 30 yards, with runs scored by boundaries off a bat two and a half inches wide and a foot shorter than usual. The difference between the two teams was the pair of boots obtained by one of England's bowlers, Captain 'Fizzer' Pearson. With them on his feet (everyone else was barefoot), he was unplayable.

Unlike Australian officers, expected to muck in on the railway with the Other Ranks, British officers were responsible only for administering the camps and building latrines and new huts. When British officers were finally ordered to work on the railway, Swanton's wound received in Singapore, and a bout of polio which hindered the use of his left arm, kept him back in the camp. The history of the Thailand–Burma Railway was written by Sibylla Jane Flower, a soldier's daughter, and she told Rayvern Allen: 'I'm afraid Jim was the subject of animosity and ridicule on the railway. A lot of the officers were not convinced that he had a genuine wound.' Flower herself remarked that Swanton was in the jungle much longer than most POWs. 'It shows a resilience which is remarkable.' He had learned the art of survival, and some of his methods attracted abusive reactions from his colleagues. Having promoted himself from acting captain to acting major, he was treated with a greater degree of respect by the Japanese officers, and given lighter administrative duties. When he was finally ordered to join the troops on the railway, he went as hospital amenities officer.

Perhaps the most profound impact of this ghastly experience was on his religious faith. Jane Flower reports: 'Jim's faith was forged, he told me, in the tragic camps … when the guards would be screaming at the men and would drive them to work with wire whips. It was then with the men that Jim tried to bring religion and faith.' He tried very hard; building an altar in a jungle clearing, taking services and officiating at funerals, he sometimes wondered whether after the war he might take holy orders.

Swanton appears in the published diaries of Lieutenant Colonel E. E. Dunlop, an Australian surgeon better known as 'Weary' Dunlop, whose inventive work in intolerable conditions saved hundreds of lives among the POWs and whom Swanton would describe as 'the most heroic figure' he had ever met. 'Maj. Swanton had many ideas,' he recorded in November 1943 after a meeting to discuss increased recreation and entertainment for the prisoners. 'The expanded activities should if possible embrace not only concerts, quizzes, competitions, talks, etc. but also an arts and crafts programme (especially for limbless men) and education activities, lectures, talks, classes and readings, since there is a great scarcity of books.' And a week later: 'Education and talks scheme is moving along well: Swanton tells me he has the programme well in hand.' Just before Christmas, discussions took a different turn. 'An amusing half hour listening to Marsh, Father Bourke, McNeilly and others after going to bed,' noted Dunlop. 'Marsh explosively and violently took exception to the fact that Maj. Swanton, Turner and one other were taking advantage of their position on the hospital welfare committee to proselytise their views as "Christian fascists" (i.e. Anglo-Catholics) and to that end depicted Franco as a knightly soldier of God!' To accompany these startling right-wing political opinions, Swanton remained an unbending stickler for order and discipline, once putting on a charge three officers who had failed to bow to Christ on the cross as they passed the altar in his makeshift church. The charges were laughingly dismissed by the commanding officer.

It may have been his religious faith and his discovery of the deep resources of the human spirit that inspired in his autobiography the last word on his years of captivity: 'From the experience, I had gained much that would always remain.' Men who served with him in the camps were entitled to their unsympathetic judgements, though those may have been exaggerated by the inhuman conditions when they were first made. But he had consciously practised the art of survival, and he had survived.

———

Swanton's harrowing story had an unforgettable conclusion. When his father went to Waterloo station to meet the boat-train bringing the troops from Southampton, he walked straight past his son, who had lost so much weight that his own father did not recognise him. But he had endured remarkably well, mentally and physically, and he seems not to have been haunted by the experience, though he could never escape it entirely. As their former commanding officer, he would years later invite old army colleagues from the Bedfordshires to join him each summer for a day's cricket at Sir Paul Getty's rural but immaculately equipped ground at Wormsley.

Before the war, Swanton had been, by his own account, an indifferent churchgoer. After it, he found that his POW-camp Catholicism could be absorbed into the Church of England's Anglo-Catholic variety. On his return in 1945, he was living at home and trying to reconstruct his career when he met a fellow survivor, who introduced Swanton to 'Freddy' Hood, principal of Pusey House, an Anglo-Catholic institution in Oxford. Hood had a penchant for celebrated high achievers and Swanton qualified. He went to live in Pusey House, along with teachers and students; it had a fine library and a church for High Mass, and it kept a good table for members and guests.

For Swanton, Pusey House provided more than a room, which he could vacate without causing any trouble when he left for a cricket tour in foreign parts. It was a further education, too; Rayvern Allen observes that Swanton would have felt he was getting the next best thing to being an undergraduate. He was allowed to behave like a member of the university, including joining Vincent's, an exclusive (100 members) all-male club. Most of its members had won a sporting Blue, but it opened its bar and restaurant to 'games-minded men' such as Swanton. Friends speculated on the likelihood of Swanton taking holy orders. He might have considered the idea during his imprisonment, though evidently on his return decided not to go ahead. But he did enjoy a happy bachelor's life in this ecclesiastical environment until 1952, when he bought a house in London. It was conveniently close to Lord's.

2

John Arlott:
The Policeman Who Wrote Poetry

The most important single person in John Arlott's life was probably his mother, Nellie. Brought up in Meads, a suburb of Eastbourne, she was one of a family of twelve, the daughter of an Irish mother and an itinerant building worker disabled with rheumatic fever. She had left school at eleven to go into service, where she sang while she did the laundry on a Monday, and became a handy cook and a needlewoman.

When the coal shovel was found wanting, her mistress sent Nellie off to the local ironmonger to buy a new one. It was her first step to acquiring a husband. Behind the counter was a short, neat, muscular young man who had come to work in Eastbourne after a spell as a repair man fixing faulty goods in the hardware department at Harrods. A colleague, intent on opening his own ironmonger's in Eastbourne, suggested Jack Arlott should join him; and Jack was helping behind the counter when Nellie came in for the shovel. They chatted, and started to walk out together – before their courtship was rudely interrupted by the shop declaring bankruptcy. Jack was unemployed, but they married anyway in 1912 and promptly left for Basingstoke, then a modest country town in north Hampshire, where Jack had been born and his family still lived.

Jack got a job as a fitter with Thornycroft's (a local company that made lorries) and a place to live, both courtesy of his father, who was the registrar for Basingstoke's two cemeteries. He told his son about an empty lodge in one of them. It had three bedrooms, a dining room, kitchen, an outside lavatory, and it was built in the style of a Swiss chalet. The garden was large, and the rent manageable. The lodge can still be glimpsed by train passengers south of Basingstoke station, situated just beyond the ruins of a thirteenth-century chapel at the entrance to the cemetery. A blue plaque on the wall now identifies it as John Arlott's birthplace.

———

Nellie became pregnant soon after they moved, and as was customary in working-class families the birth took place at home. Leslie Thomas John Arlott was delivered on 25 February 1914, a bonny baby weighing seven and a half pounds. Family life was soon upset by the war, his father being called up in 1915 to join the Royal Army Service Corps. For the rest of the conflict he was stationed in Mesopotamia – where, coincidently, the army used the Thornycroft trucks that Jack had once helped to build – and India.

Their son was to spend his formative first years with Nellie, who always called him Les. (John came later; for our purposes, he is John from the outset.) The child was brought up by his mother, and her sister, Edie, who had moved into the lodge when her own husband went to war. John was the raw material from which Nellie could, consciously or unconsciously, mould her only child. The first ingredient was love, nearly unconditional, but not quite. 'She was a happy person, and extraordinarily perceptive,' he wrote in his autobiography, *Basingstoke Boy*. 'For years she would puncture her son's deepest-laid tricks and stratagems with a broad smile and a cheerful but deadly accurate, "I know you, my son."' While according to Arlott's son Tim, the more observant and unsentimental of his biographers, 'When she did speak, it had been considered and passed as worthwhile beforehand. She never prattled or used clichés. She passed on her Liberal views and careful choice of words to her son.' However, Tim is not convinced that the enfolding love of mother and aunt was altogether healthy: 'It gave him an expectancy of attention that neither he nor anyone around him would be likely to forget, especially in his later years.' In the early 1920s, Arlott had an argument with Edie which ruptured the relationship. As a boy, he did not have a forgiving nature.

Without having any particular goal in mind, Nellie was actively ambitious for John. She belonged to the aspirational working class; by the age of four, two years before he was to go to school, he had been taught by her to read. She read eagerly herself, and like her father she honoured the memory of William Gladstone, the giant of Victorian Liberalism, and was an ardent reader of the *Daily News*, the Liberal newspaper that was a forerunner of the *News Chronicle*. Arlott's father and grandfather were of a different persuasion, helping to found a branch of the National Association of Local Government Officers (NALGO) in Basingstoke. Unable to find a job when he returned from the war – a return that had involved mother and son going to the railway station day after day, anxiously waiting for the train bringing him home – Jack was again rescued by his father, who suggested he should take over the duties as registrar of the cemetery where they lived, for the weekly wage of £2 2s 6d.

Nellie became increasingly active in local politics, taking responsibility in the local hierarchy as the secretary of Basingstoke's Women's Liberal Association. Arlott in fact could boast that his mother really did know Lloyd George. She had taken young John to the station to meet him when he came to speak in the town; Arlott remembered the great man ruffling his hair. Nellie generally remained the dominant figure in the family, growing the vegetables in the garden, cooking, and doing the laundry. As for her husband, Arlott towards the end of his life drew a vivid picture of his father. 'He was quite small and neat, most capable, superb with his hands; he could do anything in the house, indeed he furnished it in oak,' he told Mike Brearley in the course of their lengthy conversations for Channel 4. 'He used to mend our shoes, change the fuses, do the plumbing, do the carpentry, do all the repairs about the house. Of course he worked himself to death. He just worked so hard to keep the family going on a small income, that when he retired there wasn't very much left. But he was such a sweet, gentle, loving, indulgent man.'

Music was Jack's hobby; he played various instruments and delighted in the music hall. John was never much interested in music. The best thing his father did for him was to make a bookcase for his growing collection of comics and books. One of his early acquisitions, in 1924, was a copy of the 1922 *Wisden*. (Arlott, whose memory for detail was never entirely reliable, was later to claim that he discovered Neville Cardus's cricket writing in his 1922 *Wisden*. The inspiration must have come from elsewhere, for Cardus did not contribute to that year's edition.)

The prelude to the story of Arlott's love of cricket began when he started going to the local infants' school, Fairfields; it stood opposite a cricket ground, May's Bounty, to which after the war the local cricket team returned only in 1921. 'I was seven, and through the gaps in the oak palings I saw people in white moving inside there, and I went in through the gate, waiting for somebody to bawl me out, and nobody did – they were all too occupied. And I watched this, which seemed to me like magic.' His father explained that they were playing a game called cricket. The boy returned to watch. In *Basingstoke Boy* (written, somewhat archly and alienatingly, in the third person), he recalled how 'it was all puzzling and, so far as his childish brain could assimilate, beautiful'. His father shaped a piece of wood into a bat, found an old tennis ball and bowled underarm to John in the garden. The seed had been sown.

Life at the lodge had its tensions. A close schoolfriend observed that, while Arlott always appeared relaxed and capable of defending himself in an argument, few people knew how highly strung he was. Most of the time, this was camouflaged; but at home he could be surprisingly thin-skinned and mildly hysterical over perceived insults. When he could not find a small bag of copper coins he had buried in the garden, his fury was so great that his parents feared he was having a nervous breakdown. There were few psychotherapists to call on in the Basingstoke of those days, so they treated the boy with Ovaltine and some pills from the chemist.

A thin skin was also evident at school, where he believed he had been punished unjustly after a confidence had been betrayed by his teacher. Arlott remarks in his autobiography that the world was thereafter never quite the same again. As figures of authority, schoolteachers were not to be trusted; but they had recognised enough academic promise to enter him for a scholarship at the county grammar school. One crucial element was a religious knowledge test. This was administered by the chaplain to the Bishop of Winchester, who confessed astonishment at the depth of Arlott's knowledge of the Prayer Book. Arlott replied that he knew most of the Prayer Book, but that there was much of the Bible he did not understand. 'What don't you understand?' asked the chaplain. 'Lots of the Revelations of St John the Divine, sir,' he answered. 'Young man, neither do I,' said the priest. Arlott was awarded a county scholarship, with an extra pound a year for his superior religious knowledge.

At the age of eleven, Arlott went in 1925 to Queen Mary's School in Basingstoke, where his low opinion of teachers was soon confirmed. Unsurprisingly, those teachers identified Arlott as a chippy troublemaker. He read widely, Robert Graves, Conrad, Buchan, Wilkie Collins and Jerome K. Jerome all in due course being on his personal reading list; but there was no encouragement to be had from his English teacher, who compared Arlott's work with that of a friend called Jack Donovan, who, the teacher thought, might earn a living as a writer. 'As for yours, Arlott,' he went on, 'I shouldn't bother too much about it, there's nothing there.' Donovan believed Arlott was the most caned boy in the school, which may have motivated him, aged thirteen, to make at the Debating Society the case against corporal punishment in school. The motion was carried by twenty-four votes to twenty, but the headmaster did not curb his enthusiasm for the thrashings. 'He thought he could beat me into submission,' recalled Arlott.

Although he would later claim that by the age of ten he had 'studied every book I could get and every local oracle on the game' – not to mention spending 'hours on end' bowling at home on 'a tarmac garden path' – his cricket story began in earnest when he was twelve, and he saw his first Test match. In August 1926, when the family was on holiday in London, Arlott learned that the first day of the Ashes decider at The Oval coincided with the last day of their holiday. His parents were reluctant to let him go, but he pestered them with such persistence that they relented, giving him two shillings to get in at the gate and sixpence for a lemonade. 'I went by myself, solemnly warned that there were people at cricket matches who would overcharge boys for mineral waters. Ate my sandwiches at ten past eleven. Everyone stayed away because they said the crowds would be so large, they wouldn't get in, yet the ground wasn't even full.'

He watched Jack Hobbs and Herbert Sutcliffe open the innings, and saw the forty-eight-year-old Wilfred Rhodes bat. Harold Larwood bowled faster than Arlott had ever seen, and Australia were 60 for 4 in reply to England's 280 at the close of a compelling day's play. For much of his life, Arlott could describe the game from start to finish, as though he had been there each day. At home, he continued to soak up cricket history, filling a school exercise book with statistics. One curiosity was his fondness for Glamorgan, who had joined the county championship in 1921 and, as perennial underdogs, automatically engaged Arlott's sympathy. By 1929, he was lecturing the school's literary and scientific society on classic matches in the history of the game.

He was a player as well as a spectator, Donovan recalling him as 'a capable non-stroke maker'. He was also centre forward in the school football XI, and cycled to and from Reading to support the football team. Then suddenly in 1930, to the chagrin of his parents, he abruptly quit school, not long before he was to sit the School Certificate exams, which were viewed as a significant pointer to his future. The headmaster had seen Arlott roughly bundle an opposition goalkeeper into the net, and decided that punishment was required. He forbade him to play any sport for the school, ever again. Arlott lost his temper and stormed out. David Rayvern Allen, Arlott's authorised biographer, admits that the decision was irrational, impetuous and wilful, but views it as ultimately unsurprising: 'Once he had decided on a course of action, nothing could deter him.' He was permitted, however, to sit for the School Certificate; and when he did so he walked out of the geography exam after an hour, sure that he had already done enough to pass. He left early, he always boasted, so that he could travel to Reading to watch a football match. His invigilators failed him, not because of his grasp of geography, but because of arrogant ill manners. (Rayvern Allen discovered another memory failure. Reading could not have been playing when Arlott sat his exams, in July.)

His parents had taken his education seriously because it was a passport to getting a safe job, ideally in the civil service, with tenure and – the great goal of the aspirational working class – a pension. But Arlott was not interested in consequences; in his autobiography, he explained that he did not belong to the class of person who planned a career: 'His kind simply took it as it came.'

It did not come easily. The Great Depression had begun, work was scarce, and eventually it was his father who found him a job in the Basingstoke Town Planning Office at ten shillings a week. He learned to type (with four fingers) and handle the telephone; when he saw a job advertised in the local paper at £1 a week for a 'diet clerk' in Basingstoke's mental hospital, he applied for and got it, confident he could manage to calculate the amount of food that was required for the patients, and then to buy it. He became good at mental arithmetic, friendly with the butcher and the baker, and learned about life and lust from the Irish doctors and the nurses. His fondness for Basingstoke inspired a charming little poem:

> Of Basingstoke in Hampshire
> The claims to fame are small:
> A derelict canal
> And a cream and green Town Hall.
>
> At each weekend the 'locals'
> Line the Market Square,
> And as the traffic passes,
> They stand and stand and stare.

He stayed almost four years at Park Prewett Hospital, putting up with a petty disciplinary regime in return for a wage that allowed him visits to cricket in the summer – dominating his annual holiday – and to the theatre in the West End.

On leaving, he chose to become a policeman, on the face of it surprising from someone with a well-developed mistrust of authority and of unquestioning discipline. Arlott's subsequent explanation was that he had liked the idea of a job in the open air, while his father had, of course, welcomed the security and the pension. He chose Southampton to be near his mother's cooking, and the laundry.

On the verge of his twentieth birthday, in 1934, he was six foot, good-looking and charming. Leslie T. J. Arlott, now formally known as John, became PC 94 in the Southampton County Borough Police Force, at £3 2s 6d a week plus a six-shilling rent allowance: in his words, 'a princely sum by a country boy's standard'. Tim Arlott thinks that police work did not suit his father, and that he 'never developed that unthinking respect for discipline'. Arlott himself considered that he was not a very good copper; but he spent more than a decade in the force, becoming one of the youngest sergeants in the south of England and being identified as a potential high-flyer.

After being sent to a police training college in Birmingham – where he came top of the class and learned about tramping the beat, Moriarty's *Police Law*, and getting a broken nose in the boxing ring – he started for real in Southampton, a thriving port city that was tolerant of minor crimes and misdemeanours. Until the world went to war again, Arlott patrolled the streets and developed a keen eye for minor detail. When he became bored he read a book – indeed, local people noticed that he was able to read and direct traffic at the same time. His batting, meanwhile, was not good enough to secure him a place in the Southampton Police cricket team. But he never missed a chance to look in at the county ground, where he stood, uniformed, watching Hampshire batsmen in the nets. He became friendly with a contemporary, a young wicketkeeper called Leo Harrison, a future stalwart of the Hampshire team. For Arlott, it was the first of a number of close friendships with professional cricketers, but none was more intimate than this.

Arlott graduated from behind the nets to a welcome in the dressing room, and accompanied the team to the odd away game. In August 1938, he was deputed to be the substitute fielder when Hampshire were a man short in a county match at Worcester. 'I would have put my heart in front of a ball to stop it,' he recalled six years later about what had been until then 'the most exciting thing' ever to happen to him. 'I was playing cricket with the men who had seemed to me more than men in mighty setting. Now I was part of it all.' In the fullness of time, a staple story in his extensive repertoire of anecdotes would be his tragi-comic experience of fielding at third man as the home side piled on the runs. Chasing hard to prevent a boundary, Arlott slipped, turned somersault, and, as he got to his feet and was about to throw the ball in, realised that he was facing the wrong way. (Rayvern Allen discovered a match report which noted without comment that a 'PC Harlot' had fielded for Hampshire.) Otherwise, his active contribution to cricket was confined to manning the public-address system at Southampton Police games. His responsibilities included some snatches of commentary. He was told he was good at it.

When war began in September 1939, Arlott's first thought was that a more interesting job and better pay might be found in the RAF. At their recruitment office, he was confronted by a police inspector who informed Arlott that he was under arrest: it was an offence to resign from police work, which was 'restricted employment'. Back on the home beat, he faced the uncomfortable reality that Southampton as a port was proving to be a regular target for German bombing raids – 'the place reeked with fear,' he remembered. Before long, Arlott was transferred to Special Branch, where his cursory command of a few European languages picked up on the beat was considered useful in identifying enemy agents. It taught him that he had no taste for spying on people.

In May 1940 he married Dawn Rees, a nurse at the Royal South Hants Hospital. His new mother-in-law declined to join them; as a daughter of the owners of Dewhurst, the chain of butchers, she thought Dawn had married beneath herself. Photographs of Arlott's mother and his wife hint at a likeness between the two. Dawn had blue eyes, a nice smile, an optimistic outlook, and the freedom to speak sharply to her new husband in a way he had not been used to at home. Arlott had a tendency towards garrulity, and Dawn was entitled to say cheerfully, 'For Christ's sake, John, stop being so self-conscious.'

After their flat was bombed in 1941, they shared accommodation with friends until buying their own house, with enough space to shelve Arlott's growing collection of books and glass. The marriage and the move came at a decisive time in his life. Arlott was no longer a country boy: he was approaching his late twenties, and was catching up with contemporaries possessed of a far better education. His wide reading had given him an autodidact's confidence in what he knew, and his charm and enthusiasm made for good friendships. Finding that he liked reading poetry, he had to show that he could write it, too. Helpfully, a new Chief Constable, Frederick Tarry, took a liking to him, calling Arlott his 'booksie boy'. If Arlott was not at his desk, Tarry's first phone call would be to the reference section of the public library: 'If you see PC Arlott, would you kindly mention that the Chief Constable would like a word?' Tarry co-opted Arlott to write regular reports to the Home Office about the state of morale in the area, which were admired. New friends at Southampton University College, who enjoyed talking to him, suggested that he lecture in the extramural department. The subject was improbable, but he had collected enough information on the Russian army and its strategy to speak about it. He had an audience, and the extra money was useful.

He was already a dedicated collector. 'I collected people, friends all my life,' he would reflect to Brearley. 'Books, furniture, junk, pottery, engravings, water colours and drawings.' The wine came later. In Southampton, he had started to collect recent first editions, which he would send to the author or artist, asking for a signature. Recipients included T. S. Eliot, Cyril Connolly, John Piper and John Betjeman. Arlott told Brearley that Betjeman – not then the household name he would become – had been an immense influence. 'I think I would never have tried to write poetry if it hadn't been for him.' He was, Arlott said, 'always a funny man, with an immense streak of sincerity and depth of feeling, and as independent a thinker I suppose as there has been in this century in Britain.'

When he had the idea for an anthology of poetry romanticising England, he wrote to Betjeman asking whether he would like to collaborate on it. Betjeman declined, but George Rostrevor Hamilton (well-known as a high-ranking civil servant who was also a man of letters) expressed an interest. They proposed that Oxford University Press should publish *The Oxford Book of Topographical Poetry*. When OUP declined, Hamilton approached Cambridge University Press, who responded positively. It would be titled *Landmarks*; and that moment in late 1942 when CUP took it on was, remembered Arlott in *Basingstoke Boy*, like 'a blinding light': 'He was accepted as a writer – or, at least, a collaborator – to be published.'

Arlott was in luck after John Masefield, the Poet Laureate, had refused them permission to reprint a poem of his about Worcestershire cricket. Announcing that he could write just as good a poem himself, he produced 'Cricket at Worcester 1938': 'Dozing in deck-chair's gentle curve, / Through half-closed eyes I watched the cricket,/ Knowing the sporting press would say/ "Perks bowled well on a perfect wicket".' Hamilton liked it, and on Arlott's behalf sent the poem to Cyril Connolly, influential editor of the famously high-brow magazine *Horizon*. Connolly, who had watched county cricket as a boy, said he remembered it just as Arlott described it, and the poem appeared in the July 1943 issue. (The Reg Perks who had toiled hard on a batsman's wicket would become another close friend of Arlott's when the war was over.)

Arlott was confident enough now to send other poems to newspapers and magazines. Within a year some of them were being anthologised. *Landmarks* itself was extensively reviewed in December 1943, and he was asked to submit work to the BBC's poetry programme. Connolly responded generously, writing in May 1944: 'You are, in fact, original now, with a growing talent for getting crowds, groups of people, *collectiveness* into poetry. This is very rare.' Jonathan Cape agreed to publish a slim volume of Arlott's poems – in style, essentially those of a late Georgian – titled *Of Period and Place*. 'His verse is intensely English, written with affection and deep knowledge,' declared Edward Thompson in the *Observer* in February 1945. 'He cares about technique, and is at pains to make every word do full service; his use of adjectives is especially vivid.' While according to another reviewer: 'He must learn to pass from the thing seen to the thing felt, but he apprehends the way.' It was a striking debut.

At home, Dawn gave birth to a son, James, in December 1944. The child was christened by Andrew Young, a poet, formerly a canon at Chichester Cathedral, who had become another friend and mentor. George Rostrevor Hamilton was a godfather. In their new house, the Arlotts had enough room to start entertaining; and new friends, such as the artist Michael Ayrton and the Betjemans, John and Penelope, stayed there. When the Arlotts were invited back to the Betjemans near Wantage, the hostess pigeon-holed him: 'Just the man I want to move my henhouses.'

On the cricket field, Arlott had been forced to admit that he was not a good player. He was at the crease when four runs were required off the last over in a match between two divisions of Southampton's police. The bowler was a former county cricketer. Arlott tried to cut the first three balls, and missed; two more balls passed wide of the wicket. The final ball hit the wicket. It was the making of a watcher instead of a participant.

Towards the end of the war, and by now promoted to acting patrol sergeant, Arlott was chosen to go to an advanced police-training school in London. The exact chronology is unclear, but it was probably during 1944 that Betjeman told the poet Geoffrey Grigson about his new friend, describing him as 'a policeman who is mad about poetry'. Grigson's day job was as a BBC talks producer in Bristol. Perhaps prompted by Betjeman adding rather condescendingly that Arlott 'might make an amusing broadcast', and no doubt intrigued by the concept of a poetry-writing copper, Grigson asked him to give a radio talk about his addiction; to which Arlott replied that, although he would like to broadcast, he had no wish to be treated as a freak. In that case, countered Grigson, he would be required to audition. Accordingly, Arlott read a long, difficult passage from Coleridge's *Biographia Literaria*, short on verbs and punctuation. He cleared that hurdle and was asked, next, to write a script – 'a kind of lay sermon,' specified Grigson. Arlott found this a formidable challenge, and his earliest attempts were rejected. But eventually, he found a subject that suited both of them; and Arlott made his first broadcast for the BBC on 23 October 1944, in a series titled 'An Enthusiast on His Enthusiasm'.

His enthusiasm was cricket, of course, and his long, autobiographical essay was another remarkable debut. It ended with a conversation he had had with a veteran of Basingstoke cricket. 'I turned to Dick in the slips: "I suppose really good cricket is an art," I said. Dick had a real Hampshire voice … "Art," he said, "get away with ye." Then, after a pause … "But it's a damn fine game, or I wouldn't waste my Saturday afternoons at it."' Arlott himself listened to the repeat.

When he switched on, his face fell, soon accompanied by an expressive 'Dear oh dear', prompting his wife to ask him what the matter was. 'That's the script I did,' he replied, 'but they've got this country chap reading it.' Dawn could only laugh: 'That's you, fool.' It was the first time he had heard his recorded voice. 'I never dreamed it was like that.' Back home in the cemetery, one of the grass cutters asked Arlott, 'And what be this 'ere Lunnun talk you'm puttin' on then?' At the BBC, Grigson told the assistant director of talks that the Hampshire burr was just acceptable; while soon afterwards, also at the BBC, the actor Valentine Dyall caught Arlott trying to speak 'the King's English'. When he asked why, Arlott said he thought everyone at the BBC talked like that. 'I'll personally cut your tongue out if you carry on,' replied Dyall. 'Only you can speak the way you do. Stick to it.' By doing so, he saved Arlott's voice for the nation.

Arlott modestly attributed his sudden early success to the fact that most of his contemporaries were away at the war, but this new voice was quickly recognised by the BBC as a valuable acquisition. He was learning a new trade the best way, by doing whatever came up. Introducing *Country Magazine*, making programmes on the metaphysical poets, paying a tribute to President Roosevelt after his death, describing a cricket match involving New Zealand servicemen – it was all good experience. Then, as the war ended, he became a small part of British history. He was still a working policeman, studying at the training school in London, when he was informed by an incredulous course commander that the BBC had specifically requested that Arlott, a mere provincial sergeant from Southampton, should represent the nation's policemen in a radio *Tribute to the King* on VE Day, 8 May 1945. 'What right have you to speak for the police, young man?' he spluttered. Arlott's contribution to the programme went out anonymously. 'The war brought us many new tasks. We've faced them not only as officers of the law, but as the friends and protectors of Your Majesty's subjects.' That same week, Arlott wrote and presented a radio programme about *The Hampshire Giants*, in other words the eighteenth-century Hambledon Cricket Club. 'This talk was so richly English in subject, style and accent that its accidental presence in Victory Week was a triumph of fitness,' wrote the reviewer in the BBC's weekly magazine, the *Listener*. 'Mr Arlott is a fine broadcaster: I could do with some more of him.'

Soon afterwards, someone from the magazine talked with the unknown policeman. Sensing that Arlott would rather be in broadcasting than on the beat, the BBC person asked if he was intending to apply for a vacant position on the Overseas Service (successor to the old Empire Service). The job would be as producer for literary programmes, a role that during part of the war had been performed by George Orwell, until he tired of the BBC's bureaucracy. Once alerted, Arlott promptly became one of two hundred applicants for the job. For the final interview, he had a cold bath in a friend's flat, put on a silk shirt and talked his way into a new career.

It was the start of an astonishing and rapid transformation. His parents, who thought the BBC was not a secure employer, wanted him to stick with the police and the pension. But Arlott had not been happy, and he sensed that his taste in reading and writing poetry, along perhaps with his voice, might be the open sesame to a different and more

In his new job, Arlott's principal task was to produce a weekly programme called *Book of Verse*, and he brought Dylan Thomas, the boisterous Welsh poet, with him. 'I adored Dylan. We were of an age, and I used to get Dylan in to read. He'd be away and I'd get a letter from him saying "Dear John, very hard up, may I come and boom for you next week?"' Thomas contributed to more than forty programmes, and became a drinking companion. Arlott for his part swore that Thomas never did a broadcast for him when drunk. More generally, Arlott was popular among poets because he had a budget and could pay them in ready money, which was often spent without a pause in the George, the BBC's local. He met Louis MacNeice, whom he considered the best poet among his contributors. The Irish writer H. A. L. Craig wrote scripts; Cecil Day Lewis, Roy Campbell and Stephen Spender were contributors; E. M. Forster gave a book talk once a month; and that minor hero, Valentine Dyall, read the poems.

The Eastern Service's major listenership was in India; and at a planning meeting early in 1946, the Director of the Service asked whether an Indian cricket team wasn't due to visit England in the summer? Arlott confirmed that it was, and the Director judged that their games would be worth a ten-minute match report at 4.05 p.m. But who could be trusted with the commentary? The BBC's established commentators would mispronounce the names, and the Indian who would be broadcasting in Hindi did not speak good enough English. 'Have you ever done a cricket broadcast?' the Director asked Arlott. 'Yes,' he replied, without going into detail about how little he had actually done. He was commissioned then and there to provide commentary from the first two games of the Indian tour, at Worcester and Oxford. The BBC had decided that, unlike Indian accents, Arlott's was acceptable. Moreover, S. J. de Lotbinière, Swanton's old taskmaster in outside broadcasting, had officially declared that the new man had 'a vulgar voice, but an interesting mind'.

In *Indian Summer*, his first cricket book and the start of what became a series of books on the immediate post-war seasons, Arlott described the auspicious moment: 'I left for Worcester, leaving behind me a mountain of unanswered mail and a top-heavy system of laundry by post. On the morning of 4 May, 1946, I sharpened my six pencils, and congratulated myself on having left my grey suit at home in favour of a tweed suit and set off for the first real cricket match in six and a half years.' Later in 1946, Arlott contemplated his new position. 'A writer on cricket will tend either to be the coldly omniscient or the imaginatively reminiscent,' he reflected in *Indian Summer*. 'I have chosen the role of deck-chair connoisseur.' On meeting Rex Alston, the BBC's principal cricket commentator, the first thing he did was to present his credentials: a book of his poems. Arlott had performed the best trick of his life so far – putting his favourite poets on the radio and being paid to watch cricket. 'It seemed,' he would write more than forty years later, 'a combination of happinesses almost beyond his belief.'

took the game almost as seriously as he did himself. What Swanton saw and thought is contained in his archive, which is kept, suitably, in the Frank Woolley Stand at the county ground in Canterbury. Arlott's cricket journalism began more modestly with broadcasts from the Indian tour of England. The two worked at the same match for the first time at the second Test at Old Trafford, towards the end of July. Examples of Arlott's early work at the microphone are rare, but after each of the tours he covered – home and abroad – during these early post-war years, he wrote a short book, published promptly by Longmans, Green & Co., providing a full and satisfying account of his life as a cricket reporter.

The working environment for newspapermen was congenial. James Cameron, in the thick of it, recalled fondly the 'rough and tumble of the English post-war newspaper scene'. Newspapers were controlled by wealthy press barons, literally so in the cases of Beaverbrook (*Daily Express*), Rothermere (*Daily Mail*) and Camrose (*Daily Telegraph*). Competition was intense, but the business was profitable; British daily and Sunday national papers sold an average of 38.5 million copies a day in 1948. (By 2015, the daily sale had fallen to seven million.) Journalists' jobs were portable ('he'd cross the Street for 12s 6d,' shrugged the old hands, as a colleague moved on); and although few grew rich, they earned enough to buy a house in the suburbs and pay for the drink. Editorial budgets were generous, with regular tours abroad meaning that cricket writers became seasoned travellers. Their output was strictly limited, however, not just by the cost of sending cables to London, but by newsprint rationing, which had begun in 1940 and did not end until 1956. Broadsheet papers – such as *The Times*, the *Telegraph* and the *Manchester Guardian* – varied in the late 1940s between six and ten pages, while the tabloid *Daily Mirror* did not get above twelve. Reporters wrote when they had something to say, and they kept it as short as possible. Swanton rarely wrote more than half a column for the *Telegraph*; they all had plenty of time for dinner. By contrast, the BBC was more like a government department, hierarchical and faintly authoritarian. With television still in its infancy, radio was the senior service, and in his own particular 'Eastern' patch Arlott was exhilarated by the creative freedom he was allowed. He was purposeful, reliable and worked hard. He remained a producer of poetry programmes. The cricket was added value; by his name, the budget would say, 'Staff, no fee'.

For Arlott – 'the rawest of all commentators' – the disappointing quality of the cricket in 1946 did not impede his delight at watching it happen: it was 'joy beyond any conceivable ambition'. In Oxford for the university's match against the Indians, Arlott stayed with Dylan Thomas, and was to be found sitting in a bomb crater in The Parks chatting with him and Cecil Day Lewis, no mean poet himself. No such frivolity for Swanton. Judged by his expectations, the summer proved a severe disappointment. The weather was deplorable, and the quality of county cricket so uneven as to make figures and county performances 'a dangerous guide to the highest class'. Moreover, most amateur county captains were in his eyes not up to the job (despite his having declared at the outset of the season that they had, compared to professional captains, 'a truer notion of the essentials of a cricket match'); and he would have sympathised with the *New Yorker*'s London correspondent,

Mollie Panter-Downes, who on inspecting the traditional highlight of cricket's social calendar, Eton and Harrow at Lord's, lamented that 'as a parade of the upper crust, valiantly pretending that everything was still the same, the occasion was a little saddening', not least because 'the men looked an extremely shabby bunch'. On the momentous decision that professionals would at last have their initials displayed on the scorecards sold at Lord's – albeit after their surname, unlike the amateurs – Swanton was apparently silent.

After only two matches of commentary to India, Arlott was summoned to see his boss. He feared he might be criticised or disciplined. Not so; instead, he was handed a telegram from the New Delhi office which read: 'Cricket broadcasts greatest success yet East Service. Must be continued all costs.' Asked if he would be willing to carry on until the end of the tour, Arlott was delighted, despite the warning that a falling off in the quality of his regular poetry programme would not be tolerated. By working on Sundays, and in the evenings when games were in London, Arlott said he could do it. By now, the Arlott family had moved to the north London suburb of Crouch End. When he was reporting a match in the north of England, he would take a Saturday night sleeper from Manchester, arriving home for breakfast. Then he spent the day in the recording studio, returning home for a quick dinner, before catching the sleeper back to Manchester.

Arlott was learning fast. One method was to befriend the players, a privilege not permitted to cricket writers in the twenty-first century. He ingratiated himself with Indian players by recording messages to their families at home, and inviting the best of them, such as Vinoo Mankad, Vijay Merchant and V. S. Hazare, back to dinner at Crouch End. Forgetting that his guests were rigid vegetarian teetotallers, what they could eat was reduced to rice and potatoes ('how they punished the rice,' he recalled). Arlott went out of his way to get to know the Indian players better by sticking to them between games, including paying the difference to sit alongside them in first-class carriages when BBC expenses covered only third-class rail travel. 'He could not afford it,' he wrote long afterwards in his stubbornly third-person autobiography, 'but he knew, in his waking consciousness, that he would never have such a chance again, and he made the most of it ... The family did not go short.'

The Indian team's first visit to Lord's was to play MCC. 'I found Nimbalkar's googly the most baffling of all,' noted Arlott; 'it appeared to me absolutely undetectable.' He was especially pleased by Merchant's 148. 'I knew how anxious he was to make a hundred that day and I was amazed to see his stroke-play flowering under his anxiety.' A month later, he was back at Lord's for the first post-war Test, as a first-day crowd saw the debutant Alec Bedser bowl India out in a match that England won easily. Lord's itself was a place with which Arlott would have a long and complicated relationship; but at this stage, although understandably associating HQ with cricket's ruling class, it was relatively untroubled. 'The pavilion is a rare example of a large Victorian building which is warm, and, simultaneously, a complete unity: its red-brick is friendly despite its eminence,' he observed in *Indian Summer*. 'The huge score-board stand and the terraces which run from it to cover the Nursery End, are in the modern, concrete, idiom. Yet this is concrete slim, for all its strength, curving to enclose the green turf, which runs to its edge and continues the theme of green and white – white flannels, the umpires' white coats, white creases, white concrete in easy rhythms, across and against green grass, grass matured in its long occupation to the texture of velvet.' In short: 'The man who feels for cricket accepts Lord's: there is no need to convince him by argument, he senses at once that it is a natural product.'

Arlott's inexperience encouraged omniscient judgements. In India's game at Old Trafford, watching Lancashire's left-handed Jack Ikin score 'some pleasant runs' with wristy strokes through the off side prompted a grave passage about how although in principle he welcomed the sight – 'we have seen far too few such strokes in the past twenty years', in other words going back to the prelapsarian Oval of 1926 – the cautionary truth was that 'if Ikin is to become a Test Match batsman, he must not use those shots until his eye is in, and even then not to bowling too inimical to them'. Arlott then crossed the Pennines, for Len Hutton's undefeated 183 for Yorkshire against the tourists: 'An eminent literary critic once said to me, " 'Great' is a great word; one should think before using it, but once it is said no more need be said". Ever since then I have been chary of using the word "great". But of Hutton I would say most solemnly that he is a great batsman.' Arlott admired Hutton's single-mindedness; and he quoted the crowd in dialect, 'Wi've no tahme fur t' faancy stooff i' Bratford.'

'India's captain, the Nawab of Pataudi, is a mystifying person,' observed Swanton during the second Test: 'Having put England in, he placed a defensive field and bowled well wide of the off stump.' Arlott was reluctant to rush to must have been gratified by the praise of the *Times Literary Supplement*. 'Sensible and extremely well-written,' stated the anonymous reviewer (in fact Dudley Carew, author of cricket's great 'lost' novel, *The Son of Grief*). 'He is content to let the statistics look after themselves, and his primary concerns are with the quality and individuality of the players and with the game less as an end in itself than as part of the English scene.' Was he perhaps lacking on the technical side? Not according to the *TLS*: 'His notes on the bowling of Hazare are alone sufficient proof that he thoroughly understands the game's mechanics'. Even so, 'in general, he prefers the large humanitarian approach to cricket'.

By this time, his accent and approach were becoming of increasing interest to colleagues at the BBC. Compared to Swanton, who undoubtedly spoke 'the King's English', Arlott's Hampshire burr, often a little drawn out, was instantly recognisable. Rex Alston warmed to his eye for detail and humour, while also noticing Arlott's habit of talking to players in their dressing room. A strong friendship with Glamorgan's ultra-competitive future captain Wilfred Wooller was his introduction to that county's dressing room, where he immediately behaved as if he belonged. 'He was a good learner,' recalled Wooller. 'Although he always gave the illusion that he was up to the ears in first-class cricket, he wasn't really.' Alston, himself shy about going into the dressing room, was impressed by Arlott's ability to make himself one of the cricketers. Inevitably, his early commentaries (not only in the 1946 season) were littered with mistakes, but the professional cricketers tolerated him because they found him likeable, and they assisted his climb up a steep learning curve. 'It is with professional cricketers that one learns the infinite variations and refinements of cricket method and strategy – and it is only with that knowledge that one can begin to assess any aspect of a player,' Arlott would reflect in 1949. He for his part responded sympathetically to their modesty, friendliness and intelligence. His son Tim plausibly suggests that the nature of the game, with its sudden and final difference between success and failure, is what seems to make those who play it more human and individual than other sportsmen. Peter Baxter, for many years his producer on *Test Match Special*, reckoned that there were only two cricketers whom Arlott had not liked; Arlott himself thought it was four. Tantalisingly, and whatever the correct tally, their identities have yet to be revealed.

As for Swanton during 1946, he was confirming that summer – down to the last subclause – his long-term employment by the *Daily Telegraph*: monthly salary of £100, monthly expenses of £200 a month, and £52 a year for secretarial costs. The paper's executives had decided that the new man should concentrate on his job as cricket correspondent, giving up his broadcasting. Swanton disagreed, and at length. In office politics, Swanton's persistence was his most effective weapon. His strategy was to wear down the editors back in Fleet Street – and it worked.

Arlott's key discussions came immediately after the season. The BBC executive who thought he had a vulgar voice (albeit an interesting mind) asked if he would like to broadcast on national radio on the following summer's South African tour. Despite having encountered at Lord's in the first Test a certain amount of feeling among radio colleagues – Swanton among them? – that he was (in his own words) a 'down-market interloper', he could live with that. Arlott's reply was unhesitating. Of course he would, and no, he went on, the poetry programme would not suffer. Looking back, from the secure distance of an autobiography, Arlott concluded that for the second time in barely a year he had become 'a different person in experience': 'First, the policeman had become a radio producer who also broadcast talks and wrote; now he had also become something of a specialist cricket broadcaster ... He had been admitted into what Brian Sellers [Yorkshire's captain] called "the circus".'

That autumn, while Arlott went back to the recording studio, Swanton was in Australia for England's hastily arranged and – as seemed obvious even at the time – premature post-war tour. 'In civilian clothes, the greatest cricketer of history looks a frail little man full of good spirits, but struggling with ill-health,' was his first impression of Don Bradman since 1938. The impression of frailty was misleading. A month later, in stifling Brisbane heat, Bradman was batting at his customary No. 3 and providing no evidence of any loss of his will to win, especially against England. Bradman was on 28 and Australia were 74 for 2, with the Don facing Bill Voce. 'The ball seemed to fly from the outside edge into the hands of Ikin, who threw it up and looked triumphantly towards his captain, a yard or two from him,' reported Swanton in the *Telegraph* about one of the more resonant moments of cricket history. 'I am not disputing,' he added, 'the decision of the umpire when Bradman stayed his ground. But I record the occurrence as it appeared to others.'

Those 'others', especially in the *Express*, the *Mail* and the *Mirror*, had no inhibitions about disputing a decision that probably prevented Bradman's instant retirement from cricket. Indeed, over the rest of the tour, umpiring became their principal preoccupation. Swanton, who retained a reverence for authority and believed that an umpire's decisions were not a suitable subject for debate, proceeded in his most lordly fashion to judge the behaviour of his colleagues. 'We cricketers are apt to claim, with not too conspicuous modesty, that specially noble virtues are inherent in and derivable from cricket. We must seem to many a hypocritical breed when the great question of the hour seems to be not whether England can win or save the match, but whether Edrich or Compton was or was not lbw.' 'It is one of the fascinations of cricket,' he added in a lengthy piece for his paper that was reprinted in the Melbourne *Argus*, 'that it is so clear and open a test of character, and no one wants to see the natural humours of a man subdued to the point of dull anonymity; but the truth is that these tremendous sporting affairs, on which it might be thought the prestige of nations rested, can only be kept in any remote degree of perspective if all concerned, players, press, and public, do our best to see the other fellow's point of view, and, frankly, mind our manners.' Swanton's early followers warmly approved of his Olympian tone and gentlemanly sentiments. 'In these days of provocative reporting,' declared J. C. Jackson of Kensington in a letter to the *Telegraph*, 'it is refreshing to the reader to have news which is free of unhealthy criticism.'

During the series itself, Swanton's optimism miraculously survived the humiliation of the tourists losing at Brisbane by an innings and 322 runs. 'Take Bradman away from Australia,' he asserted before the second Test, 'and an analysis of the two teams, man for man, leaves the advantage with England.' But two more defeats and two draws made this forecast look ridiculous, as Swanton himself admitted, concluding that England's cricketers had still to relearn the art of waging war against the Aussies. For Swanton personally, though, it was a successful tour. Not only did he, as a clubman by choice, persuade his colleagues that they should found the Empire Cricket Writers' Club (first chairman: E. W. Swanton) in order to lobby for better press-box facilities and communications, but he got the *Telegraph* to pay Bradman £65 for an exclusive interview after the final Test – the beginning of a relationship that would continue, in person and by mail, for more than half a century. Right from the start, as Michael Down has observed in his revealing edition of their correspondence (*Calling the Shots*), Swanton in effect acted as Bradman's invaluable and largely uncritical conduit to the English cricket establishment. In April 1947 Bradman wrote saying he hoped that Swanton would give R. W. V. Robins (captain of Middlesex and an England selector) what he called the truth about the recent tour, in order to offset stories Swanton would hear from people who had an axe to grind (though he did not specify what he might be accused of). 'You may rely,' Swanton reassured him, 'on his getting a fearless and unprejudiced version of the facts from me … I feel the blame lies very largely with us.'

———

Despite a bone-chilling start – with an old man who had been on nodding terms with Bobby Abel informing Arlott that the South African tourists' visit to Worcester coincided with the onset of the fifth Ice Age – 1947 turned out to be a dazzling, unforgettable summer when the sun seemed to shine endlessly, and the rain took an extended holiday. 'In every way,' declared

Wisden's Hubert Preston, 'the season of 1947 bears favourable comparison with any in living history.' Those golden months belonged above all to Middlesex's Denis Compton and Bill Edrich, who left behind them a trail of broken batting records. 'Had they been too much alike,' Arlott wrote of their partnership, 'they would not have captured the imagination. They are not to be compared; rather, their differences should be relished for the contrast between them that made their dual performances the more absorbing.' The glamorous, crowd-pleasing Compton (scorer of eighteen centuries, beating Hobbs's record) was uncoached, intuitive, trusting his skill to sweep and glance – and for Arlott he became the symbol of the pleasures of peacetime. He defined Compton's genius as a unique ability to overcome error: playing at the end of the season for Champion County v. The Rest, he went down the pitch to drive Tom Goddard, slipped and fell far out of his crease, yet contrived, while lying on the ground, to late-cut the ball for four. Swanton added that, when the need arose, Compton's defence could be as orthodox as anyone's. He was sure that Compton was, then, the best batsman in the world: 'There can be no disputing that very few cricketers in the game's long history have given such intense and consistent pleasure as Compton has done this summer.' He added the significant, very Swantonian qualification that the level of English bowling was lower than at any time since W. G. Grace had turned cricket from a country pastime into a national institution.

The 1947 season was also the one in which Arlott began commentating on national radio and, in Rayvern Allen's words, 'really made his mark'. 'I heard you at Taunton and excellent it was,' Edmund Blunden (one of 'his' poets

and well known also for his prose work *Cricket Country*)
wrote to him appreciatively as early as May. 'I wish there
were more who could discourse on cricket matches in
your complete style.' Dylan Thomas, listening in Florence
to events at Trent Bridge, went where he was most comfortable – over the top: 'You're not only the best cricket
commentator – far and away that; but the best sports commentator I've heard, ever: exact, enthusiastic, prejudiced,
amazingly visual, authoritative, and friendly.' The fact that
Thomas was in debt to Arlott, both literally and figura-
tively, hardly blunted his ardour, but the gist was almost
certainly sincere. So, too, was Alston's enjoyment of
Arlott's 'wonderful phrase' when South Africa's 'Tufty'
Mann twice dismissed Middlesex's George Mann – a clear
case of 'Mann's inhumanity to Mann'. Yet already he
divided opinion. 'At school in 1947,' remembered Frank
Keating, 'a philistine bully boy sneered at me and said that
guy Arlott was more interested in how a bowler ran or in
the pigeons near the sightscreen than in the score.' A fan
from the start, Keating never forgot a snatch of his commentary from that year's Headingley Test: '… and Butler
[Harold Butler of Notts] turns, hitches his trousers, and
comes rolling in: one – two – three – four – five – six –
seven – eight, over she goes and – he's bowled him.'

A more mature critic that summer was J. H. Robson of
Newcastle upon Tyne. Not only, he wrote to the *Listener*,
were cricket's radio commentators 'inclined to be far too
familiar' – 'again and again players are referred to by their first
names, or even their nicknames, as though the narrator were
claiming them one and all as his own boon companions' –
but they also almost invariably forgot that it was 'neither

illuminating nor necessary to describe minutely, ball by ball, the inception of the bowler's run, his journey to the wicket, his delivery and the batsman's stroke'. What did Robson want instead? 'A much more imaginative account of events is called for: not a bare verbal reproduction of events but a significant picture with colour, emphasis, light, shade and meaning. In other words, an interpretation.' Subsequent correspondents took issue. 'What has more significance, more meaning, at a cricket match than the action of the bowler, the pitch of the ball, the response of the batsman?' asked C. J. Kaberry of Cuxham, adding that the BBC's team enabled listeners to visualise all this 'most admirably'. Alex Cooper of Aberdeen, who had seen England beat Australia by an innings at Lord's in 1886, agreed: 'What is biting the fellow? To me the commentators bring the play to the unseen spectators, of whom I am one.' The fullest response came from W. I. Gaskin of London SW11, asking Robson to 'listen more attentively' to Messrs Alston, Arlott and Swanton. Alston he praised for his 'descriptions of field placings and manoeuvres', but he mainly focused on the two others. 'Arlott's pithy non-stop remarks are not only those of a true cricket-lover, but by introducing descriptions of the surroundings of the ground, the vagaries of the weather, the relation of the crowd to the players, he supplies Mr Robson with his "significant picture with colour, emphasis, light, shade and meaning".' As for Swanton, his 'experience of the game, his knowledge of the great, past and present, his intimate details of the finer points of spin, the wickets, the stroke play, the meaning of any field changes made, dotted with recollections of matches of days gone by, supply the "interpretation" asked for'.

Swanton towards the end of his life spoke, in a measured and analytical way, about Arlott's early impact. 'My first impression of John was that he was different,' he told Rayvern Allen. 'There was no Arlott prototype, so to speak. You can imagine Alston, the schoolmaster, the steady orthodox performer. John was not orthodox – as it seemed at that time. The thing about him, of course, was that he produced a personal idiosyncracy of style – if not idiosyncratic, a very natural style of talking. He was a very good reporter with a gift for colour ... was "quick on the ball" to spot anything off or on the field, any quirk of a fielder, that sort of thing. He was unconventional in that way ...' It was a generous enough tribute, but undeniably the two men were never kindred spirits; or, as Swanton put it, 'I wouldn't say we were blood brothers' – least of all in these immediate post-war years. It may have been at Lord's in 1946, but probably at Trent Bridge in 1947, that there occurred an almost mythical episode in which they argued loudly about a disputed seat in the commentary box, culminating in Arlott threatening to throw Swanton off the top of the pavilion. Rayvern Allen adds in his account that both men were innately too sensible and too professional to let a feud develop; according to Tim Arlott, the enmity that his father felt towards Swanton never really went away, though in later years he was generally careful not to advertise it. His was an essentially unforgiving nature.

The immediate upshot to the difference of opinion was ten lines of undistinguished Arlott verse:

Stately is my manner and Swanton is the name,
And in the *Daily Telegraph*, I write about the game.

I was never at Oxford or Cambridge,
But I think my accent will pass;
And I've got a check suit and deer Michael,
And that's in the Bullingdon class.
I've dined out with all the best people,
And I thought I made quite a hit:
So why should mere cricket reporters
Declare I'm just a big journalist?

Arlott's squib was soon circulating in the press box and, according to Rayvern Allen, producing 'many a smirk', presumably especially among those colleagues wont to refer to him as 'Gentleman Jim, the Journalist'.

When winter came, Arlott was back at the BBC producing his poetry programme, while Swanton closed his door at Pusey House and left for the West Indies and another Test series. It was the start of a long affair with the islands: not only draining any residual racial prejudice he may have felt, but in turn having a profound influence on his loyalties when South African apartheid caused rifts in international cricket. For him, the first game in Barbados was a revelation, as Clyde Walcott and Everton Weekes scored memorably powerful hundreds in, as he wrote, 'the best traditions of the Colony'. (Barbados was still eighteen years away from independence.) An understrength England, led by the forty-five-year-old G. O. ('Gubby') Allen, managed to draw the first two Tests, but comfortably lost the third and fourth. 'Our side,' commented Swanton, 'is a band of very gallant triers.'

That tour was soon forgotten, as later in April 1948 the Australians under Don Bradman arrived in England amid considerable hoopla. Their first major engagement, before the actual cricket began, was entirely of Swanton's devising. The previous autumn, he had managed to get Bradman to persuade the Australian Board of Control that the tourists should attend a dinner hosted by the Cricket Writers' Club (still formally known as the Empire Cricket Writers' Club) – in order, as Swanton explained, to 'start things off on the happiest note in the important direction of publicity and press relations'. Accordingly, a distinguished company (including the recently married Duke of Edinburgh, as well as Bradman and his men) gathered in black tie at the Public Schools Club in Piccadilly and, recalled Swanton, dined pretty well; the six speakers, carefully selected by the chairman, were Swanton himself ('bowled a perfect opening over,' loyally reported the *Telegraph*), Bradman, Sir Norman Birkett (the greatest legal figure of his day), Harry Altham, the cricket writer R. C. Robertson-Glasgow, and Canon F. H. Gillingham (former Essex batsman, master of deadpan humour). In a final, crowning coup for Swanton, the BBC transmitted live at nine o'clock on the Light Programme the speeches by Bradman and Birkett.

'Before they have played a single match,' he noted next morning in the *Telegraph*, 'there can hardly be a hermit in the Shetland Islands who does not know that Don Bradman and his players are among us.' Arlott found the growing frenzy distasteful. 'Men who, in a normal year, do not know which team has won the County Championship, will utter such rubbish as will convince any sensible man that they have completely lost all sense of proportion,' he wrote crossly in Worcester's Diglis Hotel on the eve of the season. 'Because of this obsession, which flourishes in ignorance, men who love the game of cricket will be unable to play it as a game,' his journal entry continued. 'It will be pretended that victory or defeat in a Test Match proves something other than the fact that under given circumstances eleven men of one country are a better blend of batsmen, bowlers and fieldsmen than eleven of another.' Arlott was willing to take sides, but only up to a point. 'Being human and an Englishman, I hope England will win: I hope rather more that I may see great cricket played by great cricketers. I had sooner see England lose with a good team than win with a bad one ...' In practice, it soon seemed evident to Arlott that, unless it rained, the best bowlers in England could hardly hope to bowl out the 1948 Australians twice in five days for 'headable totals'. It was the prospect of rain that allowed Swanton to offer a remarkably optimistic judgement before the series began: 'Perhaps the most sanguine followers would hardly expect England to win a Test series fought without rain. But, in an English season, it does rain, and if it does so at the right time, as it did last year in the Tests versus South Africa at Leeds and Old Trafford, I hardly think we should need any incidental luck to show ourselves the better side.'

Helped by an experimental law allowing a new ball after only fifty-five overs – a regulation that might have been designed for a captain with Ray Lindwall and Keith Miller in his armoury – Bradman's 'Invincibles' won the series crushingly. A straightforward victory at Trent Bridge was followed by an overwhelming triumph at Lord's, where the older author of this book remembers Bradman batting like one of Francis Thompson's run stealers, flickering to and fro. 'Australia won by 409 runs, which was, presumably, big enough even for Bradman,' was Arlott's unhappy, rather sarcastic reaction. From the start, Swanton pushed the claims of Robins to be England's captain, instead of Norman Yardley, arguing that the former's approach would be more 'aggressive'. Robins was a good friend and golfing buddy of Bradman; and conspiracy theorists have argued, with somewhat flimsy supporting evidence, not only that the fifty-five-overs experiment was Bradman-driven (with MCC pragmatically accepting it as the price for ensuring that he definitely came on the tour), but also that those backing Robins did so in order to continue to keep Bradman sweet. Either way, Swanton did not let up, vainly – almost obsessively – pressing for Robins right to the end.

Back in July on the eve of the third Test at Old Trafford, taking stock of the post-Lord's national mood following the home side's poor start to the series, Arlott delivered one of his neo-philosophical correctives. 'Cricketing England and, more especially, non-cricketing England, which had heard or overheard the news, were full of woe and anger. Old men wagged their heads sadly, and uttered, as original, a statement to the effect that men (in this case cricketers) were not what they were. Others proposed various remedies, outstandingly "Sack the lot".' Bewilderingly, the only person who got the sack (for one match only) was Len Hutton, one of England's best two batsmen; Arlott reflected that Australia's fast men had 'worked, on every conceivable occasion, to shatter Hutton's confidence, and they had succeeded'.

In fact, England were more convincing in the third and fourth Tests. After three days at Old Trafford, Arlott concluded that England had achieved 'at least an impregnable position, probably a winning one'. Then the rains came, and stayed. The fourth Test at Headingley began with England making 496: seemingly formidable, but Swanton still wondering whether that was enough on a pitch that was playing as well as it had in the 1930s, when Bradman scored a triple century in a day. Then, on the Saturday, Miller and Neil Harvey, in his first Test, batted with such brilliance as to bring Arlott and Swanton into complete unanimity. 'Before our very eyes,' declared Arlott, 'two of the greatest innings of all Test cricket were being played ... Miller's 58 will remain in mind if every other innings I have ever seen is forgotten ... He raised cricket to a point of aesthetic beauty.' Swanton, as ever, inserted his own historical context: 'I have never seen a better short innings than Miller's 58, not even Woolley's at Lord's in 1930.' Eventually, Yardley was able to set Australia a target of 404 on the final day. Swanton was well pleased by what he had seen so far: 'Will the heroics of the past two days be sustained to the end? If they are, this may well go down as one of the greatest Test matches.' So it did, but for the wrong reason. The absence of an effective English spinner was aggravated by dreadful fielding, with eight chances missed, as, in Arlott's words, 'Bradman and Morris made their runs steadily, running like well-planned trains to their time-runs schedule'. His reaction after Australia's victory by seven wickets was harsh for him: 'None of the chances was absolutely easy, but none of them would have been remarkable if taken. They should have been accepted by Test cricketers; since they were not, the side which missed them deserved to lose.' Arlott did add that it was 'a great eleven that won'; while Swanton, though lamenting how 'the English bowling declined in length, as did the English effort in the field both in management and accuracy, to say nothing of apparent zeal', nevertheless ended his report magnanimously: 'There it is, regrets we must have, yet after all, it was indeed a grand match, and all honour to Australia.'

At The Oval in mid-August, Bradman's team truly became the Invincibles, dismissing England for 52 in the first innings and winning by an innings and 149 runs. The match was unforgettable for Bradman's farewell innings, when he needed four runs to finish his Test career averaging 100. He was applauded loudly to the wicket, late on the rain-affected first day, and the England fielders raised their caps to a chorus of three cheers. At one of cricket's most historic, emblematic moments, Arlott was at the microphone. After describing how Bradman 'gently' played out his first ball from Eric Hollies 'in the direction of the Houses of Parliament', he went on:

No run, still 117 for one. Two slips, a silly mid-off, and a forward short leg close to him, as Hollies pitches the ball up slowly. He's bowled! (*Applause and cheers, for almost a minute*) Bradman bowled Hollies nought ... bowled Hollies nought ... Now – I wonder if you see a ball very clearly on your last Test in England, on a ground where you've played out some of the biggest cricket of your life, and the opposing team have just stood round you and given you three cheers, and the crowd has clapped you all the way to the wicket – I wonder if you really see the ball at all?

Whether dry-eyed or not, but in any case defeated by a googly, Bradman had to settle for 99.94. 'After such a reception,' reflected Arlott in his journal that evening, 'a man could hardly do other than score a duck or a century – and a duck did Australia no harm.' Swanton, for his part, noted that Jack Hobbs's last Test innings had been almost exactly eighteen years earlier, also at The Oval, and that he had been bowled for nine.

'There must be many thousands of listeners unable to get to any of the Test matches who have had the fullest possible impression of them,' declared the *Manchester Guardian* even before the series had ended. 'To the little "Test team" of commentators great credit is due. Rex Alston, John Arlott, and Alan McGilvray not only record the game, ball by ball, over long periods, but they have become adept at setting the scene and slipping in all the details that make it a living picture for the listener. The additional comments and summaries by A. E. R. Gilligan and R. C. Robertson-Glasgow complete an excellent scheme of reporting.' The paper also praised Arlott for *The Old Man* – an 'exceptionally well done' radio programme which he had recently written and introduced, in honour of the centenary of Grace's birth. Particularly notable (and resourceful) was his recorded interview with the former fast bowler Charles Kortright, an old sparring partner of WG, whose 'whole account was so touched with personality and spirit and humour that it beat most "interviews" hollow'. Among Arlott's youthful fans that summer was a fifteen-year-old living in Sheffield and for much of the time in bed with pneumonia. 'I listened to the radio for 12 hours every day, waiting for the cricket commentary that edged its way on to the air between broadcasts of "The Dream of Olwen",' recalled Roy Hattersley. 'Describing the agile menace of the Australian wicketkeeper, John Arlott had a sudden revelation. "Of course, Tallon is prehensile. All talons are prehensile." In the back bedroom there were angry scenes as I demanded instant access to our aged *Chambers Dictionary*.'

Definitely not a fan was one Australian. Arlott 'did not endear himself to me,' McGilvray remembered some four decades later about the 1948 tour. 'I considered him fairly high-handed.' McGilvray told the story of how Lindwall had been annoyed by Arlott's describing one of his deliveries as 'turning from the leg'; and how, after Lindwall had explained to the Englishman that he swung the ball, sometimes cut it, but never turned it, Arlott had said, 'Just a matter of expression, dear boy. Just a matter of expression.' Another unbeliever, but for different reasons, was the *Observer*'s radio critic W. E. Williams, for many years editor-in-chief of Penguin Books, and immortalised in Wikipedia as 'an educationalist and powerhouse of popular education'. 'We are still a bit capricious, I suppose, in our likes and dislikes of wireless voices,' he wrote early in 1949. 'One which I like least is John Arlott's, whether he is annotating his Book of Verse or reporting the Test Match from Cape Town. No one can more expertly summarise the day's play [Swanton fortunately never an *Observer* reader], but, alas! those abundant diphthongs displease the ear, and the lack of cadence in his delivery makes hard listening.'

England's winter tour to South Africa still lay ahead when, in the immediate aftermath of the Ashes series, Swanton surveyed in the *Field* the state of English cricket. Admittedly, he noted, there were extenuating circumstances in austerity Britain – 'in these days when our cricketers have to last till lunch-time on a watery chunk of hotel dried egg instead of the lamb chops and plates of kidneys of their fathers, it is the hardest thing to infuse them with an ardent, combustible spirit' – but the fact was that, whether in 'the smallest village' or 'the county of Yorkshire', since the war 'the old playing standard has not been recaptured, or even closely approached'. 'Consider,' Swanton went on in thoroughly gloomy vein, 'the weakness of the amateur element nowadays – those who have played as a relaxation have always provided so much of the yeast to cricket – and add the loss of players in that vital year of their development to National Service, and the difficulty of offering wages high enough to attract them to the game as a career when they finish it, and you have a set of fairly depressing circumstances.' In short, he concluded, 'the game in England needs strong stimulation'; and he called on MCC to be less 'a benevolent godfather' to cricketers, more 'an earnest parent'. MCC did indeed respond to the post-war situation (and perhaps directly to Swanton's *cri de cœur*) by setting up soon afterwards the MCC Cricket Enquiry, that in turn led to the MCC Youth Cricket Association. Was one possible remedy conceivably the appointment of a professional to captain England? 'An England captain must essentially have the breadth and buoyancy of a leader,' observed Swanton shortly before the Oval debacle, 'and if the ranks of the professionals could supply such a man, any lurking prejudice would soon be disarmed by performance.'

Arlott's season was not yet over. 'After Test Matches,' he wrote at the time in Kiplingesque tones, 'the captains and the kings depart instantly in a swirl of dust followed by their retinue, for their business is done.' But he was now free to do what he liked best. 'Test cricket's all very well as a spectacle and all that,' he told Mike Brearley four decades later, 'but I love a county game – you know, perhaps at Glastonbury or Horsham or Neath or Ebbw Vale, where you can hear the players talking to each other. You used to be able to hear Wooller cursing the batsman ... And you feel somehow close to the players ... With a cricketer, you watch him for three days and you've got to see the kind of man he is. He's got to reveal himself.' After The Oval, Arlott made for Bournemouth's Dean Park, where men were still lingering in marquees furnished with solid Victorian armchairs. He joined them to watch an encounter between his favourite counties – Hampshire, county of his birth, against Glamorgan, both of them with players whose company he had come to enjoy. It was a contest, he anticipated, bound to be 'as keen as a Test Match': if Glamorgan beat Hampshire, and Yorkshire failed to win against Somerset, then Glamorgan, among county cricket's perpetual also-rans, would be champions. In fact, he explained in due course, it was even keener than a Test because the batsmen did not have the time and space of a five-day match. 'This was cricket played with the winged chariot at the players' backs ... Yet, after the Test Matches, here was an atmosphere that was like home after the atmosphere of business.'

Glamorgan won the toss on the Saturday (a week after Bradman's duck) and batted, though for only three overs because of rain. Monday saw them scoring 315 quickly enough to leave Hampshire with an hour and a quarter's batting that evening. Injuries had forced Glamorgan to recall J. C. Clay, who at the age of fifty – 'white-haired, tall, thin and sloping-shouldered' – would pair with Len Muncer. When these wise old off-spinners began to bowl, their quick men had already taken two wickets. They now took two more wickets each, and Hampshire were 50 for 6 at the close. Arlott was particularly impressed by Glamorgan's out-cricket: not only the fielders running to their positions with an alertness matched only by the Australians that summer, but the field then 'taut as a fiddle-string', turning 'good honest bowling into rapid match-winning bowling'.

At the start of the third and last day, Glamorgan had less than five hours to take 14 wickets on a tame track; but their spinners fairly quickly polished off Hampshire for 84, well over 200 behind. Though his friend Leo Harrison, the Hampshire wicketkeeper, did manage to stick around for a while, Arlott noted somewhat tartly that in general he had 'yet to produce scores as impressive as the appearance of his batting'. Wilf Wooller duly enforced the follow-on; Clay and Muncer took eight wickets between them, the lion's share going to the fifty-year-old; and with Hampshire all out for 116, and Yorkshire having little joy in Taunton, Glamorgan were champions for the first time. Lusty renditions ensued, by players and supporters alike, of 'Land of My Fathers' and 'Sospan Fach'. 'There are better bowling sides, there are better batting sides, but fielding I think has carried the day, that and enormous enthusiasm,' Wooller told Arlott on the radio later that day. And John Clay (who had first played for Glamorgan in 1920) chipped in: 'I can hardly believe it's true, and when I think of those old players, Norman Riches for instance, as John Arlott has said; Eddie Bates; Jack Bell; well, Dai Davies funnily enough, one of our oldest players, he was umpiring here today, so it was a great day for him – he gave the last man out (*laugh*).'

Arlott in his journal claimed that one key factor in their success had been Wooller's decision to live with the professional players, unlike most amateur captains who had different dressing rooms and stayed in smarter lodgings: 'The only way to *know* cricket, as it is the only way to know the theatre, is to live with professional players. Wooller's captaincy was not only better informed, but it was also more sympathetic and more easily applied because he knew his men.' Arlott was a fond admirer of Wooller, whose ruthlessness on the field and intemperate, often right-wing opinions were undeniably at odds with his own liberalism; but he was one of many who, while disputing Wooller's views, held him in 'respect and affection' for his 'honest and absolute loyalty'. Besides, Wooller had also been a willing collaborator in Arlott's education in the finer points of the game.

The season over, he plundered the thesaurus for his last, heartfelt, sentimental words on the memorable summer of 1948: 'Is there, I wonder, anywhere in the world such a human, generous, unenvious, shop-talking, enthusiastic, mellow, craft-versed, sporting community as English cricket professionals?' Soon afterwards, in a study of 'The Players' (in effect a close socio-economic analysis of the conditions of the professional cricketer) that was included in his 1949 collection *Concerning Cricket*, he added a coda to this encomium: 'On a sane and economic level no argument can be adduced for a man becoming a county cricketer: he is valuable to the student of social history only as an example of the incurable romantic – but it is difficult indeed to deny him sympathy, perhaps even envy.'

Concerning Cricket itself was arguably the most 'Arlottian' of all Arlott's cricket books – and certainly one of his most appealing. The introductory essay, 'Aspects of Cricket', repudiated as 'completely false' Kipling's nostrum that 'the game is greater than the player of the game'. Instead: 'The game echoes no further than it is played. Its true importance lies in the fact that men express themselves through cricket … My own attempt is, primarily, to write of men I know. I write of them in a cricket setting because that is the background I know best, and, hence, the background against which I may best judge a man and the implications of his actions.' Arlott added that 'as soon as he enters the human field, the cricket writer moves in the territory of the novelist, whose business is the presentation of humanity'; but even so, he surmised, 'while a writer may one day write a book which shall be to cricket what *The Compleat Angler* is to angling, yet the game can never give rise to a *War and Peace*'.

In essays that followed, 'The Craft So Long to Learn' (a nod to Chaucer) evoked the old-style veteran rural cricketer, ending with a description of how he 'turns back to the beginning of his run to bowl again, the ball lying in his hand as easily and naturally as the chisel in the hand of his brother the carpenter, or the cobbler's awl in the hand of Old Small' (a reference to John Small, Petersfield's champion cobbler, violinist and cricketer of the mid-to-late eighteenth century). 'A Cricket Match at Bath' was near-rhapsodic about two recent days of county cricket, as a small, quiet, sympathetic crowd watched the craftsmen diligently and patiently go about their business, though ending with a semi-ominous warning that those West Country spectators 'should remember that they have something increasingly uncommon and to be cherished'. 'About Essex' celebrated the main characters of 'a bank-holiday team – at their gayest under the sun and on hard wickets'. 'Felix and Some Aspects of Early Cricket' reflected his steadily growing interest in the pre-modern game – in some sense, in Arlott's eyes, cricket before the fall. 'The Case Against League Cricket' (in truth about a nor-thern world of which Arlott was relatively ignorant) was that the overseas professionals unhealthily dominated the matches and thereby discouraged young, local talent from developing. By contrast, a trio of sketches of Worcestershire pros – Reg Perks, Peter Jackson and Dick Howorth – was wholly positive. And a short piece on Bradman (origin-ally written for Jack Fingleton's *Brightly Fades the Don*) ended chillingly enough: 'I do not think cricket is under Bradman's skin, but I believe that it is under his skull – in close control. Therefore, he has missed something of cricket that less gifted and less memorable men have gained. How, I wonder, would Don Bradman define happiness?'

Perhaps most interesting of all in the collection was 'So Over to the Cricket at …', quite possibly a pioneer attempt – by anyone – to analyse the challenges and pitfalls of being a cricket commentator. Arlott instanced the second day of the 1947 Headingley Test, when in front of a full house and on a turning wicket after a thunderstorm, the English openers faced an unwaveringly accurate South African attack:

On the far side of the field spectators are sitting on mud, watching cricket after their own heart with the grim intentness of the Yorkshireman. How shall the commen-tator put into words this apparent inaction, this sultry heaviness of the air, the steadiness of the batting, the grim relentlessness of the bowling? Shall he do it by bald, blunt statement, which must prepare his listener for minute after minute of *numerically* dull play? Or can he show the true nature of this tug-of-war – the tightness of the bowling and fielding, the grim, experienced, technically perfect batting of Hutton and Washbrook? How can he show that the work of these two batsmen has the quality of deep knowledge and experience to be found in the oldest of the crafts of the country?

'I ought to be television receiver, a second-by-second news reporter, a painter – to capture the impressions as distinct from the photograph of the play – and a poet – to catch the atmosphere of controlled strife and deep strategic exercise of a mellow craft,' was Arlott's rather wistful conclusion. 'One day, when the picture becomes *half* complete, I shall know that I am dreaming.'

'Well up to standard,' declared the *TLS* about *Concerning Cricket*. 'As a writer Mr Arlott commands many of the qualities that make him so good, if at moments so irritatingly mannered, a commentator. That is a rare thing. For it is one thing to convey poise, rich observation, humour and passionate knowledge on the air; it is another to substantiate these by a prose style.' Admittedly, the reviewer (the discerning Alan Ross) went on, Arlott lacked the 'clean elegance' and 'artistry' of Cardus, or the 'fantasy' and 'erudite wit' of Robertson-Glasgow. Nevertheless, 'almost certainly he knows as much about cricket as either, he cares for it as deeply, and he writes with a rich, profoundly concerned allegiance'. In retrospect, 1949 may have been Arlott's authorial zenith. Everything was still fresh; there was still a sense of wonderment, whether outwardly or inwardly directed; and celebrity's inevitable coarsening effect, however much resisted, had not yet quite begun.

The winter of 1948–9 marked a turning point for Arlott professionally: his selection as a radio commentator on the English tour of South Africa announced his arrival as a bona fide cricket journalist who also did poetry programmes on the BBC. He had liked some of the South African cricketers on their tour of England in 1947, and local radio had picked up some of his BBC commentaries. As a journalist, he was still an innocent, happily discovering that it could be much better than working. On arrival, he enjoyed 'magnificent hospitality' in Johannesburg, where beer and whisky were more freely available than in still war-affected London. He was in luck with the cricket, too. 'At one match in 10,000 the ritual cricket equivalent of runs-wickets-time resolves itself into the pattern of complete drama,' he wrote in unashamedly purple prose after the first Test. 'When that happens, it is not necessary to know cricket to correlate all this data, to feel that its ingredients, like the elements of Greek drama, have compelled a balanced perfection of construction. It is in the air. It was in the Durban air.' Elsewhere in his account, he compared the contest to an orchestra 'sweeping along to the final movement of Beethoven's ninth symphony, building as it goes, heightening every sense, carrying the imagination along to the boundaries of bearing'. 'The score-book,' he added, 'can offer only figures: memory links emotions with the gradual disappearance into cloud of a distant line of hills. I am grateful to have seen that cricket match: I dare not hope to see such another.'

More prosaically expressed, England won by two wickets when at the very death Derbyshire's Cliff Gladwin, abetted by Bedser, scrambled a leg-bye. 'And he's knuckled it, and they're running, and Bedser isn't run out, and they've won on the last ball of the last over,' Arlott behind the microphone hoarsely told the world. Elsewhere on the ground, an almost equally thrilled Swanton – especially delighted by Gladwin's broad northern accent as he strode out to bat with the words, 'Coometh the hour, coometh the man' – prepared to write a *Telegraph* report that, though eschewing Sophocles and Beethoven, was quite unlike his usual style:

> The language of Mr Jingle has served before to describe a cricket match and it can perhaps do so again. Wonderful match, sir – all heroes – England hitting out – wickets falling – rain falling – light shocking – Mann, Washbrook gallant fellows. Compton a genius, sir, old head on shoulders – this Jenkins, first Test Match, Worcester sauce, Yorkshire relish, have it your own way … Half-hour to go, 31 to win, still together – 20 minutes, 18 wanted, Compton bowled behind legs, gliding. What's that? Jenkins caught wicket? – 10 to six, 13 to make – Gladwin missed mid-on by Tuckett, run two, this Gladwin has fight, sir. He'll do it yet. He will. He has …

Even so, for all this Dickensian excursion, his perspective on England's flawed performance during the match still retained a strong sense of the nuts and bolts, whatever the drama. Typically, he worried not only that England were without an off-spinner, but that, although they were reasonably fit, they were not 'hard'. Swanton always imagined himself inside a cricket captain's head; whereas Arlott, who was more familiar with the inside of the spectators' heads, focused on the players as a whole.

The next Test at Johannesburg was memorable for England's record opening stand of 359 between Hutton and Washbrook, though it ended in a draw. Matches in Cape Town and Johannesburg finished the same way; but Arlott's education was not confined to cricket tourism. Finding himself in South Africa barely half a year after the coming to power of the National Party had initiated what would become the apartheid era, he became interested in what, like others, he called 'the native problem'. In Grahamstown, shortly before the final Test, he was staying with Charles Fortune, South Africa's leading cricket commentator. On a rainy night, Arlott went along when Fortune took his 'kindly native cook' home, and described the scene in his book of the tour: 'We drove into the native quarter ... Shame, hesitation, doubt, guilt struggled in the mind ... In crawling filth, in houses made out of petrol tins hammered out flat, the people who live in that healthless quarter are fortunate if they have a dwelling with one brick wall supporting a chimney ... The conscience cannot throw it off.' This was a decisive moment – in Arlott's words, a 'violently chilling' experience.

England won the fifth Test and the series in Port Elizabeth. Arlott reported on 'gay and sad farewells', and boarded the flying boat in Cape Town. When an immigration officer asked him to fill in the box marked 'Race', Arlott replied that he belonged to 'the human race'; and he would never return to the land of apartheid. He flew north through Africa, with stops each night so that the passengers could have a decent dinner and sleep. Arlott left the flight at

1949, with New Zealand touring, was Arlott's fourth home season in his new role, and he confessed to a slight fear that some of his delights in the game might begin to pall. MCC decided that, rather than have three four-day Tests, there would be four lasting only three days; and Walter Hadlee, New Zealand's popular captain, in turn decided that he did not have the bowling to take twenty England wickets in three days and adopted a defensive strategy – so successfully that all four Tests were drawn, with Arlott in his brief account of the series calling that a moral victory for Hadlee, because New Zealand had survived against the stronger team. Even in a dullish season, Swanton's capacity for seemingly omniscient historical rankings (analogous to Roy Jenkins constructing elaborate historical league tables of politicians) seldom failed him. Of the visitors' two outstanding batsmen, he had already marked the card of Martin Donnelly, calling him back in 1946 'a great batsman in the sense that the phrase can be used of perhaps three other men in England today' after his century in the Varsity match; while a year later, also at Lord's, his undefeated 162 for the Gentlemen had prompted Swanton to announce that he was now 'accepted quite universally by cricketers as comparable to the best left-handers who ever played, that is, of course, to Woolley and Clem Hill'. The revelation in the New Zealand team was Bert Sutcliffe, another left-hander. 'I have never seen more glorious striking than Sutcliffe's,' declared Swanton after watching him score 46 in thirteen minutes in a run chase at Southampton. The only innings that rivalled it, he added, was Learie Constantine's whirlwind 57 in twenty-seven minutes at Lord's in 1933.

Because the cricket authorities in those days paid attention to the physical demands made on Test cricketers, MCC unilaterally decided that the proposed tour of India in 1949–50 would be asking too much of the players, and unceremoniously cancelled it. Accordingly, Swanton for once was able to concentrate on being the *Telegraph*'s rugby correspondent, while Arlott returned to the BBC to do the work as a staff producer he was paid to do. Even so, he was not prevented from working elsewhere; and, like many freelance journalists, he always feared that work might dry up, so he never turned it down. As a collector, his acquisitive nature was costly and depended on the supplementary income he earned outside the BBC. Arlott had begun to write regularly for the *Daily Mail*, and in April 1950 took the time to travel to Tilbury where the SS *Orontes* was sailing for Australia. On the passenger list was Harold Larwood, emigrating from the country that he believed had abandoned him after the intensely controversial Bodyline tour of 1932–3. The day before, Larwood had had lunch with Douglas Jardine, his captain who had remained loyal to him, and he had also sought out Jack Hobbs. Together, they had drunk so much champagne that he left England with a mighty hangover. Arlott had expected a crowd of reporters and photographers to mark the occasion; in fact, he was the only person on the quayside waving Larwood off. Arlott's piece suggested that, the morning after, Larwood did not have much to say when they chatted. 'As I stand on the quay,' he wrote instead, 'the sun has come out to temper the cold wind of late April, and a figure of cricket history is leaving England for Australia … Bare minutes ago, the ship cast off, and is standing out in the river, the oil smoke running out of her yellow funnels – and the man who has just turned away from the deck rail is "Lol" Larwood, who in September 1932 sailed from this same quay, and in this very same *Orontes*, to Australia and an epic Test series.'

By this time the focus was on the West Indian tourists. Swanton had seen the class of Frank Worrell, and the belligerence of Clyde Walcott and Everton Weekes, spearheading the defeat of Allen's men in 1947–8, but as usual was still broadly confident, seeing no reason why they should not be beaten 'in one Test or more'. Arlott thought the West Indies side 'looks no easy problem', though had doubts about their bowling attack – specifically, the absence of fast-bowling partnerships, as there had been in the 1930s. That said, and conceding it might be rash, he did add that, based on what he had seen in the nets, a virtually unknown twenty-year-old spinner called Ramadhin might make a significant contribution.

More generally, Swanton was still worrying about the training facilities for young cricketers. He proposed the laying of concrete wickets in the nets to reduce the impact of bad weather at the start of the season – but in this case he was an unhonoured prophet. And, of course, he continued to fret about the potentially diminished role of the amateur, and the spectre of first-class cricket becoming in England a completely professional game. Swanton's loyalty to amateurism had much to do with social class. He regarded himself as upper-middle – and that, in a class-based society, meant taking responsibility. The attitude was formed by long traditions of military experience in which the leader was an officer, and the professionals, whether soldier or professional cricketer, were the 'other ranks'. Swanton expected captains on the cricket field to behave like leaders, and over the past four years he had been disappointed by what he had seen on his return to civilian life. 'The blending of class with class, which is one of cricket's most valuable benefactions,' he now wrote in his new *Telegraph* column ('Monday Cricket Commentary'), 'has faded into the background.' From his perspective it was a justifiable concern, as all the signs during the 1950 season were that the traditional two-class system was barely hanging on. Most of the counties had captains who were either 'shamateurs' or – like Somerset's Stuart Rogers, an army officer with a disciplinarian streak who did not bowl and had a career average of under 19 with the bat – not really worth their place in the side. The only two professionals in charge were Warwickshire's Tom Dollery and Sussex's James Langridge, the latter after a fierce pre-season row, as members revolted against the committee's plan to appoint joint captains – both of them amateur, with one in effect a stand-in until the end of Cambridge's fixtures freed up the other.

In the first Test at Old Trafford, on a turning wicket, Eric Hollies and Bob Berry spun England to an emphatic victory. Swanton understandably remarked on how pleasant it was to see England win at home for the first time in three years, while Arlott judged it the most exciting Test in England since the war. He was especially struck by the sight of Evans facing Sonny Ramadhin's equally youthful co-spinner, the left-arm Alf Valentine, with a confidence he could not quite believe. It was, he wrote, 'like a man in a film, approaching a disaster of which the audience, but not the victim-to-be, is conscious', and 'there was a temptation to shout to him to be careful'. He vividly described how the bowler, taking eleven wickets in a losing cause, swung his arm over 'as if oiled on the axis of his shoulder', with his whole body seeming 'to pivot on the point of leverage which his index finger was digging beside the seam'. Later in June, at Lord's in the second Test, the worm turned as dramatically as worms can. The three Ws scored an aggregate of 405 runs; the West Indian spin twins took 18 wickets for 279 runs; and during their marathon 231 overs, the English batting fell back on what Swanton could only call 'trepidant and unconvincing defence'. Overall, he calculated, the winners had faced only 11 overs more than they had bowled themselves, and yet they scored 326 more runs. After the overwhelming victory, Arlott could not praise highly enough Ramadhin and Valentine: 'This is something more than good bowling; it is great bowling by any standard in the history of the game.'

On the final day, Arlott apparently commented on air on the quiet of the crowd and the absence of their usual cries of pleasure and surprise. 'The truth of the matter,' revealed Neville Cardus's friend Margaret Hughes, 'was that they were huddled around a portable radio listening to the commentary, and as he made this remark a cheer was given specially for his benefit.' This was also the series in which the future football writer and commentator Brian Glanville heard Arlott's commentary for the first time. 'I was at once fascinated and beguiled by it: rich and orotund, southern and rural, pregnant with images of the countryside,' he recalled. 'Who on earth was he, I wondered? A former, famous cricketer, perhaps, of whom one should have heard? Who else would be permitted to break through the barrier of standardised, middle-class English?'

In fact, at least one section of the Lord's crowd was very much not silent during the Test, as Arlott himself acknowledged in his evocative written description of the scenes at the end:

A crowd of West Indians rushed on to the field in a final skirmish of the delight which they had called out from the balcony at the Nursery End since the beginning of the game. Their happiness was such that no one in the ground could fail to notice them: it was of such quality that every spectator on the ground must have felt himself their friend. Their 'In, out, in, out, in, out,' their calypsos, their delight in every turn of the game, their applause for players on both sides, were a higher brand of spirits than Lord's has known in modern times. It is one of my major credit marks for MCC that faced with all the possible forms which a celebration of victory might take, their only step was to ensure that no portions of the wicket were seized as trophies. Otherwise, these vocal and instrumental supporters were allowed their dance and gallop of triumph which ended too soon for the interest of many of their fellow-spectators.

'Happiest of all' in Arlott's eyes was that these memorable celebrations were 'not by official guests, but by men from the West Indies, who came anonymously and paid their money to see the match and who derived from it a happiness far greater than some critics of the game have ever known'. Which critics did he have in mind? It is tempting to guess an obvious one, but here it is worth quoting Swanton's contemporary account of what happened after Worrell had 'finally despatched' Wardle 'to the unbridled joy of his countrymen':

> Some of them, armed with impromptu instruments, saluted the great occasion with strange noises, and a handful with their leader [Aldwyn Roberts, aka Lord Kitchener, who had come over on the SS *Empire Windrush* two years earlier] swayed round the field to give a first reminder to those who know the West Indian Islands of the bands at carnival time. One felt sorry that the august dignity of Lord's and perhaps the sight of many helmets and uniforms so subdued the rest. But, for them at least, it was a victory unforgettable.

Soon afterwards, Lord Kitchener's fellow calypsonian, Lord Beginner (Egbert Moore), recorded 'Victory Test Match', in effect a match report set to music:

> Cricket, lovely cricket
> At Lord's where I saw it,
> Yardley tried his best,
> But Goddard won the Test,
> They gave the crowd plenty fun,
> Second Test and West Indies won
> With those two little pals of mine
> Ramadhin and Valentine.

'Hats went in the air', Beginner sang in the last verse, as he came to the celebrations; and he added touchingly, 'People jump and shout without fear' – though in fact Kitchener had been arrested on the field, until booing by

English spectators ('They won the match, let him enjoy himself') had sufficiently embarrassed the policeman to release him.

After West Indies comfortably won the third Test at Trent Bridge (double-century for Worrell, century for Weekes, ten wickets for the two little pals), England went to The Oval needing a win to square the four-match series. The visitors' 503 (another century for Worrell) put paid to that, and England duly went down by an innings (14 wickets for R&V) despite Hutton's undefeated double-hundred. For Arlott, the most heartfelt moment came when Compton – his favourite English batsman of the era, now returning after an operation for his floating kneecap – ran himself out for 44. He thought afterwards that he had never reacted with such emotion to an event in a cricket match: 'The feeling was less than partisan ... the return of Compton had been more a symbol of our hopes than ever.' Ramadhin and Valentine, who had taken between them 59 wickets in the series, were evaluated by Arlott as 'the finest pair of spin bowlers – as a pair – to play in England since Grimmett and O'Reilly'. They were so young, and playing in a setting so novel to them, that their joint performance must 'be ranked as one of the finest cricket feats ever performed on Test level'. The only sour note on the last day in south London was the behaviour of the Metropolitan Police. Swanton, tellingly and perhaps again unexpectedly, had no sympathy for them. 'As at Lord's, the final scenes were enlivened by the spontaneous rejoicing of the West Indian supporters, and again the law brought them strictly to heel. We could well have borne another calypso, and a few hand springs, for it was a victory handsomely and sportingly earned.'

A running sub-plot through the 1950 season was the make-up of the party to tour Australia the following winter, starting with the question of the captaincy. By mid-July, when both the present captain (Yardley) and a recent captain (Mann) had declared themselves unavailable, mainly for business reasons, debate was increasingly keen. 'My own choice,' asserted Arlott in that month's issue of the short-lived *Cricketers' Magazine*, 'would be Wilfred Wooller, a useful change bowler, a fair bottom-half bat and a wonderful field (so that he would not be a passenger), but above all, a captain with heart, courage and experience and one to go for a finish.' Weighing up the situation, Swanton from his usual pulpit judged that the likely choice lay between Freddie Brown, an amateur who way back had been on the Bodyline tour and was now an inspiring captain of Northamptonshire, and Warwickshire's much-respected professional captain Tom Dollery. Rather like St Augustine and chastity, he could not quite yet – in reality – embrace the prospect of England being captained by a pro. 'Good judges and students of cricket who are by no means prejudiced against a professional captain, as such,' he wrote, 'may well ask themselves whether this particular moment is the time to experiment in this direction.'

As it happened, Brown and Dollery were soon afterwards the respective captains in the annual Gentlemen v. Players encounter at Lord's. On the first day, Brown made a superb century, reaching three figures with a straight six into the Pavilion, and altogether scoring 122 out of 131 during his hour and three-quarters at the crease. 'The more elderly were reminded of how cricket used to be played,' noted an admiring Swanton, 'and especially how the ball used to be driven before the game's descent, as many would lament, to an age of over-sophistication and a dreary philosophy of safety first.' He hardly needed to spell out the moral – namely, 'the significance of what we saw today was that it was the product of a style of play which is essentially that of a cricketer not under the restraints and taboos of one who plays the game for his living'. Next day, Dollery himself scored an admirable century, but within minutes of his declaration and the Gentlemen leaving the field, Brown had been invited to take the side to Australia. Swanton greeted the news warmly, not least perhaps on account of England's new captain having 'spent the latter part of the war in a prisoner-of-war camp', an experience which 'many people found to be no mean university in the broadest sense'.

Which men would he be leading into battle? A ponderous, piecemeal process conducted by an unwieldy selection committee eventually by the end of August resulted in a generally much-criticised touring party with, among other things, a distinctly old-fashioned, non-egalitarian flavour. In particular, there was the inclusion of three young, palpably inexperienced, Cambridge-educated amateurs: David Sheppard and J. G. Dewes had made a mountain of runs on a university wicket widely acknowledged to be a batsman's paradise, while the quick bowler J. J. Warr, likewise still an undergraduate that summer, had bowled well enough but unsensationally, coming fifty-fifth in the national averages. Significantly, their county affiliations were Sussex, Middlesex and Middlesex again – socially very acceptable. Swanton was on the whole far from unhappy. Sheppard's 'forward style', he predicted, 'should be well suited by the wickets'; Dewes he had his technical doubts about, but 'certainly has the prime quality of resolution'; Warr he described before the key meeting as having 'many good qualities', after the announcement as 'a dauntless fellow who will really look to be *hoping* for a bowl at five o'clock on the hottest day'. In addition to those largely character-based endorsements, moreover, Swanton took comfort in the choice of Compton as Brown's deputy: 'The fact that he is the first professional whom MCC have appointed as vice-captain of a touring team is evidence for any who required assurance on the matter that the Committee are interested in the man rather than his status.'

That autumn, before the Tests began, Arlott examined the whole sorry mess – a mess, tellingly, that went back to selection policy during the home series against the West Indies, including at different stages the inclusion of four promising but unproven amateur batsmen (Hubert Doggart and Doug Insole as well as Sheppard and Dewes): 'Much of the confusion of these selections was, of course, involved in the selectors' search for a young amateur to take over the captaincy at some time in the future ... Meanwhile, opportunities, not only of beating the West Indies, but also of taking a balanced and strong side to Australia, were disappearing.' It would have been much more sensible, he argued, if the selectors had instead, 'when experienced batsmen dropped out of the side', turned to Northamptonshire's 'seasoned' professional Denis Brookes as a replacement. Yet what was truly interesting and perhaps unexpected about Arlott's analysis was that, in the end, he drew back from making the obvious charge that to an undue extent the touring party's composition had been based on socially hierarchical, non-cricketing considerations. 'The virtues of the team selected for Australia – youth, a happy proportion of amateurs – such as should indicate the continuing strength of the amateur tradition in the country – enthusiasm and promise, are such,' he wrote with complicated syntax but seemingly complete sincerity, 'as we should observe with gratitude.' Perhaps he did not want to be viewed as a boat-rocker? Or perhaps he still believed, almost as much as Swanton, in a 'blending' of the two traditions?

Over the ensuing Ashes series, that youthful amateur 'promise' would go sadly unfulfilled. Sheppard and Dewes managed 74 runs between them in seven innings; Warr took 1 wicket for 281 runs. 'Will one ever know what the selectors were thinking of?' lamented the novelist-cum-classicist Rex Warner. And, writing to a moderately sympathetic Australian friend (in a correspondence collected in book form in *Ashes to Ashes*), he reckoned that 'the abolition of the dictatorship of the MCC' was the only thing that might save English cricket. Class and cricket: if mid-twentieth-century Britain was a society where accidents of birth still largely determined life chances, which in many ways it was, then the question facing cricket was whether it was going to continue to be part of the problem or start to be part of the solution.

4

1950–60: Dusty Afternoons

Following England's cricketers on Ashes tours in the decade after the war could at times seem like taking long, well-paid holidays. There is a glimpse of the life led by Swanton and his colleagues in one of the best of all cricket books, *Australia 55* by Alan Ross, poet as well as the *Observer*'s cricket correspondent. Early scenes were played on the SS *Orsova*, a newly built ocean liner taking the players and journalists to Fremantle while they recovered from the rigours of a Britain only slowly emerging out of austerity. In Naples, Ross shared a taxi with Swanton and Ian Peebles to visit Pompeii, and to consume lobsters and drink the locally produced Lacryma Christi. On board, eight of the party shared a table, where the pre-war flatmates conducted a duologue. This was a Swanton his readers had no idea existed, and Ross reflected that, if the pen should ever fail them, the music halls would be the gainers: 'I should like, from a box seat in the Chelsea Palace, to see Swanton in a Free Forester cardigan feeding Peebles with his indulgent adroitness that brings forth a spacious and weltering interior monologue.' Arriving in Perth, Ross, Swanton and *The Times*'s John Woodcock were given use of the nets after MCC had finished.

Yet for Swanton at least, these trips to Australia were far from just expenses-paid jollies. Four years earlier, in his book of the 1950–1 tour, he had noted his commitments in addition to filing his daily reports for the *Telegraph*: namely, doing close-of-play summaries for the BBC, covering the tour for a group of South African morning papers, doing some work for the *Field*, compiling a survey of the tour for *Playfair Cricket Annual*, and writing the book itself, 'much of which had necessarily to be put together while the tour was going on'. Fortunately, he had superior secretarial help – as he generally ensured was the case – in the person of the young, pre-*Times* Woodcock, who also under Swanton's patronage lugged round Australia a cumbersome camera in order to make a pioneer film of an Ashes series, sent to London in instalments and first shown on the BBC.

Elusive Victory was the title of both book (dedicated to Australia's cricket-loving PM, Robert Menzies) and film (commentary by Swanton); but that victory referred only to the final Test, not the series, which was won by Australia, albeit with greater difficulty than the previous two. For that, much of the credit lay with Brown as captain, and Swanton thoroughly approved of both the man and his image: a reassuring, rubicund presence, usually pictured in his blazer and holding a pipe. To describe Brown at the crease, Swanton quoted Arlott, something he seldom did: 'When Brown is batting well, only rolled moustaches and a silk sash round the waist are needed to recall completely a forgotten age and style.' Little was expected of Brown and his men, not least after the muddled selection process (including six openers among the seven specialist batsmen); but at Brisbane, what Swanton called 'a freak match' – featuring at the crucial stage a 'glutinous' sticky dog of a wicket – saw a 'moral victory' for the visitors, though they actually lost. Then came Melbourne, thrillingly close. 'There was never a Test among all the many in which I had longed so deeply for victory,' recalled Swanton in the 1970s; and indeed late on the penultimate day, with England's second innings peril-ously poised, 'I confess I could not steel myself to watch Hutton withstanding Iverson's last over of the day'. After England had lost narrowly, normal one-way service was resumed in the third and fourth Tests, causing Swanton to complain later that 'sometimes on this tour it seemed to me that the Australian's pride in his cricketers translated itself too easily into an irritating assumption that they were unbeatable'. Unsurprisingly, he was delighted when England won the fifth Test by eight wickets, declaring that 'this match must inevitably mark the beginning and the end of an era'. It was clearly the end of the Bradman era, but in truth the first shoots of an English recovery were not easily visible, not least in the persons of the overexposed young Cambridge cricketers.

By the time the everlasting Ashes battle was resumed, England had a new captain, following Brown's decision to step down. Hutton the old pro, or Sheppard the young amateur? That, as Swanton saw it in May 1952 shortly before the India series, was in essence the choice; and as before, he was not yet fully reconciled to the promotion of a professional. It was a matter of respect and authority, of officers and other ranks. 'When professionals have been called on to lead representative sides, they have not usually taken particularly easily to the job,' he argued. 'There is no strong reason why they should, since, whereas they have risen to the heights by concentrating all their energy and effort on succeeding in their own particular departments, the secret of captaincy lies in seeing the game as a whole, in appreciating the feelings of the other 10 players, and in always taking the unselfish part.' Yet in the end he stayed his hand, declining to endorse the theology student: 'To elect him captain this summer would indeed be a gesture of faith. Whether it would be altogether fair to him or in the selectors' best interests in the long run, is the issue for debate.' And when soon afterwards Hutton got the job, he was gracious enough. 'Thus has history been made, and a professional appointed, let it be added most deservedly and justly,' Swanton declared at a landmark moment in English social and sporting history that he had long dreaded but now reluctantly accepted. He did warn, however, that Hutton's 'attitude to the broad tactics and strategy of the game commonly said to be characteristic of the Yorkshireman sometimes has seemed to his captains and fellow players to cloud his judgement'. That 'apprehension', about Hutton's overly cautious approach, would never really go away, but for the moment there seemed to be no realistic alternative candidate.

Arlott for his part had had his doubts about a professional captain. He liked Hutton, however, and prepared a long and enthusiastic radio profile of the new man. A year later, the epic Coronation summer of 1953 would put the Yorkshireman to the sternest test. One of the radio commentators on Coronation Day itself was Arlott, describing the proceedings ('Slowly this procession makes its stately way round the great sweep of the Circus with a quality that somehow twists the heart in the chest') from a notably well-provided perch, in a room above Piccadilly Circus's Criterion Restaurant. Soon afterwards the Ashes series began – an exciting match at Trent Bridge halted in its tracks by rain – amidst intense public interest, fuelled in part by expanded television coverage (including a significant role for Swanton).

Expectations ran high before the second Test at Lord's, with much attention focused on the decision of the selectors to pick their chairman, the ageing if still vigorous and versatile Freddie Brown. Swanton had been pushing the idea – reassuring his readers in advance that the all-rounder 'would be perfectly happy to play under Hutton's captaincy' – and after the announcement he wrote that he was 'sure the cricket public will appreciate Brown's spirit in coming back to the arena at the call of his fellow-selectors and of his successor as England's captain'. Arlott by contrast was contemptuous: 'At forty-two, a man needs something near to genius to be an effective Test player, and Brown is only a good county player.' He noted pointedly that Brown had been unable to command a place in Jardine's team in the Bodyline series in Australia twenty years earlier when at his peak. Moreover, Brown had already announced his retirement at the end of the 1953 season. 'It simply does not make sense,' Arlott thundered, 'that a player retires when he is of genuine Test status.' His scorn was sharpened by the discovery that Brown did not like bowling leg spin at left-handed batsmen, at a time when three of the Australians' top seven were left-handed. All this, crucially, was magnified by the social context:

The presence of the chairman of selectors in the dressing room must, inevitably, have some effect upon the relations between the players and a captain who is being appointed from Test to Test … It seems a grudging attitude, emphasised, in many minds, by the fact that Hutton is a professional … Since the team was announced, I have heard many suggestions to the effect that, if Brown comes off at Lord's, he will take over the captaincy.

In short, Arlott smelled an establishment plot. And when on the first day, as the chairman bowled his outswingers 'at an amiable medium pace', he could not but groan, 'Why on earth did they not pick Bertie Buse, of Somerset, who does the thing so much better than Brown?'

Next day, Friday, Australia were all out for 346, with Hutton having dropped catches and been barracked. England then closed at 177 for 1, with the captain not out 83. Swanton did not dwell unduly on his fielding lapses, preferring to concentrate on how once again he had carried England's hopes on his shoulders: 'All epithets have been worn bare in praise of Hutton and perhaps the best compliment he can be paid is that he batted, unreasonable though it may be, as everyone now expects him to bat against Australia – every time.' In Arlott's case, feelings ran characteristically high:

At the end of play, I saw Len Hutton, as I always like to do. He is not a speechmaker but, in a few sentences, he can give an assessment of a game which cuts clearly through incident to its essential shape. I wanted, too, to congratulate him: to be honest, I wanted to thank him.

He was a little tired, and his face showed it. His hand, bruised in attempting to catch, was greyly flushed: there is no fat and not much flesh on him, and bruising goes to his bones. He looked ruefully at the marks. 'I have played in over sixty Tests,' he said, 'and I have dropped more catches today than in all those other games put together.' It was those catches, not the batting triumph of the afternoon, which occupied him.

'I wished with – frankly – genuine anger,' added Arlott, 'that those who had sneered in the morning and cheered in the afternoon – as if a cricketer were a puppet without memory or feeling – could have heard him and been shamed.'

After Lindwall had yorked Tom Graveney with the fourth ball, and Compton had joined his captain, Saturday morning represented some kind of cricketing apogee: one of those immortal passages of play. In their contemporary accounts, Swanton did his best – 'These two confronted and confounded some great fast bowling … It was war to the knife, though one noticed that between overs batsmen and fielders were prepared to exchange pleasantries occasionally, as decent cricketers should' – but almost inevitably it was Arlott who rose to the historic occasion:

This was what the bullfight calls 'the moment of truth'. It was a hundred years ago that William Lillywhite – 'The Nonpareil' – said 'Me bowling, Pilch batting and Tom Box keeping wicket, that's cricket, I reckon'. This was Lord's, the sun was shining on packed stands and terraces, on grass green with the fresh memory of rain. Lindwall and Miller were fresh and bowling with the new

ball: Hutton and Compton were batting and around them
stood Hole, Benaud, Davidson, Harvey, Morris, Ring –
all superb catchers of the ball. This generation could ask
no more of cricket.

England in the end managed only a narrow lead, and at
day's close Arlott wrote in appreciative, non-partisan
mood, 'What a magnificent, somersaulting, unpredictable
Test series this is.'

Monday was Australia's day, with England at stumps
already three cheap wickets down after being left 343 to
win. A 'disheartening' situation, reckoned Arlott, with the
match's outcome being 'settled as nearly as any game can
be settled before the end', not least because 'there is no
sign of rain'. Swanton essentially agreed about the state of
the match – 'unless the world is to turn completely upside
down, it has taken a decisive swing' – but he did add that,
even though an Australian win was apparently certain, 'this
has been such a remarkable, and in many ways such a magnificent, fight that against all reason, no doubt, I will not
believe that it is over until the scoreboard proclaims the
fact'. In the event, the scoreboard by the end of Tuesday was
proclaiming the fact that, largely thanks to Willie Watson
and Trevor Bailey, England had escaped with a draw. 'I
cannot remember when a crowd so revelled in defence
for defence's sake,' noted Swanton entirely happily, while
Arlott found in Watson's century 'a particular quality of
heroism which will remain a clear feeling in the recollec-
tion of everyone who saw it'. 'I have never seen a game,' he
added about the Test as a whole, 'more epically, more evenly
or more fluctuatingly fought out, nor one which so held the

attention and the imagination and the heroic vein.' Swanton broadly concurred ('the match proceeded on a plane of interest and level grappling that was sustained over almost the entire five days'), though in the interests of posterity and quality control he felt duty-bound to record that 'the level of cricket waxed and waned, sometimes below the height to be expected of a Test between England and Australia'.

The third Test at Old Trafford (with Hutton still captain) was a rain-soaked draw; the fourth at Headingley was controversial because of Bailey's bowling on the final afternoon: setting the field almost entirely on the on side, spearing the ball wide of the leg stump, and taking an age to bowl his overs (one of them timed at seven minutes), his unashamedly negative tactics (condoned by Hutton) brought Australia's promising run chase to a virtual halt. Lindsay Hassett, Australia's amiable captain, took a dim view, but not so the keepers of the flame, for once letting themselves down. Arlott merely pointed out that Bailey had 'bowled his defensive leg-theory – introduced to English cricket by Warwick Armstrong in the Test series of 1921', and left it at that. As for Swanton, there was no whisper of criticism in his match report, and a few days later he declared, 'I am not one of those who strongly censure England for their tactics on the last day'. He hardly needed to add that the series remained level and consequently that everything was still to play for at The Oval.

There, after three days of tense, taut cricket, England ended the Tuesday (the match had started on a Saturday) needing only 94 to win, with nine wickets in hand. 'The prospect of winning The Ashes after nineteen years,' confided Arlott to his journal, 'has been so distant that we have become like some small boy who has looked forward to a special treat for so long that he fears something will happen to stop it – or is himself sick with excitement so that he cannot enjoy it.' But the cup did not slip, and shortly before three o'clock Compton hit the winning runs. 'The crowd came over the ground like a wave, and stood closely jammed in front of the pavilion, calling for the players,' reported Arlott. 'Hutton and Hassett made speeches over the public address system and it was all over. The ground slowly emptied, not even leaving the usual pack of stragglers behind the pavilion, and the English side could look with happiness on the prospect of two days' rest – balm to the county cricketer in August.' The series, he went on after that typically humane thought, had been 'a wonderful rubber to watch': 'Unlike the Tests of the Bradman era, which travelled as certainly as trains to their clearly foreseen conclusion, these have been such that to take one's eyes off the game for a moment was to miss some vital and unexpected action. And now, for English watchers, it has ended on a champagne note.' Swanton assumed the even higher ground historically: 'It all took one back 27 years to the August evening when for the first time since the First War, Australia's colours were lowered in a Test rubber, and the crowd let themselves go as though a reproach had been wiped away. Then, as now, England's side was a blend of the ages, from the youthful Chapman and Larwood to the grizzled Rhodes and Strudwick ...'

He was careful to have words for the current captain: 'On Hutton has been the greatest strain. Anyone who has seen all five Tests, and who has realised how he has upheld the batting and appreciated the difficulties he has encountered in the field, three times with only four bowlers, almost always irked by the presence of a left-handed batsman and with several fieldsmen of limited mobility, will give him a high degree of praise for his efforts.' Was there perhaps a patronising tinge to this commendation? It is hard to be sure; but what was certain was national enthusiasm for the recovery of the Ashes, an enthusiasm rapidly translated into some 60,000 copies being sold of a compilation of Swanton's *Telegraph* reports, complete with prologue and epilogue by that Edwardian hero C. B. Fry. A few still remembered Fry's admiration in the 1930s for Hitler, though most were happy just to linger over this sweet taste of victory for the New Elizabethans.

———

In December 1953, four months after the Oval triumph, Hutton's England team flew to the West Indies, accompanied by Swanton. It was, he would point out in his tour book, the first time an MCC team had travelled abroad under a professional captain; the clear subtext was that Hutton's responsibilities involved more than leading the team on the field, that there was also an off-the-field diplomatic and disciplinary job to do. The captain's performance at the crease was in the event beyond reproach (677 runs in the series at an average of 96.71), but diplomacy and discipline demanded different skills – and those Hutton found agitating and distracting. Perhaps it was not so surprising. He was not a garrulous man; he was happy in his own company; he valued his sleep; and he did not drink. Instead, almost all his energies were focused on the cricket itself, and part of that steely determination was an instruction to his team that there was to be no fraternisation with the opposition, something that did not endear him to several of his colleagues. There was also the question – for Swanton a near-obsessive one – of England's manager for the tour. As it happened, it was Swanton who on MCC's behalf had sounded out Hutton about whom he wanted. The answer had been Billy Griffith, but in their wisdom the MCC committee had plumped instead for Leicestershire's Charles Palmer: a decent man, a good cricketer (who actually played in one of the Tests), but no disciplinarian; and during the tour, Swanton's disapproval of him became visceral.

As for the cricket, experienced professionals were soon complaining noisily about Hutton's defensive state of mind. In the second Test, for example, England took 150 overs to compile 181 runs in their first innings. Swanton was predictably critical, lamenting in the *Telegraph* after that match (with England already two down) that 'the futility of this exaggeratedly defensive mentality has been aired in these pages often enough'. 'There has been,' he claimed, 'a cohesion about the West Indies play that has not been faintly reflected in that of England', whom he accused of playing as if suffering from a collective depression. Nor, though Swanton was more circumspect about this, did it help the tourists' mood that umpiring decisions were consistently incorrect. Eventually, Hutton listened to his players, and agreed to become less cautious. That was in his power; imposing his authority was not, particularly in the case of a much younger Yorkshireman.

Fred Trueman, twenty-two at the start of the tour, was travelling abroad for the first time. Arlott in his subsequent biography described a young man who was 'feeling his oats, glorying in the violence of being a fast bowler, quick-tempered, and apt to make the wrong joke out of sheer excitement'. Having played with Hutton for four years, he naturally called him 'Len', but the rule on tour was that Hutton was addressed as 'skipper'. Trueman was irritated, and this was added to the list of his alleged misdemeanours. Reports of bad behaviour were attributed, almost automatically, to Trueman – guilty or not. Accused of ill-manners in a hotel lift by two expatriate ladies, Trueman and his buddy Tony Lock were hauled before the captain and the manager. 'It wasn't me,' said Fred; he was not believed; and the guilty parties (Denis Compton and Godfrey Evans apparently) did not own up. When a West Indian umpire complained that he had been called a 'black bastard' by a Yorkshire bowler, the damaging reflex response was that Trueman was that bowler, but in fact it was Johnny Wardle. Trueman believed with a measure of justification that he had become the team's scapegoat. Arlott's biography suggests that he smouldered, and over the following years some of his fury was worked off on apprehensive, unhelmeted batsmen.

Eventually, the skipper restored honour on the field, by inspiring victories in the third and fifth Tests, thereby squaring the series. But even Hutton was accused of racist ill-manners when, shattered after scoring a double-century at Sabina Park, he failed to acknowledge the congratulations of Jamaica's chief minister. Swanton judged that Hutton was not able to assert authority in the way amateur captains had taken for granted, though in his overall assessment of a fractious few months his deepest ire was reserved for Trueman: 'His need is control in all its aspects, on the field and off it,' Swanton wrote in his tour book, 'and I confess I would not be happy to see his name again in a touring team, irrespective of the number of wickets he may have got, unless I was convinced of a radical change of outlook.' *West Indian Adventure* was published in May 1954, and when some weeks later the team to visit Australia that winter was announced, the out-and-out fast bowler was Frank Tyson, not Fred Trueman. More broadly, the tour had been (in Swanton's later words) 'a diplomatic and sporting disaster of the first magnitude' – so souring relations that Swanton, who needed no excuse to travel the West Indies, was in due course encouraged to take a judiciously chosen team of his own, captained by Colin Cowdrey, to the Caribbean in 1955–6 to heal the breach, which to an extent it did. Cowdrey's subsequent thank-you letter to Swanton was a model of its kind: 'I would like to congratulate you most sincerely in putting an awful lot right, or, rather, making amends for an awful lot, in spite of the fact that they will never forgive MCC for 1953–54.'

Hutton would never recover from the burden he felt on his first overseas tour as captain, scoring only 306 runs in fifteen more Test innings. In his opinion, the experience shortened his career by 'perhaps two years'. He played in the first Test against Pakistan in 1954 before being afflicted by neuritis and taking a month off cricket. In his absence, his critics, led by Walter Robins, took the opportunity to press the claims of David Sheppard (soon to be ordained) to captain the team in Australia. Sheppard, skippering England in Hutton's absence, let it be known that he would be willing to take on the job, and once again it was a case of amateur versus professional for cricket's top position. At which point – having in his tour book described Hutton's captaincy as 'disappointing only to anyone who foolishly supposed that a shrewd technical Staff Officer could be turned overnight into a fiery, fearsome Battalion Commander' – Swanton offered his thoughts. 'There is no better fellow than the average modern cricketer,' he wrote in the *Telegraph* between the second and third Tests. 'But he does want looking after, and he will react for better or for worse according to how he is handled.' The decisive factor, in other words, was man management. There followed some sharp words on Hutton's captaincy: 'It is fair to say, that his own strong accent on defence has apparently repressed the younger English batsmen … As in batting, so in tactics, choosing the bolder of two courses does not come easily to his nature.' Sheppard, by contrast, he called 'a young cricketer of strong character and much determination to whom leadership comes naturally'. Swanton did not formally plump for either man, but it was obvious which he wanted. Yet in vain as it turned out, for a week later MCC – influenced possibly by Sheppard's double failure for the Gentlemen at Lord's, possibly also not wanting to look ungentlemanly in relation to the temporarily stricken Hutton – stuck with Pudsey's finest: unanimously according to Hutton's biographer, by one vote according to Arlott's information. 'The most probable outcome,' reflected Swanton next day, adding that he expected Hutton, with a good manager by his side, to 'do a worthy job' down under, perhaps even 'reach his peak as a captain'.

The tour itself would feature an experiment – four years after the Brisbane sticky-wicket melodrama when a hot sun dried a wet wicket and the ball spun so violently off the pitch that most batsmen were rendered incapable, and each side declared for grotesquely low scores. This time, an innovative adjustment to the game's laws would allow wickets to be covered (as opposed to being left open to the elements) during Tests. Both Arlott and Swanton feared that covered wickets would tend to emasculate the spin bowler's art. Swanton, who always studied changes in rules and regulations with care, had especially strong feelings. 'I abominate the idea on principle,' he declared. The proposal had come from his friend Bradman, who wrote to Swanton explaining that the motive was money, principally to reduce the time lost and thereby to gain the maximum financial return from Test cricket, after Brisbane's tropical storm in 1950 had cost £7,000 in lost gate money, a substantial sum then (when Australia still used pounds not dollars). Even so, Swanton opposed covered wickets because they would remove the element of chance that, he thought, was one of cricket's virtues. When MCC consulted England cricketers about the issue, they were more or less equally divided, for and against, and for the time being MCC could think of no reason to reject the proposal. Swanton insisted that artifice had triumphed over nature, but his influence did not quite stretch to making the regulations for international cricket. The 1954–5 experiment proved to be the thin end of the wedge: within a decade, covered wickets would become the norm, in England as well as Australia.

Hutton's defence of the Ashes involved Swanton's third trip to Australia, Arlott's first. Swanton liked Australians, who tended to take him at his own valuation of himself. His friends there were drawn from the Australian establishment; and if he could he would stay privately rather than in a hotel. When he eventually stepped down as the *Telegraph*'s cricket correspondent, his first 'retirement' book was *Swanton in Australia*, an account of his eight tours. It had a foreword by the former prime minister Sir Robert Menzies – and, to make sure the Australian bases were covered, an introduction by Sir Donald Bradman. By contrast, Arlott (who arrived shortly before the first Test, having been commissioned to write sketches of Karachi, Hong Kong, Tokyo and Seoul among other places) was troubled by Australians. 'Their speech, their laws, their cooking, their manners are not the same as ours,' he had written in *Concerning Cricket*. '"Australianism" means single-minded determination to win – to win within the laws but, if necessary, to the last limit within them ... It means that they have never lost a match – particularly a Test match – until the last run is scored or their last wicket has fallen.' This was the reason why Bradman offended Arlott's romanticism, which was defined by his belief that humanity and humour are greater than hundreds, that character transcends catches, and that basic truth is bigger than bowling. In its own way, though, Arlott's take on Australia was arguably no less snobbish than Swanton's. 'It is a dull country: the people much of a hearty sameness and none of the things that interest me available in more than driblets – virtually no second-hand bookshops, bare bones of worthwhile architecture, no pottery, no glass, no pictures,' he wrote to Rex Alston soon after Christmas. Nor did he relish, recalls John Woodcock, that two luminaries in the press box, Jack Fingleton and Bill O'Reilly, both very fine cricketers-turned-journalists, made him the butt of jokes about his passion for wine; while in the commentary box his style continued to meet with the disapproval of the ABC's Alan McGilvray, who insisted that the score be given three times in an eight-ball over, whereas Arlott as ever was more interested in mood and colour.

The series began with England's humiliating innings defeat in Brisbane, after Hutton had won the toss, chosen to field, and watched helplessly as his all-pace attack conceded over 600 runs. 'The balance of the side could cause trouble' had been Arlott's cautious pre-match assessment, while Swanton had merely pointed out that 'it is not, I suppose, necessarily wrong to attempt something that has virtually never been done before' – a reservation about the lack of spin that intensified once the match was under way, supplemented by Hutton's ill-fated decision (virtually against precedent at Brisbane) to put Australia in. Years later, Colin Cowdrey recalled an episode in the hotel foyer after the Test. The air-mail editions of the British papers had just arrived, with Swanton's criticism making for 'particularly strong reading'; and just as some of the English players were discussing it, 'the two men of the moment walked in':

Hutton came in at one door and Swanton, with the dynamite edition of the *Telegraph* neatly folded under his arm, entered by another. One of the senior England players chose this moment to call out: 'Oh, by the way, Len, have you seen what the *Telegraph* said?' The declaration of World War Three could have hardly had a more dramatic effect. No one moved and the silence was total until Hutton eventually said, 'No, I haven't.' Slowly he walked across the foyer and removed the newspaper from under Swanton's arm. Even more slowly he unfolded it and turned the pages until he found what he was looking for. He absorbed what he was reading in his own good time, then re-folded the paper and handed it back. 'Yes,' he said with a twinkle. 'Yes, I've seen the *Telegraph*.' The general opinion was that he had been consulting his share prices in the stock-market columns ...

The pre-Christmas Sydney Test saw a dramatic reversal of fortunes, with England winning by 38 runs and Swanton praising the selectors for 'putting their faith in two young men [Tyson and Cowdrey], neither of whom had great records and neither of whom would have been included by popular choice'. Even so, he was still unhappy. 'The party, as it seems to me,' he complained soon afterwards, 'badly needs a regular system of supervised cricket training which would include well-organised nets, fielding practice and, yes, in certain cases, physical training' – all this as opposed to the existing 'sometimes haphazard approach to practice'. 'Swanton is very pompous and opinionated,' the England manager, Geoffrey Howard, had written to his wife earlier in the tour, adding that 'he is also pretty often right'; but almost certainly, from his perspective, this was an opinion too far.

The drama of the legendary Melbourne Test, beginning on New Year's Eve, started in Hutton's hotel room on the first morning, as the captain lay in his bed, saying that he did not think he could play. As word got out, Arlott that morning noted that 'a cold, fibrositis and general malaise' was the problem. In the event, a local doctor (summoned by Howard) examined Hutton and briskly advised him to get up, have a shower and breakfast, and get down to the ground and play. He arrived there in time to tell Alec Bedser – recovered from the shingles that had kept him out of the Sydney Test, and raring to go on his favourite Australian wicket – that he was not in the team, even after the two men had inspected the wicket together. 'He has been too great a cricketer to be treated in this way,' commented Arlott, though over the next few days it would be England's younger bowlers, Frank Tyson and Brian Statham, who powered the team to victory by 128 runs. 'It is all over, after as exciting and moving a day's cricket as I have ever seen in my life,' Arlott wrote at lunchtime on the fifth day after Australia had collapsed to the speedster now instantly known as 'Typhoon Tyson'. 'Did I say day?' added Arlott. 'It was a mere eighty minutes.'

Four weeks later, after England had won the fourth Test at Adelaide by five wickets and retained the Ashes, Arlott compared the final day's play to 'the plot of a novel', representing 'the fall of power on one side, the assumption of dominance on the other'. 'England,' he added, 'have lost their inferiority complex bred by Australia's immense post-war power. They start any match now in the belief that they will win. In fact they are not a great side but Hutton has employed all their assets shrewdly.' Swanton, just about ungrudgingly, also praised the captain: 'To him must go much credit for imbuing into all his Test XI the unwavering determination which has been the basis of his own play. In the long run it is this which counts for most in battles against Australia on the cricket field.' Even so, he continued to be in the ear of the England manager. 'Jim Swanton is after Len again,' Howard wrote home near the end of the fifth Test in Sydney (a rain-affected draw). 'He never misses a chance to take a dig at him! It's all so silly: the Lord Protector of English Cricket. He has not made a great deal of progress out here, and people are beginning to tire a bit of his stuff, I think.'

Regaining and now retaining the Ashes: it had been a signal achievement by England's first professional captain. Back at Lord's, MCC decided to alter the terms of honorary membership in order to be able to award it to a professional who was still playing; and in due course, the club's secretary (Ronnie Aird) was at the dockside at Tilbury to present Hutton with his member's pass and bacon-and-egg tie. Hutton himself missed most of the 1955 season because of lumbago and announced his retirement early in 1956. Swanton in the *Telegraph* duly paid tribute to his 'tactical shrewdness' and his 'conscientiousness'; but he also noted how Hutton had captained his country 'with a quiet dignity that would have befitted any and all of his predecessors'. That indispensable blessing given, the way was now clear for the Yorkshireman's richly deserved knighthood, which followed a few months later.

'The Englishman's Cricket', published in the *Spectator* in July 1951 (and later reprinted as 'The Englishman's Game' in his 1952 collection *The Echoing Green*), was Arlott's contribution to the Festival of Britain. Essentially a paean to the depth and intimacy of cricket's English roots, it took aim at 'those who argue that the true aim of our cricket should be to win Test Matches against Australia', much though Arlott himself was longing for what at the time still appeared a distant hope:

Only the argument to which Hitler subscribed, namely, that victory in a sporting event proved some superiority in the nation of the winner, could claim the winning of Tests as the end rather than a single aspect of the game. The blindness of this argument is the failure to recognise that the most important attribute of cricket is the happiness it produces in those who subscribe to it – whose enjoyment is often in reverse proportion to their skill. Two hundred men in England play what is called 'first-class' cricket, but some hundreds of thousands are cricketers. The happiness of the 'rabbit', rather than the success of our Test team, is the touchstone of English cricket …

'The grandstands and goalposts of a football-ground stand out rawly in the landscape,' he asserted, 'but the cricket-ground belongs there as naturally as a cornfield.' Arlott's concluding passage, predictably heartfelt, included a dig at what one might call cricket's sanctimonious 'Lord Harris' tradition, a tradition that among contemporary cricket writers Swanton was especially prone to invoke:

There is beauty in the pattern and rhythms of white-flannelled players against the green grass background. The game has produced art, minor but unmistakable. Thus the phrase 'not cricket' means, in fact, something less quixotic than some moralisers have suggested and, simultaneously, something far greater than their use of the term indicates. That is 'not cricket' which denies the qualities of a game which is reasonable, skilful, carried out with the participants' full industry and effort, frequently epic, aesthetically pleasing, and native to the English soil and people.

Tellingly, Arlott in August 1953, even as England were recovering the Ashes at The Oval, came out on the radio against televising Test cricket. 'There must have been over this last Test match hundreds of little boys watching it on television,' he declared in a Home Service discussion, 'when as far as cricket and its future are concerned, they'd have been much better off playing outside with a bat and ball in the fields.' While two years later, previewing for the *Spectator* the new cricket season, he wrote warmly of how 'in the club game, from "Conference" to rustic level', there would as ever 'be found those deep and varied joys from which cricket grew, and which will outlive Test matches as surely as they are absent from them'.

What about the cricket that was neither Test nor club? Previewing the 1954 season, Arlott in a passage on county cricket evoked – indeed, celebrated – what in essence had seemingly become a semi-private, hermetic ritual:

> Before the small and drowsy crowds of a third day, many a relatively unimportant match will go down quietly to a draw … Then average county players will make sure of their thousand runs for the season – that traditional insurance of another contract – against bowling lacking the malice to deny them that security. It would be a harsh critic who would take away those dusty afternoons when the sound of a child's piano practice floats out of a nearby window to the ears of an umpire feeling the tiredness in his feet and regular bowlers strolling unhurried in the outfield against tomorrow's labours. It is, you will appreciate, a domestic matter; one which spectators may attend if they understand, or ignore if they do not.

Swanton saw things very differently. That same month, May 1954, he complained bitterly about how 'county cricket, speaking generally, has got into a pawky, dreary, defensive groove'; and how 'in most counties, the side is inclined to drift amiably along, disclosing only a proportion of its true possibilities'. Swanton's prescription was, of course, more of the right sort of amateur captains ('If we could only find a few Fenders, Robinses and Sellerses most of the weaknesses of modern first-class play would vanish very quickly'). Yet in terms of recognising that there was a problem, the contrast with Arlott's deep-dyed conservatism – in this area of life at least – was instructive.

Viewed in retrospect, county cricket by the mid-1950s was clearly displaying (even as the Test team was in its pomp) early symptoms of a nervous crisis. In August 1956, the think tank Political and Economic Planning (PEP) published a report, *The Cricket Industry*, declaring that 'in crudely economic terms, county cricket is fighting a losing battle against shortage of capital, income, and the highly skilled labour the game requires'. Although the diagnosis was sound in parts, PEP's solution was unrealistic, even laughable: that since the number of people free to watch cricket was falling, the answer was to play cricket only at weekends. Nevertheless, the very fact of the report did carry a warning that cricket was susceptible to commercial norms that could not be ignored just because it was a sport – and, that autumn, MCC set up a Special Committee under Harry Altham's chairmanship to consider the future welfare of first-class cricket. 'The MCC have for some time past been increasingly concerned with the decline in the gates of County Matches and with the tempo at which the game is played,' asserted the opening sentence of its report in February 1957. The decline by the mid-1950s in the appeal of the county championship was indeed striking: whereas between 1948 and 1951 the annual average total attendance was 1.96 million, between 1952 and 1955 it had fallen to 1.65 million, and in 1956 (admittedly a wet summer) only 1.1 million watched county matches. Arlott at this point does not seem to have written on the issue, but even he might have conceded that something needed to be done.

Filing his *Telegraph* piece from Johannesburg, Swanton broadly welcomed the report – whose key recommendations included an overs-limit to first innings of county matches and restrictions of the number of leg-side fielders – but argued that the real underlying problem of present-day English cricket was 'the batsman's mental attitude'. He quoted approvingly Gubby Allen's recent charges that 'batting is now at its lowest standard of all time' and that 'batsmen have the ability but lack the will to attack'. Swanton himself now graphically elaborated about 'the method today', with 'left-hands wrapped so far round the handle as almost to risk a broken wrist, right-hands down by the shoulder of the blade, and bodies slewed round towards the bowler, so square-on that the cover drive is virtually impossible'. And: 'There is a wide falling away from the fundamental mechanics of batsmanship which extends, great player though he is, even as far as P. B. H. May. So, it is no use expecting too much too quickly.' One area in which he criticised Altham and his colleagues was for failing to tackle 'the undue proportion of the summer given over to Test Matches', spreading their 'unwieldy shadow' over twenty-five days of each home season. 'Only the visits of Australia, South Africa and West Indies merit such an interference with the domestic programme,' he wrote. 'If the other three countries were given three five-day Tests, the fixture lists would preserve a saner balance at least two years in every five.' Yet, if that was regrettable, Swanton was wholeheartedly enthusiastic about the report's most eye-catching recommendation. 'Hurrah! for the blessing given to a knock-out competition among the counties, to be run side by side with the County Championship. This is to be a two-day hustle [but one-day unless weather intervened] with a maximum 54 overs per innings, and the only sad thing is that it apparently cannot be arranged until 1959.'

A month later, ahead of the Advisory County Cricket Committee's (ACCC's) two-day spring meeting to consider the report, a major piece by Swanton sought to spur them on. 'The people really in the dock are the captains and the county committees behind them who countenance dreary play by the cricketers on their staffs,' he insisted, whereas 'it is the MCC who, with their eyes on the rapidly dropping attendance figures, are attempting to intervene on behalf of the suffering spectator'. What about the body of professional cricketers as a whole? Swanton gave them short shrift:

> The players, judging from published remarks, are 'agin' the proposals generally, but with due respect to them I hardly feel that the views of most of them need to be given decisive weight. In fact, open-minded though they may be in other respects, county cricketers in the past have been almost always conservative as regards changes in the laws or the conduct of the game. They make their living playing in a certain way and they are understandably dubious at first about altering their technique and perhaps having to learn afresh.

He ended by asserting that 'without wishing to see the game degenerate into a slogging-match, it is the skills and graces of batsmanship, more than anything else, that the average spectator comes to see'.

In the event, the ACCC did not accept the overs-limit proposal ('too much for the counties to swallow,' noted Swanton), but did bite on Middlesex's idea of the number of points for a first-innings lead to be regulated by the speed of scoring; and it did agree to adopt various other recommendations, including standardised 75-yard boundaries plus increased powers for umpires to reduce time-wasting, in addition to a maximum of five on-side fielders (with a maximum of two behind the wicket). All in all, Swanton expected 'a wide degree of satisfaction' from the cricket world. The issue of the knockout competition was, however, deferred until the ACCC's autumn meeting – at which point, to Swanton's dismay, it was rejected. 'This has been "shelved" because of the alleged difficulties of arranging fixtures and of allocating grounds,' he reported. 'Frankly, I have little doubt the difficulties, which there undoubtedly are, could soon be resolved if suddenly the counties were deprived of their income of around £5,000 a year from Test sources and also of the much larger sums passed over to many of them by supporters' clubs obtaining their revenue from football pools.' In short: 'At the present time, "gates" to many of them are of minor importance'.

By this time, November 1957, MCC had another ad hoc committee at work on a further thorny, and in this case increasingly embarrassing, question – namely, the matter of amateur status in a changing social and economic environment, whereby ever fewer high-class cricketers from public-school backgrounds could afford to play genuinely as amateurs, or even semi-genuinely as, for example, salaried club secretaries. Even Swanton, diehard defender though he was of the amateurs and their contribution to the game, had accepted a few months earlier that 'there is a limit beyond which, if it were passed, the matter must sink into pure hypocrisy'. The Special Sub-Committee was chaired by the cricket-loving Duke of Norfolk; and Charles Williams in *Gentlemen & Players*, his valuable archivally based account of the death of amateurism in cricket, tracks its difficult discussions, culminating in a report in February 1958 that rejected 'any solution of the problem on the lines of abolishing the distinction between Amateur and Professional', on the grounds that 'the distinctive status of the amateur cricketer is not obsolete, is of great value to the game and should be preserved'. There followed all sorts of convoluted suggestions about how those amateurs could be financially enabled to stay in the game, including going on overseas tours, while yet retaining their status. 'The Shamateurs' Charter' was how one paper, the *Daily Express*, labelled the report, but Swanton for the moment stayed his hand. However, a month later, when the ACCC essentially accepted it, he offered a realistic, informed perspective:

The players and administrators of other games may be unable to suppress some amusement at the official definition of a cricket amateur, while to a cynic the whole business, of course, is meat and drink. The fact is that MCC were put in an unenviable position by the pressure, exerted chiefly by a few leading amateurs, to revise and clarify the status of the amateur. Most people close to

abolition of the amateur/pro distinction. Put another way, his political instincts, whether applied to the cricketing or the wider world, remained liberal rather than egalitarian, albeit with a healthy whiff of dislike of the establishment.

As it happened, Arlott's beloved Hampshire had from 1958 a new amateur captain in the person of Colin Ingleby-Mackenzie. An Old Etonian; aged twenty-four; a dasher on and off the field – he might have seemed altogether too 'Tallis' for Arlott's taste, but in fact proved an inspired choice. Also as it happened, Arlott had decided to keep a journal for that season that would be less Test-oriented than his previous journals (which themselves had lapsed in recent years). It was a happy formula, consciously geared to that whole world of cricket-minded men who all summer never see a ball bowled in a first-class match, but follow the game through the media and are happy to read about it during the winter. This first of what became a series of four journals (1958–61) did cover England's dull, one-sided series against New Zealand, but increasingly became preoccupied with Hampshire's stirring progress in the county championship.

By Bank Holiday Monday in August (still at the start of the month), he was at Canterbury for festival week, to watch with a packed crowd Kent recover from a poor first-innings score. At the start of the final day, Kent were 87 adrift with three wickets down; and at the end of it Arlott reported that his mouth was 'still dry from the excitements of this afternoon'. Kent had batted on stubbornly, and Hampshire were left 80 to win in 100 minutes. Wickets tumbled, and with barely half an hour to go Hampshire were 48 for 6 – at which point his old friend Leo Harrison scored 17 not out in an heroic partnership with Mike Barnard to see them home. 'Now Hampshire are 22 points ahead of Surrey in the table,' recorded Arlott, 'but I doubt they have yet recovered their breath.' A week and a half later he was at Clacton-on-Sea, where a sporting declaration by Essex's Doug Insole left Hampshire 146 to win at 80 runs an hour. Seven wickets fell before Harrison, coming in with 29 to win in twenty-two minutes, rescued his team again. Hampshire remained top; but by the time Arlott was in Bournemouth at the end of the month for the Yorkshire match, Hampshire's race for the championship had exhausted them. Surrey – in search of their seventh successive championship – had seized their chance; and by the third day of the drawn Yorkshire game, the last remote possibility that Hampshire could, at best, tie with Surrey had disappeared. Hampshire were in second place, but they had never done better.

Afterwards, Arlott joined four old sweats (including Henry Horton and Derek Shackleton as well as Harrison), plus Ingleby-Mackenzie, as they drank 'two solemn bottles of champagne to a great season', with 'the relieved footnote that the strain is over for at least another eight months'. He was not just among friends; then and there – just like at Worcester in 1938, only better – he was one of them.

———

Whether commentating on Test matches (whatever his mixed feelings about Test cricket) or county matches (mainly those played in southern and western counties), Arlott through the 1950s consolidated his reputation as radio's main man. Admittedly Somerset's Bertie Buse 'objected' (according to David Foot) to Arlott 'likening his quaint physical movements on the field to a butler dispensing the drinks', while Swanton told Rayvern Allen that Arlott's commentary was 'not everyone's' (i.e. among Swanton's acquaintance-ship) 'cup of tea'; but in terms of the broad listenership they were the exceptions. 'He made many converts, especially among women,' Swanton fairly added; and in his autobiography he wrote of how Arlott as an established commentator 'managed to weave together as much information about the progress of the game as the average listener wanted along with the fruits of his observation on players, spectators and the scene generally, all laced with humour and put across in an intimate, confidential way and a rich Hampshire accent'. 'The voice,' he added, 'evoked the village green and rustic England and leisurely days in the sun.' So indeed it did, in most listeners' ears – and it was hardly an exaggeration when in 1958 the publisher's blurb to that year's *Cricket Journal* by this incipient national treasure began with the confident statement that 'the familiar voice of John Arlott, talking about cricket with a rich Hampshire burr, has become as much part of summer as the smell of trodden grass and the taste of strawberries and cream'.

It was in fact the year before, at Edgbaston for England's first Test against the West Indies, that ball-by-ball commentary – covering the whole of each day's play – began on BBC radio. The commentators were Arlott, Alston and Kenneth Ablack, with summaries by Swanton and Gerry Gomez. Later in the series, at Headingley, Arlott was commentating when Surrey's fast bowler Peter Loader took a famous hat-trick – famous in part because of Arlott's virtuoso description. With the innings already 'collapsing about his ears' at 142 for 7, the West Indies captain John Goddard then found his off stump 'leaning drunkenly back'; next ball, Ramadhin ('swinging') skied to square leg; and for the third it was 'the luckless Gilchrist to face Loader', with 'again those seven close fieldsmen grouped round the bat': 'And Loader from the pavilion end comes in, bowls to him and he's bowled him all over the place, it's a hat-trick and Loader is jumping about like a monkey on a stick. And everyone's coming up, Fred Trueman, bless him, flung both arms round Loader ...'

Although Swanton's close-of-play summaries would become legendary, above all for the magisterial tone and unwavering confidence of their judgements, his main broad-casting preoccupation during the 1950s was television. Its coverage was as yet far from ball-by-ball – at Edgbaston in 1957 it showed most days only about an hour and a half's play, with intruders on the Thursday including *Rag, Tag and Bobtail* as well as *Champion the Wonder Horse* – but Swanton at this stage seems to have preferred TV to radio and, in typically unyielding correspondence with the BBC in 1952, made much of the fact that since post-war TV coverage of home Tests had begun in 1948 (originally covering just the two London Tests) he had missed only one. In 1955 the producer Antony Craxton discussed with Peter Dimmock (Head of Television Outside Broadcasts) the question of commentary allocation for the following summer's Ashes series. 'Swanton annoys people by his pomposity,' observed Craxton, though acknowledged that he had a greater 'knowledge of the game' than either Brian Johnston (by a long way) or Peter West (by a smaller margin). Craxton added that 'he considers he is indispens-able, and I am afraid no amount of talking will dissuade him from this view'. 'I agree with all you say about Swanton,' replied Dimmock, 'but the fact remains that he is popular' – and accordingly, he kept his allocation of three Tests.

Swanton and Arlott remained through the decade prolific book writers, though not invariably the recipients of undiluted praise. 'Mr Swanton argues and describes sensibly and eloquently; he knows the game and loves it,' reflected Neville Cardus in his *Spectator* review of *Cricket and the Clock*, a 1952 selection of his post-war journalism. 'But we are still waiting for the book that is in him, needing only the leisure and concentration essential to good and organised writing.' A year later, in the same magazine, the sports-loving Labour politician J. P. W. ('Curly') Mallalieu evaluated six rapidly produced books on the 1953 Ashes series, including Swanton's and Arlott's. 'None of them,' he regretted, 'shows either the freshness or the maturity of Cardus's daily journalism and none of them has Cardus's flair for transmitting the feel of the game and its players.' Even so, 'just occasionally John Arlott gets in those touches which make his cricket broadcasts such a delight', while Swanton's account 'provides easily the most knowledgeable commentary'. Reviewing for the *Observer*, Alan Ross praised Arlott's account for conveying 'the real excitement of the summer in vivid, impressionistic manner', but noted that 'for him, the writing is far too clumsy and occasionally inaccurate'. Ross, future editor of the *London Magazine*, was renowned for his unsparing critical standards, and in 1957 he declared of Arlott's cricket writing that 'besides some indifferent books, he has written at least three very good ones' – sadly not naming which they were (though presumably one was *Concerning Cricket*).

That same year, the *TLS*'s review of a clutch of new cricket books, including Ross's and Swanton's respective accounts of the recent MCC tour of South Africa, took the high ground: 'Cricket books seem to have sorted themselves out today into three categories. Class I, the most select, consists only of Mr Neville Cardus and Mr Alan Ross. Class II, of which the head boy is Mr E. W. Swanton, is composed of good, sound writers about the game. Class III contains the books attributed to famous cricketers but not always written by them.' The reviewer (anonymous, as usual before 1974, but in fact the well-known if now forgotten literary critic and broadcaster Eric Gillett) also commended Swanton's book as 'admirably direct and forthright'; but at the same time in the *Spectator*, the Trollope expert A. O. J. Cockshut was altogether more mixed. After praising Swanton's 'insight into strategy, his instinct for picking out the real tendency of a day's play from a mass of phenomena, his understanding of the gap, great or small, between what a player is attempting and what he achieves', he turned to what he saw as the deeply unfortunate matter of Swanton's 'prejudices': specifically, 'that Hobbs and the old players would have murdered modern bowling, that the interest of cricket depends on the rate of scoring, and that the player with the best "style" may be better than the player whom the Test match averages place at the top'. Perhaps he exaggerated slightly. Yet for better or worse, the fact essentially was that for each of those 'prejudices' Swanton would have gone to the stake.

The 1950s were Arlott's decade of fame and diversification, especially after he had left the BBC's salaried and pensioned employment in 1953 (following three years as General Instructor for staff training). His rising income was reflected in a move from Crouch End to the next-door but more fashionable Highgate. During this decade, he rarely stopped attesting, however much he might have professed to wish otherwise, to the implacability of Kipling's unforgiving minute. He was opening fetes, giving after-dinner speeches, fronting advertisements ('You're bound to like St Bruno', as he held a seemingly trusty pipe), even appearing on *Desert Island Discs* ('The prospect delights me: no telephones, no deadlines, no posts, no bills, no hurry', with the eight records largely chosen by his wife and 'the biggest second-hand bookshop in the world' as his luxury item). He also for several years wrote for the *Evening News*, particularly about wine, before crossing the Street to the more Liberal-minded *News Chronicle* as a columnist and feature writer. These were also the years in which he began to cover football almost as much as he did cricket. 'He is in a fair way to becoming a football Surtees,' declared Dingle Foot (brother of Michael) about his 1952 collection *Concerning Soccer*, published at a time when virtually no serious writer wrote seriously about football, certainly in book form. Six years later, having started reporting on matches for the *Manchester Guardian* (originally as 'Silchester', a nod to where his paternal grandfather had come from), it was only because at the last moment he had been gazumped by 'Donny' Davies, the paper's chief football correspondent, that he was not on board Manchester United's ill-fated plane at Munich.

Year in and year out, however, it was probably Arlott's regular appearances on *Any Questions?*, once his unofficial banishment had ended, that fuelled his greatest celebrity. Although seldom attaining the levels of outrageousness associated on other programmes with his friend Gilbert Harding, he equally seldom minced words. In 1953, with a government-inspired witch-hunt against practising homo-sexuals well under way, he stoutly declared that 'if a person is not sexually normal, that is not cured by punishment or the law, or by home influence, it's solely a question of the way the person is, and I don't believe that by detection, punishment, religion, or spiritual guidance, you will change a person's basic fabric ...' Five years later, just after the birth of CND, he made plain his support. 'So long as atomic weapons are competitive, everybody is going to want them,' he told the audience at Bournemouth Town Hall. 'I reckon in the end everybody will get them and sooner or later if that happens, one hot-headed maniac will drop one and that will be the end.'

Twice in the 1950s – the general elections of 1955 and 1959 – Arlott stood as Liberal candidate for Epping. He was no great shakes at canvassing and barely tried, but was his usual eloquent self at meetings and generally worked hard. 'You found,' he recalled, 'that you were going past bookshops, antique shops and good restaurants without giving them a thought'; and he promised to drop his cricket and serve his constituents full-time should the improbable – and on his part unwanted – happen. In the event, in these years before the Liberal revival of the 1960s and beyond, he fared respectably enough, saving his deposit both times and in 1959 increasing his personal vote. The diaries of the Liberal grandee Lady Violet Bonham Carter (daughter of a Liberal PM, Asquith, and also an *Any Questions?* regular) record a party post-mortem after the 1955 election revealing Arlott in an uncommonly intimate and unflattering light. 'Meandering on about appealing to "moral consciousness" etc,' she noted about his contribution to the discussion. 'He had obviously had too much to drink & interrupted everybody else throughout the evening.' Proceedings deteriorated, with a fellow Liberal bawling at him, 'Oh, John Arlott, for God's sake stop talking. J. Arlott you are the bloodiest bore I ever listened to in my life. I heard the story you are telling now 25 years ago in Australia.' There might well have been an element of snobbishness in her diary entry, but it is still a glimpse of someone who had perhaps become overused to the sound of his own voice and less inclined to listen to that of others.

An unvanquishable sense of self-importance was, of course, a Swanton speciality – certainly in the eyes of many who encountered him. Probably at its worst in the 1950s, it was often allied, unless appearances deceived, to an almost absurd pomposity. 'Does the shoddy dress of many of the undergraduate spectators, the shedding by the cricketers of part of their historic uniform [a reference to Cambridge caps and Oxford sweaters], derive from the same basic cause, a weakened sense of personal dignity and good manners?' he asked after the Varsity match in July 1955. 'Are the young gentlemen of 1955, outwardly so polite to their seniors, intentionally cocking a snook at the past?' That same month, the *Radio Times* printed a memorable letter from a Lancashire viewer. 'The end of an exciting day during the Test match, had delayed my getting baby to bed,' related Mrs E. Byron of Silverdale. 'She was expressing her disapproval of being bathed, as I listened to E. W. Swanton giving his summary of the day's play. Imagine my surprise when he stopped and, looking straight at baby, said: "Will you be quiet there, at the front?" I think she was as surprised as I was, she looked at the screen and suddenly stopped crying.' Many years having such a good time that he had never contemplated marriage; and that after the war he had not had any money and, besides, had been too busy with his career. At which point, he told Attallah, 'the greatest bit of luck in my life was meeting Ann, who became my wife'. This was Ann de Montmorency, daughter of an Eton housemaster who had been a high-class amateur golfer. Ann was a good golfer, too, and also an accomplished pianist who – according to Swanton's subsequent boast – had played duets with Noël Coward and Don Bradman. In December 1957, she attended a Golf Ball, not long after the death of her businessman husband; as she was leaving, Swanton, who had not spoken to her, peremptorily ordered her to stay behind. The masterful approach worked: a month later they were engaged, and a month after that, on Swanton's fifty-first birthday, they married. It was a convenient marriage, on both sides, but it was far from a marriage of convenience. 'I am astonished at my own peace of mind, my supreme happiness, my complete contentment and my desolation when we are parted,' she wrote to him in the summer of 1958, by which time they were making a home together in a distinguished old house in Sandwich, one of the Cinque Ports. In her love letter, she went on to itemise what she had done in return: not just 'created a new hairstyle for you, usurped your telephone, wasted your time in bed till 10 am', but also 'made you a little less prim, less embarrassed at talking of matters which have hitherto been considered shocking, resulting in a more human, lighthearted, and to me, perfect man'. He, for his part, was innocently proud of her, perhaps not least because she, as it turned out, was a bit snobbish, too. Friends, who had been astonished by the news of their marriage, would for May's benefit his thoughts on the coming tour of South Africa. These included pushing hard for John Warr to go along as vice-captain, even if he was unlikely to play in the Tests. 'Well, I've imposed rather a lot,' he admitted near the end, and it is hard to better Rayvern Allen's comment that 'behind it all, one can see an ambition that was secretly rampant, though perhaps one should omit the adverb'.

In the Ashes series itself, Swanton took stock after the second Test at Lord's had put Australia one up: 'Nothing that has happened shakes the view that there is little between the two sides, even if the uplift which the victory has given to a party hitherto dogged by much ill-luck must make Australia more formidable from now on.' Not quite so. Cyril Washbrook, the forty-one-year-old England selector chosen by his colleagues to strengthen the batting, scored 98 in the third Test at Headingley, while May (having won the toss) got a hundred. Having been well behaved for England, on the second afternoon the wicket immediately favoured the spin of Jim Laker and Tony Lock, prompting Swanton (after the visitors had closed on 81 for 6) to write about 'the dreadful apprehensions which assail the whole string of Australian cricketers once the ball is turning'. He emphasised the ill luck of the Australians 'to find the ball doing so much so soon'. 'The preparation of wickets is an intricate business,' he added, 'wherein the behaviour of the weather plays an unpredictable part. The storms of last weekend in this case seem to have been the determining factor.' The Australians naturally suspected that the groundsman might have had something to do with it, too, by preparing a wicket that would be helpful to Laker and Lock. Between them they took 18 wickets, as England, further helped by rain over the weekend, ran out easy winners. Arlott did not write a book of the series, but in his autobiography recalled that 'pleasing as it may have been for Englishmen, it was, to the unbiased, an unsatisfactory match, not only because so many of the Australian batsmen were out of their element on a wet English pitch, but also because so few of them had the ability to bowl effectively on it'.

The historic fourth Test at Old Trafford followed a somewhat similar pattern. May won the toss, and England made 459, at the time their second-highest score against Australia since the war. On the second day Australia were all out in 40.4 overs for 84 (having been 48 for 0), with Laker taking 9 for 37. Swanton used strong language to describe the day's play: it was 'grotesque'. Two days of rain could not save Australia, with Laker (10 for 53) running through their batting again on the Tuesday and finishing the match with 19 wickets – still, more than sixty years later, an unequalled feat in Test cricket. 'It was,' judged Arlott, 'a peak performance in helpful conditions by a very great bowler; probably the greatest off-spinner who ever lived.' But what about the pitch? At the end of the second day, Swanton reported that it had been 'arid and inclined to be dusty' from virtually the very start of the match; and that on the Friday, when Laker and Lock struck bare patches, 'a little puff of dust came up and the ball turned and occasionally lifted'. He noted also that there had been no official complaint from the Australians, but that 'since they are not deaf mutes, they have conveyed what they feel, that the wicket has not given them a fair deal'. And he observed about their belief that they had been 'ill-used': 'No fair-minded, reasonably impartial person can think otherwise.' During the ensuing stretch of two days, when a great storm reduced play to a couple of hours, Swanton delved into the past. 'I have now reported, I think, 112 Test matches, at home and abroad. Only twice in England, and never abroad, can I recall Tests in which the surface of the wicket had so disintegrated on the second day.' He added that the fact that Australia had batted poorly was not relevant to the issue of the wicket; and, though taking pains to insist that in neither this nor the previous Test had there been any conspiracy involved, he did call for an inquiry into pitch preparation. Sixteen years later, writing his autobiography, his retrospective pleasure remained strictly qualified: 'It mars the picture, even at such long range, that the pitches at Headingley and Old Trafford were poorly prepared.'

The Ashes retained, England duly wintered in South Africa. It proved a competitive series – 2–2 – but as spectacles the Tests failed to rise to the occasion. 'That visit was the only one of all the many [tours] I've made abroad that I failed to enjoy,' recalled Swanton in 1972. The wickets were poor and the cricket was painfully slow, which always offended him. The third day of the fifth Test, when South Africa scored only 122 runs in more than five and a half hours, was, recorded *Wisden* at the time, 'the slowest in Test history'. Worse, there was uncommon bad blood between Swanton and the England team. Hankering after Warr, he had only partially backed the selection of Doug Insole as vice-captain; and he was highly uncomplimentary about Insole's captaincy when before the first Test he stood in for May in a game in Pretoria, and also accused some of the English players of using bad language. Lord's took offence at Swanton's criticism, which MCC's assistant secretary,

Billy Griffith, described as 'virulent' in a regretful letter to Swanton. 'I am sure you have your reasons for doing this,' continued Griffith, 'but it seemed as one who is a pretty close student of the great man that this was not your normal form.' In South Africa itself, Swanton's unpopularity in the England camp was increased, as the series proceeded, by his tactless statement that anyone of intelligence in the batting line-up would long before have altered their method. 'Peter May and Colin Cowdrey and many of the rest decided that they didn't want anything to do with Jim,' recalled Insole. 'The result of it was that Jim, who always liked to get the views of the captain or vice-captain before the game – like how was the wicket going to play, or what sort of side they were going to pick – was unable to do so. That effort on his part was laudable really, but he was always lurking around shortly after the toss. Of course now he was cut off – a bit draconian really.'

Nevertheless, Swanton's principal memory of the tour did not actively involve cricket. He finished *Report from South Africa*, his customary tour book, with various reflections. He regretted that his contacts with 'the natives' had been very restricted, but they confirmed what he had learned in the West Indies: 'Whatever his faults, it seems to me the average African native has his full share of two virtues which condone much else in life. One is a fund of fun and humour, the other a natural sense of good manners.' The tone may have been patronising, but entirely tough-minded was a passage in which he recorded his 'frequent feelings of utter bewilderment at the Nationalist treatment of the dark population, whether African, Indian, or Coloured': 'Apart from moral considerations, how anyone can suppose that a persistent policy of suppression and the denial of basic rights to the labour force of a country can end in anything short of a most dangerous crisis in the long run baffles understanding.'

England disposed of the West Indies in 1957 (3–0), and New Zealand similarly in 1958 (4–0), the main interest in the latter series being a spontaneous Twenty20 after the Lord's Test had ended mid-afternoon ('a curious hybrid because the players seemed to have no common attitude towards it,' noted Arlott). Now the English cricketing world looked forward keenly to a resumption of the Ashes battle and England's well-fancied chance to make it four in a row. The touring party under May was notable for two omissions. One was Cambridge University's captain and star attacking batsman, Ted Dexter, a decision condemned by Swanton as 'disappointingly stupid' (though he did fly out mid-tour as a replacement). The other was Yorkshire's highly popular Johnny Wardle, who on recent overseas tours had been England's most successful spin bowler. After very visibly falling out with his county captain (the inexperienced amateur Ronnie Burnet), and then publicly criticising both him and the Yorkshire committee, his invitation was withdrawn by MCC on the grounds that 'the welfare of cricket as a whole in terms of loyalty and behaviour must override all other considerations'. Arlott's disappointed, rather jaded reaction was that 'the man who speaks – or publishes – his mind, in any walk of life, must expect to take the consequences'; whereas Swanton, foursquare behind the authorities, called on 'the man in the street' to 'recognise' that MCC had 'put their foot down with all possible firmness, and said in effect that the old standards of sportsmanship and good manners must be preserved, insofar as they have it in their power to preserve them'. As for the prospective series itself, Swanton defied the conventional wisdom of the English press, asserting in September 1958 that 'if pressed for a view I would say that the proper odds at this stage may be just a shade in Australia's favour'. Yet, either way, it was not the pursuit of another English victory that he saw as the tour's main purpose. The consequence of Australia's run of defeats in the mid-1950s had been, he explained in the *Telegraph*, a disenchanted Australian public. England's mission, he thought, should be accordingly to re-enchant them back from 'studying varieties of marine nature, spearing fish and caring for their lady friend'. This was his way of saying – not quite yet fully unbuttoned by marriage – that they should quit the beach for the cricket ground.

In practice, the concept of re-enchantment soon fell off the agenda. 'On every hand we heard derogatory remarks about the cricket,' Swanton informed his *Telegraph* faithful during the first Test at Brisbane, as Bailey compiled 68 in a little over seven and a half hours. He went on:

It may be said to be outside the functions of the critic to express his personal hopes and fears. His job, I dare say, is to convey the fullest possible picture and leave it to his readers to form conclusions. However, I will take the risk of censure from those far away, who, other things being equal, are naturally and properly anxious to see England win, and say I think it would be much better for the game of cricket if England were to be beaten than to succeed at the expense of the spectators on whose support and goodwill the game ultimately depends. I will only add to this that this is the 135th Test match that I have described and that I have never before held similar feelings so far as an England victory was concerned.

'I honestly think it was the dullest and most depressing Test I have ever witnessed,' Swanton wrote after it was all over, as Australia won by eight wickets. There were five wickets for Australia's little-known quick man, the left-arm Ian Meckiff, who a few weeks earlier had taken 5 for 85 when England played Victoria. England's batsmen suspected then that he was throwing, or chucking, the ball. However, they said cheerfully that he did not throw it particularly well, and no official complaint was made. Noting that chucking was not an issue in Brisbane, Swanton described that silence as important and misguided.

The second Test at Melbourne saw England all out in their second innings for a humiliating 87, with Meckiff taking 6 for 38. By this time, Swanton's attitude had changed significantly since the years after the war when he had thought it bad form ever to question umpiring decisions. Now he was sharp about several umpiring errors, but one comment in particular revealed a new ferocity: 'I never saw anything so blatant as Meckiff's action as, with the swell of the crowd in his ears, he came up at full pelt.' He reckoned that England's batsmen had been undone by feelings of indignation and resentment as much as by the intrinsic difficulties caused by someone with his tail up bowling in this unorthodox manner. But Swanton attributed equal blame to England's fragile batting, reminding his readers that for more than two years England's batsmen had been bailed out by the bowlers. After a draw in the third Test, the series became a rout, as Australia won the last two Tests by 10 wickets and 9 wickets. Swanton thought the margin of the result made this the most surprising rubber he had ever seen.

Arlott remained in London, but his *Cricket Journal* for 1959 began in April with a fatalistic, cycles-of-history post-mortem:

> Surely, in essence, the outcome was probable enough from the start. The English batting was faced by the two types of bowling against which it has had little or no practice. There has been no parallel to the left-arm pace of Davidson and Meckiff in English cricket since Bill Voce and Nobby Clark ... So it can have been no real surprise that their bowling – coming from an uncomfortable angle – struck a series of early blows from which our batting never recovered. That early damage done, Benaud took the greatest number of Test wickets with leg-spin, the classical bowling method which English county cricket, over-concerned not to yield bonus points for first innings lead, has virtually and wilfully killed in the past few seasons.

Arlott then turned to how there had been 'much talk of the questionable deliveries of at least three of the Australian bowlers', and was inclined to take a calm, moderate view, arguing that 'jerking or throwing' was far from a novel problem in cricket and that the authorities and the umpires would, between them, sort it out. However, he anticipated that 'drag' – especially associated during the recent series with Australia's Gordon Rorke – was 'likely to prove a more complicated problem'. And he finished by quoting what Leo

Harrison had said to him the day before: 'Either you must enforce the law or else let everybody chuck from eighteen yards and make fair bowling a waste of time.'

The 1959 home series, with England crushing a weak Indian side, was probably of lasting significance only to those who happened (like the younger author) to be eight years old at the time and for whom cricket in any shape was a new, entrancing game. Still, a noteworthy moment came on the Friday of the first Test at Trent Bridge, when the wicket was covered after rain had meant there would be no more play that day. Arlott, who shared Swanton's suspicions of covered wickets, had already predicted earlier in the season that the new, time-saving regulation was 'bound to reduce the number of spin-bowlers' wickets'. In any case, the era of the great Surrey spinners was more or less over: Laker's indiscretions in a newspaper serialisation of a bad-tempered autobiography would soon so vex MCC that it would withdraw his honorary membership, and he did not play for England again; while Lock, compelled to remodel his action because of his notoriously suspect quicker ball, was seemingly a spent force. It would be another half-century before a spin bowler – Graeme Swann – consistently won Tests for England again.

Peter May's tour of the West Indies in 1959–60 was also almost the end of his era. Narrowly won (1–0) by England, the series featured bad behaviour common on both sides. Having won the second Test, England took time-wasting to a new level; while short-pitched bowling was an essential part of the home fast bowlers' armoury, with throwing endemic (*Wisden* claimed that at least six West Indian bowlers, two of them Test regulars, were throwers). Even worse, in Swanton's eyes, was that although umpires agreed about the prevalence of chucking, they did not act because they feared the authorities would not support them. For Swanton, the good news was that his friend R. W. V. Robins was the tour manager. He did not succeed in dismantling England's defensive strategy, but there were no egregious diplomatic blunders to displease the *Daily Telegraph*. For Arlott, the good news was that Trueman, with twenty-one wickets, was England's leading bowler. Six years earlier, Swanton could not contain his distaste for Trueman's personality; now his reformation glittered o'er his fault. *West Indies Revisited* was the title of Swanton's tour book, praised by the *TLS* in July 1960 as 'the most expansive and, therefore, the most interesting' of his efforts. 'Normally he ties himself down too rigidly to the matter in hand and so gives the impression that, apart from cricket, he lives in a vacuum, but here he allows himself some comments on the West Indian way of life, on the differences between the islands, and in consequence his writing, always competent and sensible, grows in status.' Another favourable review appeared in *Punch*; and its cricket-loving editor, Bernard Hollowood, took the opportunity to offer a more general assessment:

The blurb describes Mr Swanton as 'the doyen of cricket writers'. Accurately. E. W. Swanton's standards of comment and analysis are exemplary: he is utterly reliable and always busily constructive. He is apt to eschew the more florid strokes of the cricket reporter, so that his commentary lacks the dash and literary facility of Cardus or Alan Ross; but day-in-day-out he is the most satisfying performer and his pen is classically straight.

'Cricket Writing and the Press' was the title of a chapter in Doug Insole's *Cricket from the Middle*, an autobiography-cum-survey. Published at the start of what would in some ways be a decade of greater frankness, its author was willing here – if not invariably elsewhere in the book – to name names. On Frank Rostron: 'Seldom allows himself to become too occupied by events on the field.' Crawford White: 'Has an eye for the "story" and often makes a meal of it.' Brian Chapman: 'Grey has no part in his colour scheme.' Alan Ross: 'I am not sure that his knowledge is very profound.' And Swanton: 'Perhaps the most disappointing of the present crop of cricket journalists, because in riding his particular hobby horses he fails to make the most constructive use of his wide experience of the game.' Swanton, added Insole, 'tends to regard all modern players as intellectual pygmies and lives, as far as cricket is concerned, in the past rather than the present'. To his credit, Swanton in July 1960 gave Essex's captain (amateur, but grammar school) a good review, describing his book as 'modest, humorous, kindly, informative, critical in a constructive way, and withal written exclusively by the author's own hand!' As for Arlott, he was, in Insole's appraisal, 'a most pleasing writer who has recently surfaced from beneath the sea of theory which at one time threatened to engulf him, and his tremendous liking for cricket and his insatiable appetite for learning about it have sharpened his judgement'. That was a more generous perspective than that of the *TLS* reviewer who, later in the year, tackled Arlott's account of the 1960 season, *Cricket on Trial*:

This is the third volume in Mr Arlott's 'Cricket Journal', which suggests that Mr Arlott writes as much about

cricket as James Agate wrote about the theatre. He does –
but without Agate's gusto, his sheer ability as an author.
Mr Arlott's love for the game is never in question, but his
accounts ... read at times as though they were little more
than printed versions of spoken commentaries. What is
set down is sensible and sound enough, but there is little
vitality or imagination at work.

'Mr Arlott, who talks like a writer, writes as engagingly as
he talks,' was, more happily, the verdict of the *Observer*'s
Geoffrey Nicholson. Tellingly, he noted the considerable amount of space that, compared to Arlott's previous
two journals, was devoted to 'cricket politics – throwing,
umpiring, gates'. 'But then,' he added, 'that was the salt of
last season.'

Indeed it was. 'Has cricket lost its attraction? Has it
fallen out of date, out of tune with modern demands and
public interest?' Those, reckoned Arlott in *Cricket on Trial*,
were the key questions; and, writing on the eve of the 1960
season, he identified four large, disquieting clouds.

The first, inevitably, was that of ever-declining crowds.
Altham's report a few years earlier had traced the steady fall
in attendances at county matches, while Arlott would note
later in his journal that on the Saturday of the Trent Bridge
Test the number paying at the gate to see England against
South Africa was a disappointing 5,000. He offered a broad
analysis, couched in typically human terms. The cause of
dwindling attendances could not, he asserted, be 1930s-
style poverty or joblessness, given that 'we have a standard
of employment, income and general prosperity such as this
country has not known before'. He then canvassed other

causes – including rapidly increasing family car ownership ('mother, understandably enough, wants a trip into the country, down to the seaside or to relations, so the family sends no member to the cricket') and less entertaining play ('the spectator nowadays must be satisfied with a hard game – the avoidance of defeat often placed above the risky bid for a win – or stay away') – before following the new orthodoxy and pinning most of the blame on television. He compared the discomfort at a crowded Test ground, where during the intervals 'only lukewarm drink and indifferent snacks wait at the end of the long, slow queues at the refreshment bars', with the ease of a comfortable chair in the sitting room, and a clear view from behind the bowler's arm such as 'less than one per cent of the people on the ground can hope to have'. Arlott played with the idea that TV (and by implication radio) had 'increased the number of cricket followers': less money at the gate, admittedly, but commentary by experts such as Denis Compton providing greater enlightenment – 'an authoritative point of view which not even membership of the most august clubs could guarantee for the ordinary cricket follower'. Addressing (and flattering) the reader directly, Arlott finished mischievously enough, by imagining that ideal time in the future when cricket was 'completely solvent' through broadcasting income and other sources, while simultaneously 'even the greatest matches are being played before crowds so scanty that there is ample space for you and me to find a seat, buy a drink and talk to our friends in the relaxed ease and comfort that ought to characterise cricket-watching'.

His second concern arose from bowlers' apparent recent freedom to throw deliveries without being no-balled by the umpires. He questioned whether the administrators who made the laws wished to eradicate unfair bowling. On the face of it, no official action had been taken against Meckiff. In 1960 itself, when South Africa's Geoff Griffin was no-balled for throwing during the tourists' game against MCC at Lord's and again against Hampshire, he was persuaded to remodel his action. Griffin was picked for the Lord's Test, where the umpires judged that the remodelling had not been nearly drastic enough. Griffin took the first ever hat-trick in a Lord's Test; but having also been no-balled eleven times, he gave up playing Test cricket – a melodramatic if sad last hurrah. Arlott's own approach to the throwing contro-versy was to outline the historical context, just as Swanton would normally do. He claimed that since the war he had seen thirteen bowlers whose actions – sometimes, but not always – justified being called no balls; and there might have been four more. 'There has been dangerous laxity since 1946,' he declared; and he remained sceptical about indi-vidual members of the Imperial Cricket Conference, who, he feared, would be unwilling to sacrifice their own team's throwers for the general welfare of Test cricket. Certainly, England's recent experience in the West Indies had borne him out. In the event, though, he underestimated the administrators: Bradman flew to London to agree a com-promise with MCC's Gubby Allen. The new law stated that a bowler's arm must not be bent as the ball was delivered. When Australia's touring team was chosen for the 1961 Ashes series, there was no Meckiff, nor any other bowler with a suspect action.

Arlott was also concerned by the potentially damaging impact of scurrilous, gossipy memoirs such as Wardle's and

Laker's. Presumably, it was the indiscipline that worried him, because he was not censorious by nature. He worried, too, that the welfare of cricket was not on the agenda of popular 'red top' newspapers; moreover, he thought players did not warm to intrusion into their personal lives. The response of the papers, he noted, was that cricket should be grateful for all the publicity it was able to get. Arlott's well-developed scepticism took over: 'That the situation should be resolved to the satisfaction of both camps is the most improbable of all contingencies in the future of cricket.'

His final concern just ahead of the 1960 season was the threat that politics might inhibit or interrupt the tour by the South Africans. 'Some of the many British people who have been roused to indignation by Sharpeville and all it represents are now – in the absence of anyone at hand more immediately culpable – prepared to make McGlew's cricketers the object and sounding board of their disapproval,' he observed a few weeks after the massacre by armed police of nearly seventy black Africans, with many more badly wounded. 'It is to be hoped – but is by no means certain – that common sense will show the cricketers to be an inappropriate target.' These were not exactly stirring words on behalf of the anti-apartheid cause; but Arlott insisted that if the South Africans' tour 'were to collapse – because of demonstrations, political exploitation of their presence here, or crisis in their own country – English cricket would find itself in a very awkward financial position'. In fact, the anti-tour protests fairly soon petered out. Yet even if he did not say so, Arlott must have known that the serious possibility of a future South African tour having significant political implications was hardly likely to go away.

More generally, it would be fair enough to say that by 1960 both Arlott and Swanton were in tacit agreement that, one way or another, the rot was setting in. However, the means of getting rid of that rot remained – to borrow from Churchill on Russia – 'a riddle, wrapped in a mystery, inside an enigma'.

5

1961: An Orderly World

Once upon a time – before one-day cricket, before the proliferation of Test matches, before the ECB did to our summers what zealous planners and greedy developers had done to our towns and cities – the unfolding shape of the first-class season was seemingly immutable. Seventeen counties, each playing thirty-two or twenty-eight county championship matches; Tests beginning on Thursdays; other matches (three days only) beginning on Saturdays or Wednesdays; no cricket on Sundays; an almost absurdly long fixture list for the tourists (only one touring party a year); and, across the season, a plethora of festival weeks – Weston-super-Mare, Bath, Stroud, Gloucester, Cheltenham, Guildford, Worthing, Eastbourne, Dover, Canterbury, Tunbridge Wells, Gravesend, Westcliff, Clacton, Colchester, Leyton – culminating in full-blown September festivities at Hastings and Scarborough. The penultimate such season, although no one knew it at the time, was 1961. Arlott (who had just left London and moved to the Old Sun at Alresford) was entering his late forties, Swanton was in his mid-fifties: two men in their prime, reporting and commentating on a cherished but insecure national pastime, no longer quite sure of its place in unsentimental modernity Britain.

———

'Today the 1961 Australians landed at Tilbury,' recorded Arlott on 21 April in the opening sentence of his fourth-successive *Cricket Journal*. 'They have been eagerly – and anxiously – awaited, for upon them may depend not only the periodic high season which their visit traditionally creates in English cricket, but the entire public image of the game in England.' During the winter, Richie Benaud's Australia and Frank Worrell's West Indies had competed in a wonderfully inspiriting series, hailed by MCC in its congratulatory cable to the captains as 'a pattern for everyone to follow'; while in March, confronted by falling attendances and almost decade-long complaints about sterile cricket, the county captains had met at Lord's to commit themselves to a less defensive, more entertaining approach. 'Cricket in search of its Character' was the title on 29 April of J. J. Warr's *Daily Telegraph* piece, where the recently retired Middlesex amateur described county cricket as 'a professional circus restricted to a few participants and watched by even fewer spectators'. That same day, ensconced in Worcester for the traditional tour opener, Swanton identified Benaud's 'shrewd and sympathetic' captaincy as the 'best insurance' for 'the whole company of cricket-lovers' to enjoy 'a happy and exciting summer'.

The Saturday proved an understandable struggle for the Australian batting. 'So far as my memory stretches – which in respect of touring teams opening on this fair ground is back to 1930 – they have never been confronted with such a heavy pudding of a wicket,' pronounced Swanton. But by the evening Tom Graveney (who, having left Gloucestershire for Worcestershire, was not permitted by the rigid rules of the transfer system to play championship cricket that year) was 24 not out and 'stroking the ball gracefully enough to make every one regret anew his melancholy situation'. On Monday, however, he found it hard to recover his touch, prompting Arlott to reflect – in the context of this being the thirty-three-year-old's 'one remote chance of staking his Test claim' – that 'anxiety shackles such men, turns their normal, natural grace to laborious effort'; and he condemned MCC's refusal to give Graveney a special registration as 'more legalistic than applicable to a game'. Scoring was low all day, while on Tuesday, just after lunch, 'a violent storm put a depressing end to a match played in conditions too bleak for any Australian to believe that cricket was possible'.

Over the next three and a half weeks, Arlott did radio commentary at Old Trafford, Cardiff and Bristol for county matches against the tourists (his journal nicely describing Glamorgan's Ossie Wheatley as 'hardly number ten to *anyone's* number eleven'), while always doing his best to fit in Hampshire. 'It was not thrilling cricket,' he observed about their visit to Northampton, 'but there was much to relish in the craftsmanlike approach of both sides.' Swanton caught up with Hampshire at Portsmouth, albeit arriving late on the first morning. 'It was a damping start to the day's enjoyment to find, on arrival, Marshall unbuckling his pads, caught at second slip apparently off a beauty from Higgs that pitched straight and left the bat.' As almost always, whether in match accounts or his 'Monday Cricket Commentary', his strong voice did not waver. The South

African wicketkeeper John Waite had recently claimed that the no-balling of Griffin the previous summer had been 'engineered' by Gubby Allen (chairman of the England selectors) 'to keep Meckiff and other dubious Australian bowlers out of the present series'. Swanton found the case 'muddled', adding his 'belief' that 'the cricket public is heartily sick of this sort of behind-the-scenes stuff'.

By late May the forthcoming Ashes battle was starting to come into focus. 'A game that is inevitably, and quite properly, regarded as some sort of dress rehearsal for the Test series' was how Swanton on the 27th previewed MCC v. the Australians at Lord's. His special favourite among the tourists was the aggressive Norman O'Neill ('Here at last is a player fit to rank with the great'), who obliged with a century, notwithstanding a lukewarm reception when he came in to bat: 'Perhaps it is rather much to expect a Lord's crowd in a chill May wind to engender the warmth of the Opera House. But this present habit of niggardly applause for distinguished players is irrespective of weather and nationality.' The Australians won, following a typically bold declaration by Benaud, while soon afterwards, in much warmer weather at Hove, he and his opposite number Ted Dexter oversaw a nail-biting draw that left Arlott to conclude that 'if cricket is to go down in public esteem, it is doing so, on this evidence, with all guns firing'.

The first Test began at Edgbaston on 8 June. Arlott declined to commit himself to a prediction, but Swanton thought that from an English point of view there was 'absolutely no need to be despondent', pinning his hopes on the largely untested Australian attack. Above all, his greatest wish was that England would emulate Benaud's attacking approach, and that between them the teams would avoid 'the awful dull solemnity which characterised, for instance, the last English series in Australia'. Even so, he could not but reflect that 'no one will quite expect, or want to see, frivolous cricket or hazardous declarations in a Test match'.

A disappointing, rain-affected encounter was redeemed, for home supporters, by match-saving centuries from Raman Subba Row and Dexter. 'The responsible straightness and care of his defence impressed even those who knew his play well,' observed Arlott about Dexter; but as for the burdened Cowdrey, England's captain in the absence of the not-quite-fit May, he 'batted with his consciousness of peril implicit in every stroke, miserable with anxiety, playing every ball as if it were a bomb likely to explode at the slightest hint of violence'. As usual since 1957, radio brought ball-by-ball commentary (Arlott and Alston as well as the two Australian commentators Bob Richardson and Alan McGilvray), with Jack Fingleton and Freddie Brown providing the expert analysis and Swanton responsible for lunch, teatime and close-of-play summaries; while on TV, it was still far from every ball covered on the BBC's sole channel – especially on the first day, clashing as it did with the Duke of Kent's marriage at York Minster to Katharine Worsley (daughter of MCC's president-elect). For Swanton, until the English batsmen at last did their stuff, praise was reserved almost entirely for the Australians ('it was a joy to watch Harvey and O'Neill – the old hero and the new') and criticism for the English ('I cannot remember seeing so much fumbling and slow-footedness since the blackest of all dark days at Leeds in '48'), especially for Fred Trueman as the visitors on the Saturday piled on the runs: 'He actually bowled his first spell of the day from a shortened run, and it was not until his 32nd over that he got a wicket. To be honest, he had not often looked like it.' Still, the latest Ashes series was up and running, and Swanton's paper had been compelled as early as the Friday to announce that, 'because of the extreme pressure exerted on the telephone switchboard', it would be 'unable to answer inquiries requesting the latest Test match scores'. Instead, GPO subscribers – provided they lived in London, Birmingham, Manchester, Liverpool or Glasgow – could get the latest by dialling 'UMP'.

Over and above the immediate issue this summer of whether England could metaphorically regain the coveted urn, there loomed in international cricket the rather bigger question of the Test-playing future of South Africa: apartheid-implementing, no longer in the Commonwealth, and thus no longer a member of the Imperial Cricket Conference (as it was still called). 'There is,' asserted Swanton on 19 June ahead of the ICC's annual meeting at Lord's scheduled for a month later, 'a natural distaste for allowing politics to obtrude into cricket, and, I think, an instinctive desire to retain kinship with the South African cricket community, the vast bulk of whom have no sympathy with the politics of the Verwoerd government.' Accordingly, he hoped that the ICC would 'decide to re-admit South Africa subject to an affirmation by the SACA [South African Cricket Association] that in principle it approved multi-racial cricket'. 'Doctor Verwoerd,' he added hopefully, 'will not live for ever, and his policies may well pre-decease him.'

That same Monday, he was at Canterbury for the second day of the tourists' match against Kent, where 'in blissful weather, another fine crowd [25,000] spilled higgledy-piggledy over this ancient home of cricket, in stands, motor-cars, and deckchairs, on benches, and just sprawled on the grass'. They saw a century by Cowdrey ('alternated beautiful strokes with periods almost of somnolence'), followed next day by another one ('a more flamboyant continuation of the first'), as Kent fell just short of a famous victory. 'What a halo,' declared Swanton, 'for England's extraordinarily modest captain to wear when he takes the field at Lord's!' With the second Test due to start there on Thursday, intensive scrutiny attached to the likely state of the wicket – and thus the composition of the England attack. 'This year the Lord's wicket is reputedly slower, less inclined to be "green" and more helpful to spinners,' reflected Arlott on the Sunday before. 'That seems a remarkable change, but clearly it has dictated the inclusion [in the party] of Tony Lock.' A hint of scepticism perhaps on Arlott's part, but there was none on Swanton's in his preview on the morning of the match. 'There has been some thinning of the thick grass mat which has too often made the Lord's wicket a paradise for the faster bowlers; scarifying is, perhaps, the appropriate word. The hope is for a true wicket reasonably fast, and if it becomes a little dusty by next Tuesday there should be no complaints.' Accordingly, he expected England to plump for 'a balanced attack', which in practice meant including both Lock and Ray Illingworth, with no third specialist quick bowler.

That Thursday (with Swanton replacing Peter West in the TV box) should have been perfect for the home followers: Australia at Lord's, a full house, the Queen due to visit after lunch, a balanced attack, May back in the batting line-up, Cowdrey (still captain) winning the toss ... In the event, however, the main batting flopped badly, so that by the time Murray and Illingworth got together, noted Swanton, 'the stand proceeded in an atmosphere of melancholy disappointment', before the England keeper 'aimed the fashionable sweep at a straight ball [from 'Slasher' Mackay, his run-up described by Arlott earlier in the season as 'mock-sinister'] and was rather ignominiously lbw'. Yet if an anti-climactic flop it undoubtedly was (all out 206), perhaps it was a pardonable one? 'The Lord's "ridge" may be, as some claim, no more than a figment of the imagination,' observed Arlott, 'but without doubt one ball in every two overs or so of pace bowling from the pavilion end lifted quickly and steeply enough to cheat the middle of some very accomplished bats.' Swanton, too, emphasised the extenuating fact of a fast pitch combined with variable bounce: 'It is easy to say that several fell to indifferent strokes. This was indeed true, and some of the batting was below Test class. But these are the circumstances from which such strokes are bred. If any batsman had looked comfortable one would be more ready to censure others, but none really did.' Indeed, among the top order, Swanton's main implicit censure was for Dexter's gum-chewing while at the crease – 'a recent habit this, that somehow does not accord with his public image'.

Friday belonged to the angular, jaw-jutting Bill Lawry, whose obdurate 130 did much to put Australia 80 in front with two wickets left. Inevitably the bulk of the work fell to Trueman and Statham – 'lacking the "unbalanced" Australian attack of four seam-bowlers,' dryly noted Arlott, 'England had only Dexter as relief for the opening pair' – and in the end they could only do so much. According to Swanton (full of praise for Lawry, comparing him to 'that master of temperament, Herbert Sutcliffe'), 'the wicket grew tamer as the day wore on and the sun sucked the last residue of moisture from it', though 'it was never quite plumb'; and during the afternoon session, 'it was pleasant to see the grip that Cowdrey exercised after the loose cricket at Edgbaston', an improvement marred only by Lancashire's Geoff Pullar, whose 'reactions were slower than a young man's ought to be'. What lay ahead? Swanton was not too downhearted, calling for 'a thoroughly resolute approach' from England's batsmen.

It did not happen. On Saturday, in front of another full house, England's major batsmen failed again – 'for the third time,' noted Swanton, 'in four innings'. His disappointment was palpable: not just over England's performance, but that because of the continuing uncertainties of the wicket it had been, for the third day running, a day for the grafters, not the stylists. 'Certain virtues of the game were shown well enough: determination, patience, physical courage. But for most of the more attractive arts of the game there was no place.' Certainly, it was an incontrovertible fact that England's three great stylists – May, Cowdrey and Dexter, amateurs to a man – had made only 46 between them on *the* showpiece day of the English cricketing calendar. The saddest case was Cowdrey. 'Every spectator on the ground suffered with him,' wrote Arlott, 'while he played as if, instead of one of the master batsmen of his time, he was as humanly fallible as those who watched him.' By contrast, later in the afternoon, Ken Barrington – 'chunky, earthy, and workmanlike', the professional's professional – batted through to the close for 59. England finished 44 runs on, with four wickets left.

'England Make Defiant Last-Ditch Fight' would be the *Telegraph*'s headline, but there was no Monday miracle, as the Australians won by five wickets. At the truly 'last ditch' stage, just conceivably England might have squeaked home if, the last ball before lunch and Australia (needing 69) slightly rocking at 33 for 4, the most dramatic single moment of the match had gone the other way. Statham bounced Peter Burge, the aggressive Australian went for the hook, and the ball hit the splice and went up in the air towards the square-leg umpire, with Lock at backward short leg the nearest fielder. 'The Tony Lock of a few years ago – before he developed this troublesome knee – would have started a yard quicker, moved much faster and all but swallowed the catch,' reckoned Arlott. 'Lock of today set off and, with all his old enthusiasm, launched himself horizontally through the air, got a hand to it and fell. The impact of the fall jolted the ball from his one-handed grip ...' In any case, defending the Ashes, Australia were now one up with three to play.

The following Sunday – 2 July, the day after Arlott had been at Cowes to commentate on Hampshire v. Essex – the selectors announced that May would be captain for the rest of the series and that Yorkshire's Brian Close (six Tests and a dozen years after his youthful England debut) would be in the party of twelve for the imminent third Test at Leeds. Arlott was happy enough with both decisions, Swanton with only one, calling Close 'unpredictable' and declaring that 'Titmus's all-round credentials would on the whole have appealed more to many people'. Two days later came the news that Derbyshire's Les Jackson, whose sole Test had been in 1949, was likely to replace the injured Statham.

'One's reaction to the choice,' recorded Swanton, 'is pleasure that an admirable bowler will be given the accolade of an appearance for England v Australia, and some regret that a younger man should not have been thought worthy.'

Yet, more than individuals, it was the Headingley pitch that preoccupied pundits and others (including the players themselves) during the build-up. 'We have been told, semi-officially, that it is "full of runs" and "will last a good five days",' noted Arlott on the Wednesday, before explaining why such confident predictions were 'hard to swallow': 'Such grass as there is has been cropped extremely closely – far too closely, one would think, for it to hold the soil together for five days. But if there were grass – however short – all over, it would not seem so threatening; there are whole wide spaces of earth totally bare and already, if the human eye can be trusted, on the verge of becoming dust. It is all very perplexing.' Swanton agreed it was a rum affair: 'The wicket has a strange piebald look, grassy in some places and bare in others'; accordingly, with 'an easy-paced wicket' expected at the start, 'the side that goes in first will probably win'.

There ensued (Swanton still on TV duties, Arlott as ever on radio) a three-day wonder. 'The wicket, as I explained yesterday, was most dangerously bare and dry,' declared Swanton – with a slight exaggeration of his perspicuity – after the first day, when Australian wickets tumbled to Trueman and Jackson in the final session. 'There are going to be post-mortems on this Headingley wicket from now on so long as the game is played … It might yet be a subject for a Royal Commission, certainly if England win and Australia withdraw their diplomatic representatives in consequence.'

England finished the Friday on top, largely thanks to Cowdrey, who after a slow period, noted Swanton, 'eventually stilled the clamour of a not very knowledgeable section of spectators by forcing Davidson to the leg boundary'. He was out for 93 after glancing McKenzie down the leg side. 'Grout, taking the ball, appealed for a catch,' recorded Arlott, 'but, as umpire John Langridge hesitated, Cowdrey turned and walked to the pavilion.' Swanton entirely approved: 'Such is the excellent habit of the modern cricketer. The episode, of course, was completely in character. But such a gesture cannot be wholly easy to make when one is seven runs short of a century against Australia.' The contest was settled either side of Saturday's tea interval: a phenomenal spell by Trueman ('controlled and fierce,' in Swanton's words), bowling quick off-cutters from his short run, of five wickets for no runs, was part of his eventual match figures of 11 for 88 as England cruised that evening to an eight-wicket win.

'What tale could be happier to tell?' asked Swanton in Monday's *Telegraph*. 'Unfortunately, of course, the Australians, accustomed as they are to true wickets, were handicapped so greatly by this treacherous one as to modify, or even destroy, any elation in the victory. It leaves a taste of ashes in the mouth, rather than any immediate thought of our recapturing those in the urn.' Indeed, a genuinely displeased Swanton added in a further piece next day, 'on Saturday night one could hardly look an Australian fairly in the eye'. So, too, Arlott on the Headingley 'dust-bowl': 'There was, certainly, immense excitement. But no proper game of cricket can be played on a pitch where a batsman cannot play an ordinary drive, even to a near half-volley, without putting his wicket in jeopardy. English batsmen, from long experience of slow, turning wickets, can hang on, with a reduced range of strokes in such circumstances ... For the Australians, bred on fast, true wickets, such conditions are utterly inhibiting.' Altogether, it was a thoroughly disappointing state of affairs for 'a shop-window event such as a Test with Australia'.

A different sort of shop window began at Lord's the following Saturday: the annual Varsity match, with Arlott absent (commentating on the tourists at Trent Bridge) but Swanton his usual indispensable, judgemental presence. Praise for at least one Cambridge batsman ('Brearley's bat swings in close union with his front leg, while he has the habit of making a lateral movement of the right leg at the instant of the stroke, as though to further bolt and bar the door'); praise, too, for the young man who helped the ancient C. M. Wells, a Blue during Gladstone's third ministry, down the Pavilion stairs ('What is more, the undergraduate concerned knew something about Mr Wells as a sportsman: good marks to him!'); and praise even for the abuse coming from the Tavern as Cambridge batted on at the end to a dull, unadventurous draw ('a welcome intervention, this, that recalled old times'). Commendation was absent, though, for Oxford's headgear on the Monday: 'Pithey and Green arrived to bat wearing blue caps with badges that had no relation with Oxford. Finally, to horrified eyes, there emerged Neate in a green cap that was said to symbolise Berkshire – the cricket, I believe, not the golf club ...' After a sarcastic reference to 'the heroes of 1961', he continued in what was becoming the time-honoured vein on these occasions: 'One wonders whether it is some strange neurosis or just common-or-garden lack of respect for their elders and betters that is responsible for this cocking of a snook at tradition. Whatever the cause, it made a melancholy sight.'

Gentlemen v. Players, also at Lord's and with Swanton in the radio commentary box at the top of the Pavilion, followed immediately afterwards – its first day coinciding with ICC's annual meeting, where the South African question was tamely shelved for a year. The cricket itself, 'on a good wicket' according to Swanton, saw the Players making 203 in a little over four hours, prompting a predictable barb about 'professional batsmanship not shown in a flattering light' – whereas later in the day came batting from May 'in a class somewhat isolated from all others'. On Thursday, young Brearley behind the stumps missed a couple of chances ('A. C. Smith's greater experience might have served the Gentlemen better'), before next day the Players won for the first time in six years, much helped by Close's 94 not out and five wickets. 'Enlisting the hearts of the old and middle-aged by making ground to the faster bowlers,' noted an appreciative Swanton about his innings, 'and hitting them on the rise.' The Yorkshireman had been left out of the Headingley team, but no one now questioned his inclusion in the party for Old Trafford, where the fourth Test was due to start on 27 July.

Swanton on the eve weighed it all up. He was confident enough about the wicket ('a good foundation and a true surface'), but less so about the weather (albeit 'the forecast is reasonable, by Manchester standards'). As to two key individuals, 'Benaud at last is back to something like health and strength', while 'Dexter, it is said, is distressing his head with theory, which for so fine a natural striker of the ball is strange indeed'. As for Close, there was 'much to be said' for giving him 'a chance to prove that at the age of 30 he has outgrown the accusations of irresponsibility that were not unjustified in his precocious youth'. Overall, if wicket and weather remained good, he did not expect Australia to lose. What ultimately transpired was a drama on the final day that followers of English cricket could recall vividly – how it happened, where they were – half a century later.

The first two days – Thursday rain-affected, Friday sunny, Cowdrey unable to play because of a throat infection, Close playing, Arlott and Swanton fulfilling their customary radio and TV roles – could hardly have gone better for England, finishing the second day three runs behind on first innings with seven wickets left. 'May called upon Statham for a flat-out effort,' wrote Arlott about the key passage of play that Friday morning. 'Statham knows his home wicket as well as anyone and, apart from his invariable loyalty and will-ingness, he was obviously prepared to give his fullest effort to exploit the last drains of sap in the drying pitch.' He finished with 5 for 53; and when England batted, not only did May contribute an undefeated 90, but Close negotiated the final three-quarters of an hour – having 'so far given,' noted Swanton, 'no cause whatever for anxiety'. Naturally, Swanton hoped to see 'runs flowing' on the Saturday.

That desire was only fitfully realised, as England secured a first-innings lead of 177 mainly thanks to the obdurate Barrington, who with successive partners was generally, in Arlott's words, 'satisfied to stay and nudge the score along with runs that could be made without risk'. Swanton's report for Monday's *Telegraph* was distinctly muted. 'One cannot help wondering whether England may not have loosened their grip on a golden chance'; and, 'watching the England batting against what, by Test reckoning, is this so-limited Australian attack one could not suppress the feeling that they were let off all too lightly'. Similarly ominous was his evaluation of Benaud's o for 80: 'He has bowled in something nearer his old form, though rarely able to turn the ball very much. No doubt he may do so on the last day, if the skies remain clear, and Australia bat well enough.'

On the fourth day, indeed, the tourists' batting flourished to the extent of finishing on 331 for 6, with a century for Lawry, 67 for O'Neill, and Swanton purring that 'this day's cricket, watched by a capacity crowd, has been infinitely the best of the series'. He took particular pleasure in O'Neill's innings. 'No one likes to see a brilliant young cricketer persecuted by the spotlight. The penalties of fame grow more onerous series by series, and we now have to endure such unpalatable phrases as "flop" to describe some unfortunate having a bad run. Well, O'Neill did not flop today and for the sake of the game itself I hope he does not go on flopping.' Who was now in the box seat? 'Both sides can still win,' thought Swanton, adding, 'there are the possibilities of great deeds to come'; while according to Arlott, 'any result is possible but an English win seems as probable as any'.

Old Trafford on Tuesday 1 August proved an agony-and-ecstasy day, watched by a crowd of some 12,000, mainly men in ties. 'It would be hard to imagine a morning's cricket,' wrote Swanton about the first session, 'wherein fortune shifted so excitingly, where collapse and recovery were so clear-cut and the saving act more admirably done.' Or put more prosaically, three early Australian wickets fell before Davidson and McKenzie put on 98 in almost even time for the last wicket. Their partnership was only a quarter of an hour old when two disastrous overs from Close – including, noted Arlott, 'the uneconomic number of five full-tosses' – gifted 15 runs, so that in Swanton's words, 'Australian morale rose many points'. Lunch was taken with England facing the prospect of scoring 256 in just under four hours in order to take a 2–1 lead in the series. 'We will lose three or four wickets chasing the runs,' *The Times*'s John Woodcock predicted in the press box, 'and then come to grief against Richie.'

So, in fact, following a magnificent 76 by Dexter ('driving through the covers,' observed an admiring Arlott, 'like some reverberant echo of the Golden Age'), it more or less panned out, as Australia won by 54 runs with twenty minutes to spare. Immediately, and for many anguished years later, there were three critical questions:

1. What came over May, in just the second ball of his innings, to try to sweep Benaud out of the bowler's footmarks (and be bowled behind his legs)? He would subsequently chastise himself for not playing straight early on; but on the day, whereas Swanton merely recorded that he had left his leg stump uncovered and was otherwise uncritical, Arlott not only made that point, but additionally noted that the sweep was 'a stroke not normally in his game' and that 'his stroke was crooked'.

2. What came over Close during his slightly longer stay at the crease? Here, Swanton did let himself go:

> To describe Close's innings taxes charity beyond endurance, as indeed it taxed credibility to behold. To

Benaud's first ball, a yard wide of the off-stump, he aimed a sweep, legs askew, which sent the ball skirling over backward short-leg off the shoulder of the bat for two. Close had 10 balls, all from Benaud. He played this stroke, if such it can be called, five times, mostly without connection. The fifth time he scooped a catch to the man waiting to receive it some 20 yards behind the square-leg umpire. Midway through this nightmare Close had stepped down the wicket and, aiming straight for the only time, driven Benaud grandly for six. Could irony stretch farther?

Arlott was little kinder about what would be retrospectively defended by Close as 'a calculated risk': 'That grotesque stroke ... that hideous sweep ... a nightmare.'

3. Why did England, after their rapid loss of four wickets just before tea (taken at 163 for 5), not then systematically shut up shop and thereby keep the Ashes alive? The historical truth about *that* has never quite been established. Swanton at the time discerned muddle and had specially hard words for Trueman, who 'when all hope of victory had gone aimed a wild swing against a leg-spinner from Simpson'; while Arlott likewise declared that 'it was not possible to distinguish any policy in their batting after tea: were they continuing to attack, or trying to save the game?'

Both men, like May himself, were generous in defeat. 'Twice England seemed to have the game in their grasp,' wrote Arlott, 'but twice Australia, by gallant yet essentially skilful effort, wrested it from them – to retain The Ashes as gloriously as any side has ever done.' And Swanton was at his dignified best, especially about Benaud's decisive attacking spell either side of tea: 'It was fine bowling, and in many ways this has been a magnificent game of cricket. It is better to concentrate on this aspect, just as it is only proper to offer due congratulations to Australia, rather than to dwell unduly on a glorious English opportunity thrown away by misjudgement and plain poor batting.'

Arlott presumably wrote up his journal on the evening train, because next day he was on the south coast doing Home Service commentary on Hampshire v. Sussex. Hampshire, who had just gone top of the table, were without their adventurous amateur captain Colin Ingleby-Mackenzie (broken finger), so Roy Marshall – buccaneer batsman, but a dour captain – deputised. On 'a typically well-grassed Portsmouth wicket' (in Arlott's journal words), it was always likely to be a low-scoring affair. Five wickets each for Derek Shackleton ('tireless with his easy run and well-lubricated arm-swing') and Jimmy Gray ('finding some help in the atmosphere and a little from the pitch, ground away accurately') saw Sussex all out for 141. Dexter quickly claimed Marshall's wicket – 'an outswinger which straightened off the pitch and twanged the top of his off-stump' – and Hampshire finished the first day on 91 for 4. Thursday was largely a day of attrition, as Hampshire chipped out a lead of 38 and 'then, grimly and on a grim day – a gusty, chilly wind blew off the sea – Sussex set to work to play themselves back into the game'. This culminated by late afternoon in 'almost wilfully defensive batting' from Dexter, accompanied by an equally stonewall Jim Parks. 'It was odd indeed to see Sainsbury, with three men on the boundary, bowling for half an hour for one run; and odder still to hear the crowd – such of it as remained – giving the slow hand-clap to two of the best reputed attacking batsmen in the game.' Then, in the last over of the day, came a wholly unexpected burst of action, as 'Butch' White, watched by Dexter at the non-striker's end, blew away the Sussex middle order with four wickets, including a hat-trick. 'His mother and father, who always take their holiday to coincide with the Portsmouth cricket week, were beside themselves with joy': 179 for 4 had become 179 for 8, and on Friday morning only a single was added, leaving Hampshire with 143 to win. Marshall took the initiative, and by early afternoon they were home by six wickets.

It was a significant victory, especially as Yorkshire failed to win, but news of its progress was not to Swanton's satisfaction. In his next Monday column, he examined whether the county captains' commitment back in March to faster over-rates and more aggressive batting had in fact been fulfilled. Yes, in the former respect, he concluded; but for the latter, 'the evidence is much more mixed' – and, as a prime piece of negative evidence, he cited the Portsmouth match, where during the first thirteen hours, 'on a uniformly firm wicket', the scoring rate had been less than 40 runs an hour, 'a tempo ordinarily associated with the Roses matches of between 30 and 40 years ago'. He also noted that, during those trying hours, only one slow bowler had been used. In sum: 'I was glad not to be there.'

Over the next few weeks, having so far reported on only one county championship match this season, Swanton did report on three more, though hardly going far afield: Sussex v. Middlesex at Hove, Middlesex v. Surrey at Lord's ('some Surrey batting rather nearer the old standards today'), and Kent v. Yorkshire at Dover. Arlott, meanwhile, was at

Bristol for Gloucestershire v. Somerset ('a refreshingly happy air'), and at Derby for Derbyshire v. Hampshire (the visitors winning after two Ingleby-Mackenzie declarations – 'the Championship pace is becoming killing'); then at Southampton for the tourists' visit (a 'pleasantly relaxed' atmosphere during 'three days of sunshine'). By that time, the Australians had played the final Test at The Oval – an unremarkable, rain-affected affair (Swanton back on radio-summarising duties, the Arlott/Fingleton relationship distinctly uneasy) in which the series, in Arlott's unenthusiastic words, 'ended on the old, grimly defensive note, with the English batsmen demonstrating that they are better at saving Tests than winning them'. Swanton's main despair came after England's 210 for 8 on the first day: 'As a technical performance England's batting could be faulted in many ways. As an expression of character it failed equally. As an advertisement for cricket the day was likewise extremely unfortunate.'

The final stages of the county season began at the end of August, with Hampshire needing to take seven points from their last two matches, both at Bournemouth, to deprive Yorkshire of a third title in succession and to win their own first ever. Given that their second match was against Yorkshire, a powerful and highly motivated outfit, Hampshire must have hoped to get over the line against their first opponents, Derbyshire. One might have expected Swanton to make his way to Dean Park, but instead the *Telegraph*'s match reports came from A. S. R. Winlaw. Arlott was there for the Home Service – though, as his son Tim later observed, he would have been there even if he had not been broadcasting. His loyalty to the county ran deep;

many of the players were his friends; and this was potentially an historic moment.

The ten pages that Arlott devoted to the match in his *Cricket Journal* still make tense reading. After Ingleby-Mackenzie had won a good toss, Hampshire on the first day made only 'middling progress' (a total of 306) towards winning the match. But the real slough of despond was Thursday. 'Hampshire have had a hard and unrewarding day,' recorded Arlott after close of play. 'They dropped catches, and Derbyshire, playing with the bold confidence of good cricketers for whom the match is not crucial, deservedly took a first-innings lead and bonus points. Marshall, with Sainsbury entrenched beside him, gave Hampshire a fighting chance this evening, but only some major performance can now reshape the match and take them to a win ...' His detailed account nodded generously enough to the visitors – including their twenty-year-old wicketkeeper Bob Taylor, 'a young man with cricket temperament and touch in him' – but the hero was Marshall, 81 not out in barely two hours. 'On many days we have sat in awed, excited anxiety as Marshall threw his wicket into the hazard with strokes of a heady brilliance. Now he seemed utterly safe, even while he scored faster than any other batsman in England today could do without taking risks.'

Marshall went early on the final morning, but other batsmen stepped up to the plate; and at just before one o'clock Ingleby-Mackenzie declared, leaving Derbyshire to score 252 in 192 minutes. The decisive spell came soon after lunch from Shackleton, knocking over the top order. 'It was remarkable because the pitch was useless to him. Talking

afterwards, he said, "I did all I could – I just bowled straight."
He did indeed bowl remarkably accurately and to a perfect
length.' Soon, Derbyshire were 52 for 8, and that seemed
almost that – until Taylor and Harold Rhodes. 'Together
they doubled the score in three quarters of an hour. A chilly
tinge of doubt crept in … surely …' Eventually, with just
under an hour to spare, the honours fell to Sainsbury and
his slow left-arms. 'He caught-and-bowled Rhodes and
then tossed up a half-volley to Taylor who, two runs short
of his fifty, pull-drove it high towards long-on. [Danny]
Livingstone, out on that boundary, sighted it for a moment,
moved in, caught it chest-high and ran on to the pavilion.
There the Derbyshire players, as well as the Hampshire
crowd, were waiting to cheer in the new Champions.'

Speeches and lengthy celebrations followed. Arlott
being Arlott, even with emotions running high, he had
his tape recorder at the ready and – as fully documented
in David Rayvern Allen's anthology *Another Word from
Arlott* – recorded on-the-spot interviews with all of the
team as well as the club's president, Harry Altham ('I
couldn't have had a happier day'), for a programme to go
out on the Home Service. In addition to 'champagne and
more champagne', he wrote in his *Cricket Journal*, 'there
were memories, too, and gratitude, and nostalgic, sad-glad
thoughts of Hampshire cricketers who will never tread a
cricket pitch again. Their healths were drunk without stint.'
Next day, hung-over Saturday, he added some thoughts.
'For Hampshire the triumph was unique; the county's first
Championship after sixty-six years in the competition. In
another sense it was a bridge across almost two hundred
years since, through the Hambledon club, Hampshire last

stood at the top of English cricket.' Swanton, too, picked up on that connection in his congratulatory piece: 'The more historically minded may recall that Broad-Halfpenny Down is the very cradle of cricket. We can imagine William Beldham chanting a Te Deum somewhere aloft, John Small striking triumphant chords on the violin.' Even so, for all his generally warm tone, Swanton was at some pains to add a little sober perspective. 'Those who regard Ingleby-Mackenzie as a tactical cavalier are not wholly on the mark,' he argued. 'In the field, at least, this is scarcely so. Equally it is a slight exaggeration to imagine the Hampshire dressing room is a focus for trainers and tipsters, with private wires to Newmarket and Burlington Street.'

The rest of the season played out on shortening September days. Yorkshire beat Hampshire comfortably enough, despite a boundary-laden century by Marshall on the Tuesday afternoon which Arlott judged as fine as any of his innings; while along the coast at Hastings, Swanton reported on A. E. R. Gilligan's XI's encounter with the Australians, finding himself gratified by 'the right note of, so to speak, authentic gaiety': 'No one wants to see Festival games conducted like a funeral – or for that matter like a circus.' At the end, he bade his own farewell to the Australians, describing them as 'one of the most popular sides – perhaps the most popular – with spectators and opposing players that have ever come to England'.

———

Benaud's men would eventually take the liner SS *Strathmore* back to Fremantle, arriving more than six months after their original departure. The extent of the journey seemed to dictate the length of the tour. Wives

were complaining, and the next year England would fly
to Aden to reduce the sea voyage. Thereafter, as travel got
quicker, tours became shorter and county matches against
the tourists diminished in both number and consequence.
By 1963, moreover, there would be no Gentlemen to
take on the Players; and at about this time, Oxford and
Cambridge finally decided that academic standards of
candidates were more important than cricketing ability,
so that the historic status of the Varsity match began to
crumble. In September 1961, as the Australians near the
end of their marathon tour were at Jesmond playing
against the Minor Counties (captained by Jack Ikin, now
of Staffordshire), Swanton deployed one of his occasional
'From the Pavilion' pieces in the recently established
Sunday Telegraph to tackle *the* great question – only temporarily shelved – facing English cricket: should it attempt
to boost its flagging appeal and finances by introducing
some one-day games? 'If tried for a couple of seasons,'
he reflected in almost wholly sanguine fashion, 'it would
provide evidence, without altering the basic structure, as
to which type of cricket the public preferred to watch.'
Moreover, he went on, not only would this innovation
'induce a greater flexibility in the first-class player', but
'amateurs could make themselves available for a single
day'. On that latter score, Swanton was positively enthusiastic: 'Next year Denis Compton will be 42, Sir Leonard
Hutton 46. Having had the honour of playing with both
[in charity matches] this summer, I have little doubt they
are capable of giving much pleasure and instruction to all
in one-day cricket for a while yet.' And he summed up: 'I
am inclined to think the plunge is worth making. After

all, the Australians are brought up on cricket of both sorts and the system suits them well enough.' At the end of a season in which Australian vim had so painfully exposed the English lack of it, and in which the game in its country of birth had proceeded in its entrenched groove, this traditionalist accepted more readily than some what the direction of travel had to be.

6

1962–70: Tectonic Plates Shifting

The 1960s would prove to be English cricket's most challenging decade since the 1860s and the fortuitous emergence from the West Country of a youthful saviour called Grace. Cricket and class; the start of the one-day revolution; cricket and apartheid – on all these issues, during a decade of largely anti-climactic Ashes encounters, Arlott and Swanton provided an engaged, articulate and sometimes surprising journalistic commentary that not only mattered at the time, but can now be seen as a major historical source.

In November 1962, the England team and its followers were in Brisbane preparing for the first Test – four amateurs in the side, Ted Dexter as captain, the Duke of Norfolk as manager – when the shock news came through from Lord's that the ACCC had decided to recommend the abolition of amateur status in English first-class cricket. The news reached Swanton in the form of a breakfast-time cable (laconically announcing 'Amateurs abolished'), at once prompting a heartfelt piece for the *Telegraph*. 'The change strikes me as not only unnecessary but deplorable,' he declared almost at the outset, before setting out the reasons for his dismay:

> Cricket professionalism has been an honourable estate ever since the first-class game took more or less its present form in the middle of the 'nineties. But it is, of its nature, dependent, and the essence of leadership is independence …
>
> It has been said, of course, that the word amateur is an anachronism, that to preserve the status is mere humbug. I wonder.
>
> As soon as the broken-time principle was sanctioned [i.e. compensation, since 1958, for loss of salary or wages if going on a major overseas tour], and advertising restrictions removed, a distinction was created between the few who cashed in on various perquisites of their fame, and the Simon-Pure amateur.
>
> But the latter category was far from extinct …
>
> Is not the pattern likely to be one of the suppression of individuality in favour of a somewhat colourless uniformity? …
>
> Although I disliked the amateur anomalies as much as the abolitionists, the time when the future structure of the first-class game was precariously in the balance was surely the wrong one to introduce a classless society on the cricket field …
>
> Whom will the change include? Whom will it exclude [i.e. from playing county cricket]? I only hope that time proves me a pessimist as well as, patently, a crusted reactionary.

Swanton was in a minority. Far more typical was the response of the *Daily Mail*, happy to see the end of 'humbug and the need for petty deception, a blot on cricket for years'. In Brisbane itself, considerate Australian colleagues planted on Swanton's desk in the press box what he recalled as 'a wreath and a droll cartoon or two'. The ACCC vote (10–7) was only advisory, but the recommendation was unanimously confirmed by the full MCC Committee on 31 January 1963 – a day after the death of Plum Warner (historian of the Gents and Players), a fortnight before Harold Wilson became leader of the Labour Party, a month before the first Beatles number one ('Please Please Me'). Swanton, stranded in Australia, could do little about it. 'MCC could have declined to accept the verdict,' he reflected, still regretful, in the 1970s. 'Looking back, it was a pity they didn't at least fulfil a delaying function, for more mature consideration, rather in the manner of the House of Lords.'

Of course, contrary to some deceptive surface appearances, neither cricket nor Britain suddenly became classless in the 1960s. 'A zeal for the game' and 'a shrewd knowledge of its practical politics' was how Swanton in July 1962 had applauded the 'odd appointment' (Arlott's mild retrospective words) of the Duke of Norfolk to manage England in Australia, and Swanton looked forward to the Earl Marshal's 'brave adventure'. Over the ensuing years, he reserved much of his warmest praise for those from the right side of the tracks: after fine batting by Dexter, Cowdrey and Sheppard had helped England win at Melbourne in January 1963, he noted how 'three distinguished schools – Radley, Tonbridge and Sherborne – may bask in brightly reflected glory', but was silent about Maltby Hall Secondary School (Trueman, eight wickets), Manchester Central Grammar School (Statham, three wickets) and William Ellis School

(Titmus, five wickets); three years later, on the same ground, nothing could have been better than Bob Barber's undeniably magnificent 185 ('a superb disdain ... blissful watching'). Naturally, Swanton much regretted the enforced absence of the annual G versus P encounter at Lord's; but in that first empty summer, after a keen and attractive Varsity contest, he pinned his hopes – vainly as it turned out – on how 'people will gradually come back to the University Match granted a continuation of the spirit of 1963'.

Three years later saw the publication of the mammoth, multi-authored, Swanton-edited *The World of Cricket*, generously praised by Arlott as 'the most ambitious book on the subject ever published', but conspicuous for (in the sober judgement of Peter Wynne-Thomas) 'the amount of space given to public school and amateur clubs, at the expense of the professional game'. Public schools indeed ... When the Cricketer Cup for old boys' sides began in 1967, very much under Swanton's auspices, all sixteen schools were private (Repton the first winners), as remained the case two years later when the competition was expanded to thirty-two schools. As for Swanton's own teams, above all the Arabs, Henry Blofeld did not exaggerate when he noted the chief's marked preference for members 'to have been to smart public schools like Eton, Winchester or Harrow, and to have gone on to Oxford or Cambridge'; and a glance at the Arabs' abbreviated scores for 1968 reveals such names as C. A. Fry, G. H. G. Doggart, P. D. Hill-Wood, H. C. Blofeld, A. C. D. Ingleby-Mackenzie and the Earl of Cottenham. A disappointment was J. M. Brearley (City of London School and Cambridge). Writing to Field Marshal Viscount Montgomery in 1964, Swanton correctly identified him as a future England captain (albeit his 'in two or three years' proved a little out); but when, around that time, he tried to persuade Brearley to join the Free Foresters, and the young Middlesex batsman disobligingly said that he wasn't sure he wanted to play 'that kind of cricket, with ex-colonels and so forth', Swanton could only draw himself up and pronounce: 'Michael, there is such a thing as inverted snobbery.' The story went back to the Middlesex dressing room. 'It's not the kind of snobbery he knows very much about,' remarked the Shoreditch-born Ron Hooker.

Arlott seldom, if ever, had an outright go at the amateurs as such, but instinctively almost all his sympathies were with the professionals. 'He liked cricketers as a breed,' remembered his son Tim. 'He never turned down a request to write an introduction for someone's benefit or retirement brochure, and he never asked for any money for those pieces.' In 1965 he paid characteristic tribute in the *Cricketer* to an opening batsman who had made his county debut fifteen years earlier and had seldom troubled the headline writers. After noting that 'the amateur–professional distinction has been abolished but, in cricket, as in any other walk of life, the term "a good professional" remains a compliment', he went on:

Brian Reynolds is cast in the mould of the traditional 'senior pro', that non-commissioned officer of the game whose duty it was to see that the side functioned efficiently. In fact he *is* the Northants senior professional, but he would be the same man if the appointment had never been made. He thinks in team terms, watches a game wisely, and is the kind of man any captain can turn to with trust.

His turn-out – from well-brushed cap and neatly trimmed hair, to freshly blancoed boots, bespeaks a respect for his work. His jaw and his steady look are those of a man of purpose. Fresh-faced and as honest as he looks, the word that best sums him up is 'reliable': let us say *utterly* reliable.

Over and above the human aspect, it was the notion of the professional cricketer as *craftsman* that continued to make the deepest appeal to Arlott. 'The matches between these two counties are absorbing as a family game of rummy,' he reported in the *Guardian* in May 1968 on the first day of Gloucestershire v. Hampshire at Bristol. 'The established players are as familiar with the wrinkles of each other's cricket as with the backs of their own hands, and the young are quickly initiated. Yesterday's play drew only a thin overcoated line of observers yet it was full of all the delights of every skill in the game.' One moment was particularly emblematic: 'A day's bowling was only a twitch of the calendar for Shackleton and he showed no emotion when a stamp of his left foot on the delivery stride made a ball lift high on Nicholls's bat for Turner to fall boldly forward at square short leg and take the catch.'

What about the material lot of the average county pro? It is hard to find much trace of concern in Swanton's writings, but Arlott by the 1960s was very much on the case. 'Is County Cricket A Luxury?' was the title of his *Cricketer* article in 1964, arguing that, because the pay was so low, many people were unable to afford to play it and therefore much talent went to waste. Moreover: 'How many parents, at a time of full employment, are prepared to consider allowing their sons to risk the uncertainties of the – inevitably short – career of a professional cricketer?' Three years later, in August 1967, a lengthy piece in the *Guardian* examined closely the economic situation: huge variations between the counties in their sizes and methods of payment; capricious calculations of talent money; benefits or testimonials varying 'with public temper and favour'; decreasing winter work available on ground maintenance; and too many counties striving 'desperately to eke out an utterly inadequate revenue in a manner to keep both members and players relatively content'.

Significantly, Arlott in his analysis noted 'the absence of any employee's organisation': 'Until Fred Rumsey's recent suggestion, there has never been any serious thought of a cricketers' trade union. Perhaps as a legacy of the virtually feudal organisation of the last century, cricketers tend to be conservative in outlook.' There was indeed talk at last of a cricketers' trade union, but most pros were as yet apathetic or even hostile to the prospect. Arlott's final paragraph in effect sought to explain why it would take time to bring them round:

Cricketers rarely admit to being romantic. They are less inclined than those on the other side to compare their lives with those of clerks, production-line mechanics or shop assistants. But they do enjoy their five months a year in the sunshine – with luck an occasional winter tour overseas – playing a game they excel at, winning a place constantly in the local and often the national press;

it means a more varied social life for them than for most in their income-bracket in a world of pleasant companionship and excitement: and with the carrot of playing for England always dangling just ahead.

During the following winter the Cricketers' Association took shape – and Arlott was unanimously asked to become its honorary president. He gladly accepted; its membership and clout gradually increased; and over the next decade and a half he chaired around six meetings a year, as well as using his press pulpit to campaign for better pay and conditions.

Arlott's article in August 1967 coincided with an intense focus that month on 'professionalism' in cricket more generally. In politics, the two main party leaders (Wilson and Heath) were very far removed from the gentlemanly statesmen of yesteryear; in business, the cult of unsentimental, American-style management was on the rise; and in football, Don Revie's Leeds United were taking few prisoners. Should cricket follow suit, even if the result was increasingly dour or even unsportsmanlike play that turned off the spectators? Arlott, for all his empathy with the pros, had already in July written strong words, noting the high proportion of draws despite favourable weather. 'It seems that the players cannot see the wood for the trees,' he reflected. 'In fact, they are pricing themselves out of business.'

Yet inevitably it was Swanton to the fore, reporting in the *Telegraph* in mid-August on Ken Barrington's undefeated 109 in almost seven hours against Pakistan at Trent Bridge: 'As Barrington grafted away, an automatic slow-motion accumulator, it was remarked that what we were watching was the personification of the modern coldly-efficient hyper-professional performance.' Two days later, Percy Fender riposted with a letter to the paper. Barrington, argued the old Surrey captain, had on a difficult wicket played a team innings; and, furthermore, it was 'just not playing the game to slang a man who cannot answer back if he has put up the shutters in the interests of his side'. Swanton in turn then defended himself, not only noting that despite his 'many virtues' Barrington could be 'very tedious', but broadening the case to the professional cricketer generally: 'What is demanded of him is that he shall play the game in a positive and intelligent way. In this sense the professional cricketer is an entertainer, and if he cannot satisfy his audience, in the same way as an actor or any other artist, the house will soon be empty and he will be out of a job.' In essence, it was the same argument as Arlott's the previous month; but as to Barrington specifically, Arlott observed in his weekly journal (subsequently published in the *Cricketer*) that 'his colleagues went no faster and scored less', while fully conceding that it had been 'deadly slow going'.

Then came The Close Affair. Brian Close had been England's captain for the past year and had done well; but now, on the 18th, three days after the end of the Trent Bridge Test, occurred the fateful Friday afternoon, as blatant time-wasting tactics by Yorkshire under Close's leadership prevented a win by Warwickshire, and secured the addition to the visitors' tally of what *Wisden* would call 'two ill-gotten points'. The storm was immediate: boos as they left the field, the *Telegraph*'s Michael Melford calling it a 'petty, unworthy performance', and few disagreeing. 'Close has been condemned by every established critic,' noted Swanton on the Monday, 'and not least by those responsible critic-writers who follow their team day by day for the Yorkshire press.' Two days later he took the high ground: 'In these days, when almost every first-class player plays for his livelihood, the temptation is becoming the greater to over-step the line that separates the utmost keenness – which is the essence of all good cricket – from sharp practice, which is a different thing altogether.' Next day, Thursday the 24th, he fully backed the unanimous vote of the Counties Executive Committee to censure Close severely: 'If the game were to be allowed to descend to such tactics ... it would quickly forfeit the mass of goodwill that still surrounds it, despite the parlous state of country cricket and despite its denigration by some who have only the vaguest notion of its history and character.'

The timing was piquant. The final Test, at The Oval, was due to start that day; Close and Cowdrey were due to open for England; and everyone knew that shortly after the end of the match a decision would be announced as to which of those two men would that winter be taking England to the West Indies. England duly won by eight wickets on the Monday, not significantly helped by opening partnerships of 16 and 17, and the cricketing world waited for the announcement on the Wednesday. That Tuesday evening, straight after *Dusty* on BBC1, was *Sportsview* – on which, with notably ill-disguised pleasure, Peter West (quintessential public-school southerner) broke the as yet unofficial news that it was going to be Cowdrey. Next morning in the *Telegraph*, Swanton solemnly assessed the situation. Noting that Cowdrey was now the favourite, he sought to

Arlott with his mother, Nellie:
'She moulded her only child'

The infant Arlott:
'An expectancy of attention'

'Sunny Jim' Swanton, aged six, with his sister Ruth:
'We got on very well'

Swanton in the late 1930s with his father:
'Something in the City'

Arlott aged twenty-one:
'Not as good a cricketer as he looked'

Captain Swanton of the Bedfordshire Yeomanr
'Not many men liked him, but he was respecte

The only known photograph of Arlott and Swanton together: *TMS* team, Edgbaston, 1957: Arlott,
Michael Tuke-Hastings (producer), Norman Yardley, Freddie Brown, Kenneth Ablack, Rex Alsto
Swanton, A. N. Other (scorer)

Arlott, the front man at an early gathering of his fan club, late 1940s

On duty at The Oval, 1955: Peter West, Swanton, Roy Webber, Brian Johnston

Arlott: the image chosen to sell a hair tonic

Arlott's briefcase: his mobile cellar

John Arlott OBE, 1970: with Valerie and his sons Tim (right) and Robert (front)

oint authors of the history of cricket:
wanton with Harry Altham, an early patron, 1962

Old animosities put to rest: Swanton with
Len Hutton, Hovingham, Yorkshire, 1956/7

Swanton, his wife Ann, and Ian Peebles:
'Like a box-seat at the Chelsea Palace'

Rare memorabilia:
Swanton with his
1939 *Wisden* that
survived the death
camps with him

Arlott's final
farewell: Edgbaston,
September 1980

Arlott in his study at Alresford, 1980: where a two-fingered typist belonged

An Establishment man: Andrew Festing's 1992 portrait of Swanton hangs in the Pavilion at Lord's

Two archbishops and a bishop: Robert Runcie (Canterbury), right; David Sheppard (Liverpool); and Jim Swanton (Lord's), left; 1988

dispose of the canard that 'Close is being sacrificed on the altar of the old school tie', calling it 'a depressing manifest-ation of inverted snobbery surely, seeing that cricket alone among national games has abolished, for better or worse, the distinction between amateur and professional, and has an equal representation of these two former divisions on the Selection Committee'. Though careful not explicitly to come down on one side or the other, he emphasised that Cowdrey was 'held in high personal regard in every country in which the game is played', adding that his 'reputation as a captain has been perhaps undeservedly eclipsed by his so-called "dynamic" successor of a year ago'.

That day it was confirmed that Cowdrey indeed had the job – but, importantly, only as a direct result of the MCC Committee overriding the selectors' preference for Close. Arlott, writing his journal later that week, did not dissent, especially given Close's obstinate refusal to apologise for his Edgbaston tactics, even saying that he would do it again in the same circumstances: 'This is tantamount to denying the right of authority to define unfair play or to find him guilty of it. This was an impossible position for the MCC Committee faced with a recommendation from the selectors that he should take the MCC team to the West Indies, and it is hard to see that they could have done otherwise than reject the recommendation.' A last word, however, went on the Saturday to a letter writer to the *Telegraph*:

Your paper has been noted over the years for its damning with faint praise cricketers from north of the Trent and Humber, led, of course, in print and on the air, by E. W. Swanton who once, on a long-ago West Indian tour, came out with a classic example of this when he said England could only do with one Len Hutton ...

Close is of outstanding talent as a cricket captain. It is utter stupidity not to have chosen him as captain for the West Indies tour.

What should be 'out' – thrown out – is the effete, inefficient, old-school-tie-cum-vicar's-tea-party mentality which haunts the MCC and its committees and bedevils this wonderful game in England.

The writer was C. B. Collins of Staines, Middlesex: a long way from the Ridings, but perhaps he was that archetype most hot for certainties, a Yorkshireman in exile.

Indeed, though Close may have lost the battle, the war was going the other way. 'In Defence of Professionalism' was the title of a piece published in the *Cricketer*'s spring annual for 1968. The writer was the magazine's assistant editor, Christopher Martin-Jenkins; and after an obligatory reference to Close's 'notorious tactics' the previous summer, he made his case:

No one would deny the wealth of the amateur's contribution to cricket, nor would many suggest that the passing of the great English amateurs is not a sad thing, but amateurism is too often used almost as a synonym for good-sportsmanship, professionalism as a by-word for the lack of it. As a result English cricket seems afraid to exploit the reality of professionalism to the best ends. Blinded by the bad implications of the professional, legislators have been petrified into the misconception that there are no good ones.

Accordingly, 'the great problem' ahead for cricket's authorities was how 'to make a successful business out of sport without polluting its best traditions'. And: 'Perhaps the one thing that will restore the image of county cricket as a game of high excitement is – heresy of heresies – money. The professional game in England has become staid and stultified. It needs to be transfused with its own blood.' What did that mean in practice? Calling the recent decision (in November 1967) to allow one overseas player to be immediately registered for county cricket 'a cautious step in the necessary direction', Martin-Jenkins then set out his bracing vision for professional cricket's future:

> We need bigger stakes. We need more of the top overseas players. If the money is good they will come. We need a leavening of talent; the best players in the best teams. It may mean a transfer system. It does not matter. There is nothing immoral or wrong about buying a player. If his purchase injects new life into an ailing club, apparently doomed to stereotyped mediocrity, it can only be a change for the better. Anything for variety.

The article was accompanied by a printed caveat from the editor. 'The author is a young, keen, competent cricketer,' noted Swanton (who had assumed overall editorial responsibilities a few years earlier) in his best *ex cathedra* style. 'As he has recently joined the staff of this paper, I should point out that while approving his general line of argument one does not necessarily subscribe to all his conclusions.'

In fact, neither Swanton nor Arlott had been opposed the previous autumn to the instant registration of overseas players – in Swanton's case quite the reverse. 'I believe that, in the long run, even the counties who oppose the change may live to bless it,' he predicted. 'We may look forward to a general lifting of the technical level of Championship cricket. May the spirit normally associated with the cricket of such Commonwealth countries as Australia and the West Indies permeate our less adventurous natives like-wise!' Arlott was perhaps more ambivalent. 'We shall gain nothing,' he argued about the prospect of an increasing flow of overseas players into the English game, 'by trying to stem the tide – until England can produce enough outstanding players to staff seventeen county teams.' And a year later, looking back on the first season of instant registration, he offered a nicely balanced judgement: 'The new players considerably increased the power of several county sides, yet many who approved the step will not be ill-content that Yorkshire, who firmly maintain their traditional policy of playing only men born within the county, retained the championship.' In retrospect, it was a turning point – even for Yorkshire, in the end – from which there could be no turning back. For every overseas player, there would be one place less in a county team for a Brian Reynolds; and ultimately, the latter sort of pro was for Arlott the soul of the English game.

———

'It is to be hoped that they will be more sympathetic than was the case four years ago when the Altham Special Committee recommended a knock-out cup, and the counties duly rejected it,' wrote Swanton in the *Telegraph* shortly before a special meeting in December 1961 of the ACCC to decide whether or not to support this time the idea of a one-day knock-out competition, starting in 1963. In the event the counties did support it: against the background of falling attendances and increasing financial difficulties, it marked the starting gun for one-day cricket played on a professional basis. Arlott was unimpressed:

It seems [he wrote in the January 1962 issue of *Playfair Cricket Monthly*] that there is, somewhere in the administrators' minds, the picture of a man hesitating as to whether or not he shall go to a county cricket match. But he eventually decides, 'No, the scoring will be five runs an hour too slow; I will go and get drunk (or married) instead.' I, for my part, do not believe that man exists – certainly not in such numbers as to make county cricket clubs self-supporting through gate-money. Yet one day, I fear, cricket may damage itself in trying to woo this non-existent marginal voter. Aesop's dog, seeing the bone in its mouth reflected in the water and losing the reality in trying to snatch the reflection, should be an abiding warning.

He then turned specifically to the new competition:

To many it will savour of the dog with the bone: or another attempt to woo that unwooable – indeed, barely existent, man. It may attract a few people but, surely, not enough, after the novelty has worn off, to make any appreciable, or sustained, difference to county finances. If it is 'successful', then, presumably, our entire cricket play and economy must be geared to it. That would alter the entire method and character of our first-class cricket.

What then would happen to England in the Test field? For the difference between knock-out cricket and first-class cricket is vast. The players know it, and so does anyone who watched the travesty of the game in the over-limit match fill-ins after early Test finishes – a completely unhappy experiment.

The final paragraph was near-apocalyptic:

Cricket is a game for enthusiasts; it always has been. It would be a shame if, for the sake of the non-enthusiast's (problematical) gate-money, the game the enthusiast follows were ever debased. The marginal spectator might come once to see cover point fielding on roller skates, but he would not return. And when he went out, he would be followed by the old regulars.

Arlott probably did speak for many traditionalists; but by the end of 1962 the new competition had a sponsor – Gillette – and in May 1963, as it got under way, Swanton looked ahead optimistically to how 'if one-day county cricket in England can defeat the cynics and rise above the initial disadvantages of mid-week dates, it could breed in time a race of stroke-makers':

It may gradually dawn on more and more county players that, within reason, it pays to attack, and that the batsman who seeks to impose his will on the bowler gives himself an automatic advantage.

This is the basic fact that is often passed by in the countless pleas for 'brighter cricket'. The paid player will not be inclined to alter his routine for an ideal; but if he is intelligent he will revise his ideas if events persuade him that the bolder course pays.

Swanton also continued to indulge his pipe-dream of one-day cricket as a way of bringing back some 'older favourites' no longer able to play on a regular basis. 'Best of all is the prospect of Denis Compton [now approaching his forty-fifth birthday] fining down a bit, getting a little net and match play, and appearing for Middlesex.'

For the first round proper later that month, Swanton made an unlucky choice. 'While great deeds were in train at such places as Bournemouth and Cardiff,' he reported from Northampton, 'the game here had rather more of the flavour of a school house match than of a race against the clock with considered risks balanced and exchanged.' Indeed, after Warwickshire had made a ponderous 140 in just over fifty-six overs, it had been easy enough going (Reynolds taking an hour and three-quarters over 34) for the home side to win comfortably. The visitors' last chance went when Prideaux swept Hitchcock in the air to deep square leg: 'Such is the genius of modern field-placing that Amiss was fashionably stationed some 15 yards inside the 75-yard boundary board, and the ball just cleared his head. If he had been back it would have been a sitting catch.' Nevertheless, Swanton was in upbeat mood a few days later in his overall progress report on 'the Gillette Cup':

Generally speaking there is no doubt that the idea has caught on, and the only surprising thing is that this fact seems itself to have surprised many people. One finds those who look in a rather patronising way on the notion of getting a genuine result on one innings in somewhere around seven hours' play as though there were some sacred mystique about three-day cricket, with all else beyond the pale.

Altogether, he proclaimed confidently, 'far from being a gimmick, one-innings cricket – on which all the best cricketers of all the other countries are mostly reared – will help to restore essential values, certain of which have been so much in eclipse'.

Over the rest of the summer, this new form of professional cricket thrived, with Sussex under Dexter's captaincy emerging as the glamour team. 'A crowd of 15,000 who sat through an exciting game until quarter to eight saw the home county deservedly triumph with nine balls of the 65 overs' allotment to spare,' recorded *Wisden* about the victory over Yorkshire at Hove, where 'the match was played with waves of sea mist sweeping over the ground all day'. By the time of the final at Lord's, in early September, the two men took stock. Swanton was struck by how the rate of scoring of 57.71 per 100 balls had not been so hugely greater than the 1962 first-class average of 44.44. 'What grips in fact is not so much any vast acceleration of the action, though there certainly is some, but an atmosphere of concentrated purpose and intensity.' Arlott for his part was now singing a somewhat different tune from a year and a half earlier. Whatever might transpire in the final, he declared, 'the competition is already a success'. And he went on:

When a knock-out competition was first mooted, some suggested that it would never come into being and that, even if it did, it would produce poor play – '*bun-fight stuff*' as one player called it. In the event it has produced some absorbing games, with little hint of reckless batting …

The one-day shape has been extremely happy. Many spectators have been able to see, for the first time in their lives, a hard-played match between two first-class sides from beginning to end. For the players themselves, the brevity has had a tonic effect.

Even so, Arlott was careful to sound a note of caution:

Just as, before the competition began, some people were not prepared to go far enough with it, so now, there are some who want to go too far, and who suggest that the future of the game may lie in one-day cricket.

The answer to that is, with little doubt, that while a few of these games give a sparkle to the season, an unrelieved diet of them would be likely to cloy – and would certainly not produce Test cricketers.

Still, the undeniable probability was that of 'even greater enthusiasm and larger crowds for next year's ties'.

The pioneer final itself, naturally at Lord's, was a tight, lowish-scoring affair: Worcestershire, pursuing a target of 169, losing to Sussex by fourteen runs, with ten balls left and the light increasingly stygian. Arlott shared commentary duties (far from ball-by-ball) with Robert Hudson, and also covered the match for the *Observer*. 'Kenyon has sent Flavell away, kept him up his sleeve, and he's bringing Slade on,' he told radio listeners near the end of Sussex's innings. 'Now he's worked this little trick with the utmost cunning.

This means that if Sussex cut loose at the end, he's still got two overs of Flavell to use to shut them up, and for a man with only two seam bowlers he's contrived this quite magnificently ...' Swanton's main regret was that the defeated team was the one with 'a balanced attack', as opposed to Sussex's 'lopsided array of fastish and medium-paced bowlers, all individually admirable, such as *en masse* make the modern game so dull and stereotyped to watch'; but surprisingly, neither he nor Arlott dwelt on the encounter's closing stages, when Dexter displeased many neutral observers by taking advantage of a loophole in the regulations to place his nine fielders around the boundary.

What made this Saturday historic, of course, was neither the outcome nor the tactics, but instead the full house of some 25,000 – in *Wisden*'s words, 'the first all-ticket cricket match with a sell-out before the first ball was bowled' – and the boisterous atmosphere. 'A sell-out with rosettes, singing, cheers, jeers and counter-cheers,' wrote Peter Wilson (the self-proclaimed 'Voice of Sport') in the *Daily Mirror*. Swanton more mildly observed that 'everyone seemed to be "with it"'; and according to Arlott, the game's traditionally dignified, rather staid headquarters 'had an "Up for the Cup" atmosphere it had never known before, with a brave display of Wembley-type favours and a boundary bye being cheered to the echo, to suggest that a proportion of spectators had preferred this occasion to their more normal September Saturday afternoon of following the fortunes of Brighton or the Wolves'. All in all, he reckoned it to have been 'a happy triumph' of an occasion, while Swanton took pleasure in his calculation that 'the bulk of the crowd' was formed not by 'the patriots with their banners and their rosettes', but by 'practising cricketers, past and present, of all ages and types'.

In the event, neither Swanton nor Arlott was an out-and-out cheerleader the following summer – that difficult second time round for anything new. Too much defensive medium-paced bowling was Swanton's concern by July 1964: 'I think that the most successful way to play is, with some modifications, the normal way – with some ginger added. If I am right this idea will go from strength to strength, if wrong it might only be a stunt with a temporary appeal, until the novelty wears off.' Arlott, reporting on the final (another triumph for Sussex), offered a measured verdict:

This match emphasised that the Knock-Out final ensures that the cricket season no longer fades away in gentle nostalgias and festival fleshpots. Now, it goes out with a flourish of team favours, the honk of the fans' motor-horns and cheers and counter-cheers like a soccer Cup-tie.

Knock-Out cricket can never be *real* cricket. It is a contradiction of that game when the fielding side do better to confine their opponents to 100 for no wicket than to bowl them out for 101. But to fill Lord's on a Saturday in the football season is a mighty argument for it.

However, over the next few years, as the tournament settled down and the final became one of English cricket's greatly looked-forward-to set pieces – arguably *the* annual set piece – neither man found much to quarrel with. 'A victory for *cricket*', with Yorkshire 'underlining its trad-itional virtues in a way that did the heart good.' (Swanton on the 1965 final.) 'A strongly partisan crowd of more than 20,000 emphasised the standing of cricket's newest annual occasion.' (Arlott on the 1966 final.) 'A pleasing day, partisan feeling tempered by good humour.' (Arlott on the 1967 final.) 'The weather was blissful, the Test pitch extremely good, the sides well matched, with the result in dispute until close on seven o'clock, and every item of the cricket (to coin a phrase) razor-keen.' (Swanton on the 1968 final, in which Sussex were narrowly pipped by Warwickshire.) Indeed, a few months earlier, it had been left to an altogether more junior critic to issue a warning to the game's administrators. 'Like all special dishes it should not be made banal by too frequent appearances,' reflected Martin-Jenkins on the one-day game in his *Cricketer* preview of the 1968 Gillette Cup. Even so, he did not deny that whatever 'its disadvantages', it had 'the outstanding virtue of ensuring "vital" cricket'.

The one-day revolution had in fact barely begun. That same year, following on from the success since 1965 of the televised International Cavaliers matches, played against counties on Sunday afternoons (most often to boost a cricketer's benefit), the authorities laid plans and reached agreements for the start in 1969 of the John Player's County League: forty overs a side, played through the season on Sunday afternoons, with one match each week to be fully covered by BBC2.

'There is a general feeling that the case has already been argued and proved,' noted Arlott, adding that 'if the kind of cricket which has attracted many spectators and a wide television audience is given the added piquancy of inter-county competition, it will surely draw greater crowds than those who found so little satisfaction in the counties' Sunday play of 1967 [itself an innovation] – the short middle session of a three-day match.' But understandably – given his presidency of the recently formed Cricketers' Association – his concern was at least as much with the cricketers themselves as with the actual cricket they might play. 'It has proved difficult to fit the Sunday League fixtures into the pattern of the three-day weekend championship fixtures,' he observed. 'So some teams must travel to a match on Friday night, to the Sunday game on Saturday night or Sunday morning, and back again for the Monday of the first game – a pattern of five journeys a week.' And: 'The players will expect, and the county committees must provide, extra payment for the Sunday League.' For Swanton, by predictable contrast, it was the cricket alone that mattered, as he pondered at the start of the 1969 season 'what sort of fist' the counties would make of the new competition that 'is introducing them through television to such a vast new public':

> What they must hope to do is not only to keep uppermost the more positive aspects of 'instant cricket', but so to project themselves as men of wit and character that they will also bring new followers to the championship fold … The Sunday League will have proved far too expensive an injection if it simply whets unsophisticated appetites for the highly flavoured variant at the expense of the full game, with all its subtleties and ripe skills, its contrasts and its charms.

Ultimately, though, he did not doubt the necessity of the ambitious, high-profile new venture. 'Yes, the face of cricket is changing, in a way that traditionalists certainly find startling, not to say alarming,' concluded Swanton. 'But its heart beats as strongly as ever ...'

The first Sunday was 27 April. Eight matches were played, including on BBC2 (1.50–6.30) Middlesex v. Yorkshire at Lord's – the channel's warm-up to episode 10 of Kenneth Clark's *Civilisation*, 'The Smile of Reason'. Arlott was in the commentary box, along with Brian Johnston and Jim Laker. 'The match convinced me completely,' he wrote in his weekly journal, 'of the immense entertainment potential of this type of game when it is played by first-class cricketers. It is not so profound as the three-day game but it is in tune with modern public taste – and that must constitute the main argument for its success.' Over the rest of the summer it was almost always Laker and him doing most of the TV commentary. After the third televised match, the free-speaking 'Bomber' Wells accused Arlott in his *Cricketer* column of 'making excuses for some of the poor cricket'; but the general early response was accurately caught in the *Daily Sketch*'s headline, 'It's a swingalong'. The eventual champions were Lancashire; Peter Willey topped the batting averages; Tom Cartwright, who even in a novel format gave the impression of having seen it all before, the bowling averages; and Keith Boyce hit the most sixes, earning him £44 11s 4d from John Player and Sons.

The whole thing was on the face of it a swingalong indeed, including satisfactory viewing figures and total attendances of 280,000, not far short of those who paid at the gate for the whole of the season's Monday-to-Saturday county championship. 'The Sunday League has proved an immense success with all but the reactionaries who did not want it to succeed,' declared Arlott:

It is admirable that the crowds have come in satisfactory, though not in any way sensational, numbers to these Sunday games. They have a public, and they are helping maybe to free the County players from that rigidity of method that has alienated many brought up in a less inhibited, more individual age. They have made a place for themselves.

Swanton was not so sure. 'Interest in the Championship has been diluted by the instant Sunday stuff,' he complained. 'I am not at all against the 40-over league, but, under the present arrangement, the price to be paid for it could be too heavy':

It is common ground, surely, that the quality of our cricket – the game in all its subtlety and variety of skills – can only be maintained by the preservation of the two-innings match. The variant can be exciting, amusing, but if it is the real thing so far as it goes, it is not the full thing.

Henry James once wrote a short story called 'The Real Thing', essentially about how an imitation of something could somehow be more 'real' than the thing itself; but it is unlikely that Swanton, admittedly an improbable Jamesian, would have agreed.

———

During the 1960s the voice of Swanton – unflustered, pontifical, seemingly omniscient – was heard increasingly less often on television, increasingly more on the radio. Above all, he became ever more closely identified with what Trevor Bailey (who joined the *Test Match Special* team in 1966) called his 'daily close-of-play sermon': a sermon that was not so far different from his subsequent *Telegraph* report and often started with the words 'I shall begin by reading the scorecard', or sometimes 'But first, the scorecard'. The producer Peter Baxter (like Bailey, from the *TMS* class of 1966, and in charge from 1973) recalled the elaborate ritual that led up to the great moment:

He would come armed with a thermos flask which he would set down on the commentary desk with his notes, after a courteous, 'Do you want me here?' to the young producer. He would probably have to endure an irreverent comment or two from Brian Johnston [who joined the radio commentary team in the early 1970s], either on the air or off it. 'Always fourth form, Johnston,' he might protest, with a long-suffering and almost avuncular smile. The jacket would come off and be arranged on the back of the chair, revealing braces that would in themselves be far too tempting a target for the commentary-box prankster.

While the commentator entrusted with the last twenty-minute session, aware of the preparations for the end of his day's work, was describing the final overs, Jim would be reaching across to receive Bill Frindall's scorecard and make sure that it was understood that he would be reading it out at close of play.

Two more things were required of the young producer: stopwatch set on the precise clock time and a card inscribed in large figures with the time he must finish, would be set down in front of him. There was an instruction for the young producer, to be repeated every evening until the great man was sure of them. 'No signals!' This was delivered in a tone that brooked no discussion. Not for Jim the indifferently manicured finger raised before his eyes to indicate that he had a minute to go.

'Now, with his summary of the day's play, here's E. W. Swanton of the *Daily Telegraph*.' And he was away …

'It was delivered with no more than the odd word to prompt him,' added Baxter. 'And he always finished bang on time.'

By contrast, ball-by-ball commentary remained Arlott's undoubted métier. The 1960s were probably his radio prime: he still had the energy, still for the most part the enthusiasm, and by now possessed a mastery of his craft. If inspired by an occasion or a match situation or an individual cricketer, no one could touch him for making the listener feel that he or she was actually there in the ground. Take, from a single twenty-minute commentary spell on England v. West Indies, a trio of snatches from that intensely fluctuating, utterly tense final afternoon at Lord's in June 1963:

Hall turns and walks back. Close again goes out and prods the pitch. The trees away in the distance heaving under this strong wind, which in fact would help Hall to swing the ball into Close. The wind is coming in from about cover point, say extra cover; the trees heaving and bending under it, the light murky …

And now it's Hall, again from the Pavilion end, in. Bowls to Close, oh (*gasp*) tried to cut outside the off stump, through to the wicket-keeper – and about six rows of members down here fidget as if their ants were full of pants … pants were full of ants. Absolutely unable to stay still there. This awful moment when you see a batsman play outside the off stump at pace, and it goes through ...

Close 56, Titmus 11, and that grotesque tower away in the distance [possibly the Post Office Tower, in the process of being built], suddenly catching the sun like a beacon. The ground in bloom as Gibbs comes in, bowls, and Close steers him to short third man (*applause*) and takes a quick single. 202 for 5, Close 57 – every Englishman in the ground with him. Every West Indian in the ground after his blood ...

Three years later, as the West Indies closed in for victory at Trent Bridge, Arlott was commentating as Charlie Griffith bowled to England's last man, the young debutant Derek Underwood. 'No, no, no, no,' went the horrified voice, with longish pauses between each 'no' – and eventually he ' '' a still appalled tone, that a particularly fast and ... short-pitched ball had felled the tailender.

Perhaps inevitably, the experts in the box did not always see eye to eye with him on technical or tactical matters, for instance at Lord's in July 1967, when Close set Pakistan 257 to win in three and a half hours – prompting Arlott to argue on behalf of the spectators that Pakistan should have gone for it (as Hanif's men crawled to a draw), but Bailey to insist that it was never realistically on. Bailey himself would describe Arlott as 'easily the best painter of verbal pictures I have encountered', but add the rider that though his 'knowledge of cricket history and players was extensive', he was 'less expert on the game's technicalities which, as a limited player himself, had to be second hand'. They did not mind that in the Caribbean. 'He was non-Oxbridge, you see,' fondly remembered a Trinidadian listener, Trevor McDonald. 'People from Hampshire could also broadcast cricket. We embraced him for that.' While in Antigua, the young Vivian Richards would get up early to tune in before going to school: 'His commentary painted a picture in my mind that stayed with me and made me yearn for the day I could play in England.' Arlott's radio work rightly earned many plaudits over the years, with arguably the most insightful observation coming – perhaps surprisingly, perhaps not – from the *TMS*'s long-time scorer, Bill Frindall. 'The core of his whole broadcasting was the brain behind the man batting and bowling and how it would relate to the others,' he told David Rayvern Allen in the 1990s. 'So many commentators now don't think about that. They just describe the bare picture without the workings of what's going on behind.'

On the writing side, it was not until 1968 that Arlott became a daily newspaper's chief cricket correspondent, some five years after C. L. R. James had noted that he preferred Arlott's 'written description of cricket matches' to 'all others'. Even so, it could not have been a more welcome or auspicious berth: the *Guardian*, following the death of Denys Rowbotham, and in a direct line of succession to Neville Cardus. To read him in his early weeks is to get a clear sense of a cricket writer consciously and enjoyably upping his game:

The most confirmed reactionary will find it hard to fault the new stand which has now been completed on the site of the old Lord's Tavern and Clock-tower block. It has a clean, light, springing quality and, even in the dismal light of a wet Saturday afternoon, the long, simple uncluttered bar on the ground floor, with its sharp, internal lighting, has the bright air of an Italian piazza. (*6 May*)

Roope, whose future probably lies in his batting, bowled two overs of amiable pace but little accuracy, and Gibbs and Page 'worked him', as the latest dressing-room phrase has it, for a dozen runs. He took his sweater disconsolately. (*17 May, on the second day of Surrey v. Derbyshire at The Oval*)

The sun shone and, within the ring of Edwardian buildings their influence unaffected by the flats outside which are too large to belong in this private world, children stretched out, half-watching and waiting to start their own games on overlapping improvised pitches during the interval; their elders leant back in their deck chairs and sometimes dozed; here and there a large figure lay, sleeping off the morning's beer and acquiring unwanted sunburn; and the cricketers gave it all diverting, and often absorbing, point and unity. (*17 June, on the first day of Sussex v. the Australians at Hove*)

Next day, amidst 'an island of deck chairs, panama hats, picnic baskets and linen jackets in a sea of parked cars', it was 'a slim, relaxed, fair-haired young man of 21' who caught the attention; and Arlott noted how Tony Greig's 'length of arm' gave him such 'immense leverage' that 'the strokes apparently powered by no more than a turn of the wrist, travelled with high speed'.

So it went on, and a month later C. L. R. James in a letter praised him for having added 'a new dimension' to his *Guardian* reports: 'You seem to have made a sharp distinction between talking during the day on television and radio, and writing a column and a half for a more serious daily paper.' The following May, he had dinner with Colin Milburn only hours before the crash that cost that thrilling right-handed batsman his left eye; and in a moving piece written almost immediately afterwards, Arlott declared that 'as he took a match in his hands and by vivid power reshaped it according to his own unique designs, he lifted the heart as perhaps no other batsman has ever done'; and that, further, he was 'not simply a cricketer to admire but a man to enjoy'.

During the winters, Arlott continued to report regularly on football for the *Observer*. When in early 1969 the younger author, who with friends at school had started a very small-circulation magazine called *Soccer Digest*, wrote to Arlott, nervously asking if he might contribute (unpaid of course), the response was an article on 'A Great Forward Line'. 'Our sporting heroes are dictated by our age: no one ever again seems quite so far above life-size as the giants of our boyhood,' it began. 'To a boy of twelve, the Middlesbrough forwards of 1926–27 were the greatest attacking combination there could ever be; and whatever subsequent experience and objective judgement may argue, so it remains in his memory.' It was a remarkably generous (and hero-creating) thing to have done; while tellingly, he was already using the third person for a slice of autobiography.

During the mid-1960s Swanton stopped reporting on rugby union for the *Telegraph* – disenchanted by the game's increasingly thuggish tendencies – but it would never have occurred to him at this stage to step down as cricket's 'reigning chief scribe' (in Rayvern Allen's felicitous phrase).

Throughout the decade the Swantonian flavour seldom faltered. Take almost at random a trio of moments in July 1962. At Bristol for Cambridge University's match against Gloucestershire, he bigged up the young man who had scored 96: 'There are such obvious signs of class in [A. R.] Lewis that one can imagine few limits to his possibilities.' As for the Oxbridge summit itself, 'the first day of the 118th University match was not perhaps in the chateau-bottled class but for the connoisseur it was agreeable enough'. The day featured a century by Brearley, batting at number 3 and initially with E. J. Craig: 'We now had a First in Classics joining the First in Moral Sciences, but this massive intellectual combination was obviously occupied with higher things than the mundane matter of running between wickets.' Then the following week came what turned out to be the last Gentlemen v. Players, including either side of lunch on the final day some slow batting by the amateurs, ahead of a declaration:

> Our first-class cricketers, so admirable in some ways, are indeed peculiar in others. Lord's was full of practising players, past and present, as it always is for this match, and in any cricketer's company when a declaration is imminent and half the wickets are in hand batsmen aim to make a few gay strokes and end things with a flourish.
>
> When spectators are denied this pleasure they can only ascribe the reason to selfishness or cynicism or a mixture of both. I doubt if this is the right diagnosis in either case: so far as I am concerned the reason is unfathomable.

'The one certain thing is,' he concluded, 'it is bad cricket.'

Two years later, Swanton eloquently spelled out in the *Cricketer* what *really* bugged him about the class of 1964:

> So many of the present-day cricketers, and especially perhaps so many of the captains, seem complacently to suppose that they are playing not in the very dullest age since county cricket grew up a century or so ago but at a time when the game has reached its most skilful and advanced point ...
>
> What indeed many of my generation in their fifties and sixties find hard to forgive is the present lack of humility. The great players of our youth were, for the most part, modest and generous men whose manners tended to be reflected by cricketers of all classes. They enjoyed their cricket, and their pleasure likewise was communicated. Instead today we have an unsmiling ritual.

In July 1966, reporting from Trent Bridge in similarly condemnatory vein, Swanton lamented England's out-cricket ('lack of anticipation and speed ... apparent absence of some real all-out effort ...') against the West Indies. 'Milburn, of course, lacks mobility, but he is far from the only one,' he reflected. 'There were times, if those concerned will excuse the slur, when one might have been watching Aldershot Command after lunch and a free circulation of the port. I am thinking by way of the 'thirties: I dare say nowadays they are all lean and fit.'

Yet arguably there were limits to his critical fearlessness – notably, in the mid-1960s, an unwillingness to call out Charlie Griffith for his action, one that by June 1965 had prompted O'Neill, Dexter, Barrington and Benaud publicly to query it. Strikingly, Swanton *did* admit in an article in January 1965 that on many occasions, while watching Griffith bowl against England in 1963, he had said 'no ball' to himself under his breath; but in 1963 itself, no reader would have known that. Three years later, when the West Indies returned to England, he did allow himself the odd comment – the bouncer that felled Underwood was 'one of two balls bowled by Griffith during the day where cricketers' eyebrows were raised' – but little more. Later that same summer, the leading umpire Syd Buller made it clear, officiating in a county match at Burton-on-Trent, that he still found unacceptable the action of Derbyshire's fast bowler Harold Rhodes. Swanton in his 'Monday Cricket Commentary' two days later wrote sympathetically about the umpire's unenviable lot. 'If any umpire – when he is in an adjudicating position – says that Rhodes throws, then he does throw'; and he added that 'as I have admitted before, I do not count myself as a reliable judge of a throw, at any rate from beyond the boundary'.

More generally, though marriage had undoubtedly improved Swanton as a person, it could still at times seem – not least to subeditors at the *Telegraph* – like a work in progress. The young Henry Blofeld experienced him close up in the West Indies in the early months of 1968. 'One of my jobs on that tour,' he recalled, 'was to "help" Jim Swanton, the fate of many a budding cricket writer, which meant, roughly, doing everything he didn't want to do. He was a tough, not to say bullying, taskmaster.' On one occasion, in Port of Spain, Blofeld overslept and failed to perform his duties; not only did Swanton refuse to accept an apology, but 'for several days communicated with me only by message'. The tour also featured a legendary epi-sode involving one of Blofeld's bag-carrying predecessors, *The Times*'s John Woodcock. In his report of the first day of the Georgetown Test, he had criticised one of the home umpires for failing to give Sobers out leg-before at an early stage of his innings of 150. Two days later the airmail edition of *The Times* arrived and was passed to Swanton – who, having read Woodcock's account, then handed it over to the tour manager Les Ames, with the words, 'In your day, Les, responsible journalists did not make imputations of this sort.' Whereupon Woodcock, a close friend, declared loudly to Swanton, 'There are a lot of people in the box who think you are a shit, and you can count me among them.' Strong words, never mentioned again; and Woodcock even-tually became one of Swanton's literary executors.

As for the cricketers themselves, some stood up to Swanton, others less so. Presumably the more circum-spect category included those carefully chosen Glamorgan players invited on a Saturday evening in May 1969, when the team was playing at Folkestone, to Swanton's home in Sandwich – with dress, naturally, being dinner jackets. On occasion, the temptation to prick the pomposity proved irresistible, never quite so famously – deservedly so – as at Canterbury on Tuesday 6 August 1963. Kent were playing Hampshire, the TV cameras were present (Swanton, West and the injured Cowdrey doing the commentary, Johnston in charge of interviews), and the practical joker-in-chief was Kent's opener Peter Richardson, who over the years was wont to send invented match reports to the *Telegraph* for inclusion in Rex Alston's public schools round-up. That day he batted for several hours, and Swanton in his written report referred obliquely to the left-hander's 'liberties' and 'manipulations', but otherwise said nothing about what had happened. If *Telegraph* readers were kept in the dark, the *Daily Mail*'s were not. A story by its cricket correspondent, Alex Bannister, made the front page:

> England and Kent batsman Peter Richardson protested about a 'booming noise' during the Kent v Hampshire match at Canterbury yesterday. He said it was distracting him.
>
> The umpire, Bill Copson, walked over to the television commentator's box and appealed for quiet.
>
> The 'booming noise' was the voice of commentator E. W. Swanton. He said later: 'I think it was all a gag. I did not deem it necessary to subdue my voice.'
>
> But Richardson claimed he could hear every word of the commentary. 'I heard amid the boom that I was not making any shots in front of the wicket,' he said. He scored 172.

A few days later, in his Monday column, Swanton wondered whether Richardson, in his capacity as acting captain, might, 'with so many young cricketers round the ring', have had 'a slight twinge of conscience' about the whole prearranged set-up (with Copson very much in on it). Inevitably, the episode became one of Brian Johnston's classic, oft-repeated anecdotes. In an early version, for the *Cricketer*, he noted with understandable amusement how the practical joke was timed to coincide with Swanton taking over the commentary (at five minutes to one); and how, when Copson, after his grave discussion with Richardson, made his way solemnly to the TV commentary position above the sight screen, 'Jim, suspecting nothing, said the umpire must be coming to say something about the camera lights being too bright and putting the batsmen off, and must have been very surprised when Copson cupped his hands to his mouth and shouted "There's a booming noise up there which is putting the batsmen off!"'

Richardson was not the only heretic. 'I used to lead him on and try to tease him,' Ted Dexter many years later told Rayvern Allen about his relationship with Swanton. 'I liked to pinprick that old school attitude that a house match at Eton was as important as a Test Match in Australia. You know, something was wrong with the world if you weren't paying lip-service to the clubby traditions. But really, I admired him enormously in many ways. To carry on caring for cricket as much as he did and for as long as he did was quite remarkable.'

For Arlott the man, one event would come to dominate the decade – and to some degree, the rest of his life. His son Tim describes movingly in his evocative memoir, *John Arlott*, the death on the road in the early hours of 1965 of his elder brother Jim, aged twenty. Characteristically, Arlott reacted by throwing himself ever deeper into his work; but early next season, in May at a hotel in Northampton, he stayed up most of the Saturday night with some of the senior Glamorgan players, among them Tony Lewis, who would quote (on the basis of notes he took that weekend) his almost obsessive monologue: 'Why had the lorry no light or marker at the end of its extended load? Why was the lorry moving so slowly? I shall campaign for signs on long loads. Poor Jimmy, with his life ahead of him.' Until his dying day, over a quarter of a century later, Arlott wore a black tie. Was there something hammed up, friends occasionally wondered, about the ostentatious grief, about the lack of moderation that sometimes entered into his conversation? Yet, as with Swanton and his prisoner-of-war experience, it behoves no one who has not been through the same ordeal to judge. Arlott's faith is perhaps best described as that of an uncommitted Christian; in 1969, when a producer in the BBC's religious affairs department asked whether he could kindly write three hymns for their new Hymnal, he was happy to respond, telling her that she would have them next day. So she did, and one of the three, for Harvest Festival, is still in the repertoire almost half a century later. The twelve lines comprising 'God, whose Farm is all Creation' proved, he once remarked, more remunerative than almost anything else he had written in his entire life.

If there was therapy after his son's death, it perhaps came in the form of writing a solid piece of cricket history that was also very personal. Dedicated 'To Valerie for Everything', Arlott's *Vintage Summer: 1947* was published in 1967 and remains one of his most cherishable books. 'It was my good fortune to watch cricket, up and down England, on almost every day of that bright summer,' he recalled in his preface. 'But everywhere throughout the country there were men who saw every moment of play they could contrive. There was a warmth of feeling and an enthusiasm abroad which has never since been recaptured in any English cricket season.' In short, to have been present that season 'is to count one-self a member of a club within which there is no disagreement, only a consciousness of riches shared'. And at the end of the book, having taken the reader through the season of

Compton, Edrich et al., including South African tourists not yet shadowed by politically institutionalised apartheid, he described how after the last match at The Oval (the sun 'in automatic attendance' as Middlesex took on Rest of England), 'many of us felt strangely reluctant to go home':

> The Oval bars were by no means over-stocked but, by some kindly oversight, they did not close with undue haste. We could lean on the counter and talk. Many thought more than they talked. We had known and felt the untrammelled delight of cricket and, if we could not define it – and who has ever been able to do so with precision? – we knew it the more surely for our realization that it was too richly complex for analysis. We had felt that sun on our backs: we had seen cricketing feats of such happy gallantry that we had, at times, been glutted with richness ... This, we thought, is something we shall never forget. We were right.

That early post-war summer, irrespective of questions of the overall quality of play, would for Arlott always be the gold standard. At heart a traditionalist, albeit a non-establishment traditionalist, he never conceived that any of cricket's brave new worlds could possibly match his own remembrance of things past.

'Forgive me for chasing you again,' read the letter of 27 August 1959, penned in green ink on cheap, lined paper. 'I suppose you will be infuriated with me for writing yet another letter to you.' The story has been told often – of how Basil D'Oliveira, the outstanding 'Cape Coloured' cricketer of the 1950s (but, of course, ineligible to play for all-white South Africa), sent a series of letters to Arlott between 1958 and 1960, asking if he could help him to become a professional cricketer in England; how Arlott got in touch with the Manchester cricket journalist John Kay, who in turn in early 1960 found D'Oliveira a position with Middleton in the Central Lancashire League; and how by 1964 D'Oliveira was playing for Worcestershire, by 1966 for England. It still retains a compelling quality. 'I feel that if he could get an appointment here it might be a great thing for non-white sport in South Africa,' Arlott wrote to Kay shortly before the Middleton post came up (following the withdrawal of Wes Hall). 'I think that asking him over here might change the sporting and to some extent the political face of South Africa which seems to me very well worthwhile.' Six years later, in June 1966 soon after D'Oliveira's successful Test debut at Lord's against the West Indies, Arlott described him in the *Observer* as 'the most accomplished all-rounder in English cricket'; and added that he was 'far too accomplished to be left out of any fully representative English team for South Africa in 1968–69'.

By the spring of 1968, that intended tour the following winter – to a country against which England had continued to play despite South Africa's 1961 departure from the Imperial (renamed International in 1965) Cricket Conference – was increasingly on the collective mind of English cricket administrators, notwithstanding the more immediate prospect of an Ashes series. Importantly, questions of race relations and non-white immigration were becoming ever more high-profile in British politics, and indeed in everyday conversation. In *Any Questions?* broadcast on

12 April from Liphook in Hampshire, the panel discussed whether legislation – as opposed to 'evangelism' – was the right way to go in terms of improving race relations. 'He had known a lot of very nasty white men, but never met a nasty black man' was how his fellow panellist Lady Violet Bonham Carter paraphrased the response from Arlott, who 'then launched into a violent attack on the T.U.s [trade unions] – saying they pretended to be left wing & to fight for justice for the oppressed etc. & they were now trying to keep black men out of jobs & block their promotion as Inspectors on busses etc.'. 'All this,' she added, 'was well received by the audience, I was relieved to see', though it made her 'shudder' to 'think of the post' that Arlott would be receiving.

Barely a week later, Enoch Powell made his notorious 'rivers of blood' speech; soon afterwards, a Conservative MP, Patrick Wall, declared in the *Telegraph* that Powell's speech had been a clarion call to all Britons who had a pride in their country; and by early May, just over a year after he had given at Westminster Abbey the memorial address to Sir Frank Worrell, Swanton was writing a memorable letter to the *Spectator* in outright condemnation of Powell. It had been – he insisted in explicit contradiction to Wall, after detailing recent attacks on non-whites and students (to chants of 'Enoch, Enoch') – 'a bloodthirsty, hateful speech, lacking a single compassionate phrase towards fellow-members of our Commonwealth'. Swanton finished:

If 'Enoch' knew what passions he was about to unleash, he was guilty of an act that was the complete negation of patriotism. It is possibly more charitable to suppose that his frothy speech was a bid for future political power which, pray God, he may never achieve.

If 'Enochism' were ever to win through, there would surely be a migration from this once-great land of white as well as black.

The Conservative leader Edward Heath had almost immediately dismissed Powell from the shadow Cabinet; but opinion polls taken during the month or so after the speech found that between 67 and 82 per cent of people broadly agreed with its anti-immigrant thrust.

A few weeks later, D'Oliveira was in the England team for the first Test at Old Trafford. England lost heavily, but he was his side's highest scorer (96 for once out) and bowled with notable accuracy (match figures of 2 for 45 from 30 overs). The 1969 *Wisden*, in its report of the match, would include two distinctly grudging sentences about his overall contribution: 'He demonstrated the value of the straight bat and drove cleanly, but with the issue a foregone conclusion the value of his belated effort was difficult to appraise. England needed him as an all-rounder and he had failed as a first-change bowler.' There has been understandable speculation that that verdict was, in the wake of subsequent events during 1968, a doctored rather than a genuine one. That must remain a possibility; but it is noteworthy that when Arlott at the end of the match looked ahead to possible changes for Lord's, he contended that, in addition to the near-certain dropping of Amiss, 'Barber and D'Oliveira are the players to whom thought must be given. Their batting in the second innings gave good grounds for their retention, but neither is a bowler of full Test stature and the ultimate weakness in this match was the inclusion of half bowlers.' In the event, D'Oliveira was included in the party of thirteen for Lord's, but failed to make the cut on the day itself – and, in his report, Arlott made no complaint about the omission.

The politics, meanwhile, were becoming more complicated. We owe much to the forensic, pioneering analysis by Peter Oborne, whose 2004 study, *Basil D'Oliveira*, convincingly argues that by the early summer MCC privately knew that if it chose to include D'Oliveira in the forthcoming tour of South Africa, then that tour would not go ahead. Such a prospect dismayed many, including Swanton, his ear as ever close to the ground; and according to Oborne, on the day of the Lord's Test, only hours after MCC's secretary, Billy Griffith, had dangled a similar prospect before D'Oliveira, Swanton sought to persuade the all-rounder to declare himself unavailable for England – but not for South Africa. That, urged Griffith/Swanton, was the only way to salvage the tour. D'Oliveira's reply to Swanton is unrecorded, but to Griffith he said angrily, 'Either you respect me as an England player or you don't', and presumably his gist was the same the second time round. Oborne emphasises that 'there is no evidence' that the Griffith/Swanton initiative 'had the support of the South African government'; he also emphasises that neither man was a racist (Swanton, indeed, because of his distaste for apartheid, had skipped England's 1964–5 tour of South Africa) and that Swanton had been notably positive about D'Oliveira's inclusion in the England team in 1966; but he also, entirely plausibly, argues that Swanton 'was at heart an MCC man, eager for the 1968/69 tour to go ahead', and that 'he probably saw himself as trying out a solution that would suit all parties', including those wanting to break down racial barriers in South African sport.

Over the next two months or so, D'Oliveira's form largely deserted him; but at the last moment, after Roger Prideaux had gone down with bronchitis, he was called up for the final Test at The Oval, starting on 22 August. The rest would truly be history, with D'Oliveira scoring a magnificent 158, mainly on the Friday. 'Test century puts tour in jeopardy' was the title of a short piece (accompanying his main report) written by Swanton that evening: declaring it 'hardly conceivable' that D'Oliveira 'will not find a place on merit', he nevertheless noted sombrely 'a persistent rumour' from South Africa that, despite Prime Minister Vorster having announced in March a relaxation of apartheid principles for visiting overseas countries with which South Africa had traditional sporting ties, the government there had 'had second thoughts, and that D'Oliveira would not be persona grata'. 'This for many,' concluded Swanton, 'was the vague shadow that overhung an otherwise cloudless day at The Oval. Let it be hoped that it may prove a mirage induced by gossip and the heat.' The following Tuesday, England won a thrilling victory against Australia on the final afternoon, significantly helped by D'Oliveira breaking the stubborn Jarman/Inverarity partnership with, in Swanton's words, 'a very good one that beat Jarman and clipped the outside of the off stump'. The touring party was due to be announced the next evening, Wednesday the 28th. 'Whatever happens,' predicted Swanton that morning about the D'Oliveira aspect of a process necessitating (he explained) the MCC Committee giving its approval to the selectors' decision, 'there will, alas, be those who read into the decision considerations unconnected with cricket. Such people will undoubtedly be wrong to assume ulterior motives, but they may be nonetheless vocal for that.'

To general astonishment, given his Oval performance, D'Oliveira was omitted. Next day the critics were split. 'The right decision,' pronounced *The Times*'s John Woodcock. 'As the selectors saw it, he does not rate as a Test match bowler overseas; he is an indifferent fielder, and besides the other batsmen he failed to make the grade.' In short, 'had he been chosen, he could have considered himself lucky'. By contrast, Trevor Bailey in the *Financial Times* was adamant that, 'leaving aside entirely any political considerations, there is no doubt he is unlucky not to be chosen', with the Boil pointing particularly to his 'ability' and 'temperament' as a batsman. What about Arlott and Swanton? 'MCC have never made a sadder, more dramatic, or potentially more damaging selection than in omitting D'Oliveira,' the former declared. 'There is no case for leaving him out on cricketing grounds.' And he went on to argue that the player precisely met England's 'tactical need' for 'a Test-class batsman who is a reliable bowler at medium pace, or above, to make the fourth seam bowler'. Then came the crucial, big-picture passage about why the selectors had got it wrong:

In the first place, no one of open mind will believe that he was left out for valid cricket reasons ... This may prove, perhaps to the surprise of the MCC, far more than a sporting matter. It could have such repercussions on British relations with the coloured races of the world that the cancellation of a cricket tour would seem a trifling matter compared with an apparent British acceptance of Apartheid. This was a case where justice had to be seen to be done.

Secondly, within a few years, the British-born children of West Indian, Indian, Pakistani and African immigrants will be worth places in the English county and national teams. It seems hard to discourage them now for, however the MCC's case may be argued, the club's ultimate decision must be a complete deterrent to any young coloured cricketer in this country.

Eloquent and wide-ranging though it was, Arlott's perspective was broadly predictable. In this unique situation, the judgement that carried the most weight in the cricket world and beyond was probably that of Swanton. In his *Telegraph* piece, he did not deny that the selectors had 'done their best to view the situation objectively'; but in response to various self-justifying comments by them, he firmly stated that 'the paradoxical – some would say even ludicrous – theory has been put forward that this cricketer, who learned the game under the shadow of Table Mountain, is essentially a man for English conditions'. D'Oliveira, insisted Swanton, had been 'profoundly unlucky not to have been chosen'; and he declared that 'if justice has been done it has scarcely been seen to be done'. Significantly, the paper's leading article that same day went further: 'The MCC appears to have bowed to non-existent pressures. If it did, it should bow again, in shame.' Of course, 'non-existent' was at best a moot point; but, either way, the immediate widespread suspicion was that a degree of bowing had taken place.

That impression strengthened over the next few days, particularly after a rash of allegations appeared on 1 September in the Sunday press, especially the *Sunday Times*. 'They stand today in the eyes of many white men and many more coloured men condemned as racialists of the worst kind and we are all tarnished by their shadow,' proclaimed that paper's Michael Parkinson about 'the MCC selectors who made the decision and the MCC Committee that blessed it'; while soon afterwards, he fronted a television programme that included a filmed interview with the chairman of the selectors, Doug Insole, prompting Parkinson to comment on screen, 'Well, in spite of Mr Insole's obvious sincerity very few people believe him.' Very few indeed did, to judge by Swanton's overview on 4 September. MCC's decision had been, he noted, 'almost universally condemned', in turn bringing 'the great Club itself into disrepute'. And he went on:

> I have scarcely met anyone, nor have I had a single letter, that has attempted to make a case for the selectors. One reader seems to sum up a general feeling when he writes of 'the grotesque casuistry of the attempt to explain the omission of D'Oliveira on cricketing grounds' …
>
> As a cricket historian, I believe that the game has generally been wisely and selflessly guided from Lord's, and that its collective judgement comes [out] well from scrutiny over the span of a century or more. There are, however, moments that call for reform in all institutions, and such a one must surely have arrived for MCC.

Unsurprisingly, against this backdrop of widespread condemnation, including from a range of politicians, some MCC members felt distinctly unhappy about the club's conduct. A young academic, Charles Barr (future historian of Ealing Films), set the ball rolling for what quickly mutated into what Swanton would call 'the Sheppard group', with the now retired – and fiercely anti-apartheid – David Sheppard at the movement's core as it urged MCC to hold a special meeting. Swanton, writing to Sheppard in the course of the autumn, would call himself 'a very pale pink revolutionary'; but to have criticised MCC as trenchantly as he had was in its own way a storming of the barricades.

By then the tour was definitively off. The denouement began on 16 September, when D'Oliveira was chosen to replace the injured Tom Cartwright in the touring team: a moment of 'profound relief' to Swanton, while Arlott on the *Guardian*'s front page interpreted the selection as MCC's belated recognition of 'the liberalising and reforming forces in this country in a fashion which confirms the old argument that cricket reflects its social background'. 'It would be easy for the supporters of D'Oliveira,' he went on, 'to resurrect past statements which now stand revealed in all their fatuity. But it would be uncharitable to do so. It is happier to recognise that, supported – and probably astonished – by the weight and extent of feeling in this country, MCC have acted in tune with it.' All feelings of relief, let alone happiness, would prove brief indeed. 'Mr Vorster bans tour by MCC's "political" team' was the *Guardian*'s main headline on the 18th, this time with no accompanying piece by Arlott, whereas in the *Telegraph* it was Swanton on the front page for the second day running, declaring – despite the palpable fact of a batting all-rounder having replaced a bowling all-rounder – that 'Mr Vorster's contention that the choice of D'Oliveira has been "forced" upon MCC is an insult to the ruling body of cricket in this country.'

A long two and a half months then followed, before MCC's special meeting scheduled for 5 December. 'I hated every day of the autumn of 1968,' Swanton recalled a few years later, adding that 'I tried to fulfil, but with scant success, some sort of catalyst function between the Establishment and its critics.' Both he and Arlott naturally attended the eventual meeting at Church House, Westminster, where the main focus was on the resolution by Sheppard that was in effect a vote of no confidence in the MCC Committee. Among those speaking on Sheppard's behalf was the twenty-six-year-old Mike Brearley, 'nervously' according to Arlott; among those defending the Committee was one of its members, Dennis Silk, who not only stated that 'we do not stand as the social conscience of this country', but (in Arlott's words) 'introduced a note of personal acrimony towards David Sheppard'. Helped by a postal vote heavily in its favour, the MCC Committee emerged unscathed, the motion being defeated by 4,357 to 1,570. 'Loyalty to a body that by and large has served the game and the club so well was the prevalent emotion with the majority,' reflected Swanton at the time on the outcome, having probably abstained himself. Neither he nor Arlott found it an uplifting occasion. 'The level of much of the argument was terribly second-rate,' noted Swanton in his autobiography, as exemplified by the 'gentleman in a red and yellow tie' who 'indignantly queried Sheppard's right to continue as a member'; while Arlott was thoroughly dismayed by the 'all too great a parade of prejudice':

Texts were bandied, irrelevancies introduced and meta-phors muddled. The members ere never more eloquent in their spontaneous monosyllables of disapproval. One speaker referred to the extent of British exports to South Africa as a reason for giving that country no offence. In the end most of the members seemed to be exactly where they were when they came in.

The Committee who were referred to by the chairman [the club's president, Ronny Aird], without apparent irony, as 'the establishment', refused to admit the remotest possibility of error, or that they proposed to be influenced in their future relations with South African cricket by what had been said at the meeting ...

'From a lack of flexibility that was shown it may sadly have been quite unprofitable,' concluded Arlott regretfully. 'One can only hope that the evidence of this degree of dissatisfaction will lead to the searching of a few consciences before the next crisis, forecast by Robin Marlar, when a South African cricket team are due in England in 1970.'

Over the next year and a half, that prospect drew inexorably nearer. '*Can* South Africa Come to England in 1970?' was the title of Swanton's *Cricketer* piece as early as May 1969 after the English cricket authorities had confirmed that the invitation still stood. His concern was whether, if demonstrations against the tour multiplied, 'the point would soon be reached when the tour's justification as a sporting event, enjoyed by players and spectators, would disappear in an atmosphere of mutual embarrassment and resentment'; and he called on the South African Cricket Association to work towards 'multi-racial tours outside South Africa'. Six months later, in November 1969, the television cameras were at the Cambridge Union. In the context of sustained attempts by anti-apartheid campaigners to disrupt the current Springboks rugby tour, as well as the prospect of serious disruption of the following summer's cricket tour, the motion under consideration was that 'Political commitment should not intrude upon sporting contacts' – a motion supported by Ted Dexter and Wilfred Wooller, opposed by Denis Howell (the Labour sports minister) and Arlott. 'The "pièce de résistance" of the evening, and the only lasting impression one has of it, was undoubtedly the deep conviction which permeated John Arlott's stirring speech,' reported Graham Cottrell for the *Cricketer*. 'The only man to eschew notes, he thrust his hands deep in his pockets and treated the audience to fifteen minutes not only of his inimitable and dulcet tones but also of thoughts and beliefs which came from the heart and made a deep impression on all present.' A few sentences give the flavour of the speech itself:

> I cannot believe that any gentleman on the other side of the house would happily have played a round of golf with Hitler or Goering ... Political commitment is a personal matter so deep and so profound that when the split is at its deepest then the breaking of sporting contacts is only a trifling casualty ... Mr President, sir, anyone who cares to support this motion will not exclude politics from sport but will in fact be attempting to exclude sport from life ...

'For all that John Arlott says,' countered Dexter, 'my experience is that if you go out into the street and you ask somebody, what is his political commitment about this matter or another matter, he is a very confused individual.

Day by day there are the great mass of people in the world who just *live* from day to day…' The former England captain perhaps had a point, but it was Arlott who (in Cottrell's words) 'swayed the voting to his side of the house', and the motion was defeated by 344 votes to 160.

Early in 1970 – as the Cricketers' Association voted overwhelmingly (surely to Arlott's disappointment if perhaps not surprise) in favour of the tour proceeding – the situation rapidly escalated: overnight, a dozen county grounds being damaged by protesters; MCC procuring 300 reels of barbed wire to protect Lord's; and the MCC-dominated Cricket Council announcing that the tour would still be going ahead, but in a truncated form. Although Arlott did not condone direct action, his real ire was reserved for the cricket authorities. 'So far as Lord's are now concerned the issue is not England v. South Africa but the cricket establishment against the protesting Left,' he reflected in the *Guardian* in February. 'The prime consideration is that they will not be intimidated by protesters: and this issue, undoubtedly in their minds, supersedes all others.' And as a result: 'The coming season in this country must be like two parents tugging for a child so hard that eventually the child is torn in half to its destruction, and the victory of neither parent. The child in this case is cricket …' The March issue of the *Cricketer* had a Swanton editorial quoting approvingly an anonymous 'sportsman' – 'I'm furious both ways: furious that we should be dictated to by the violent minority, and furious that we can now be accused of giving comfort to the beastly doctrine of Apartheid' – while the April issue (with Swanton away, managing the Duke of Norfolk's team in the West Indies) temporarily gave the editorial pen to

Arlott. 'It seems that the best to be hoped for is a series of Tests completed, at vast expense for protection, before meagre crowds of screened spectators, in an abrasive atmosphere and at a financial loss which the game has never been worse prepared to shoulder.' As for the Cricket Council:

> It has taken determined steps, in which it will have the sympathy of every reasonable person, against those who would disrupt play by violent means, and who may be assumed to have little feeling for cricket. They have devoted less attention to friends whom they can ill spare ... The Council has admitted entitlement to peaceful protest but it has not recognised the weight of the reasonable protesters' attitude. Thus it has set at risk a substantial proportion of public support and goodwill not only for the coming season but for the entire future.

Then on 17 April came Arlott's much-publicised announcement, in the *Guardian*, that if the tour went ahead he would not be broadcasting on the matches. He explained why:

> It is my limitation, or advantage, that I can only broadcast as I feel. Commentary on any game demands, in my professional belief, the ingredient of pleasure: it can only be satisfactorily broadcast in terms of shared enjoyment. This series cannot, to my mind, be enjoyable. There are three justifiable reasons for playing cricket – performance, pleasure and profit – and I do not believe that this tour will produce any of them.
>
> The terms of the BBC's charter do not permit expression of editorial opinion. It would not be professional or

polite to disagree with my fellow commentators on the significance of the tour within the hearing of listeners. It therefore seems to me unfair, on both sides, for me to broadcast about the tour in a manner uncritical of its major issues, while retaining the right to be critical of them in this newspaper.

It is my hope to write and talk about cricket in which the minor issue of a game is not overshadowed by the major issue of principle.

Years later, Arlott commented that he would not have wanted his friends to wonder which side he was on; but according to Rayvern Allen, there was also a more pragmatic motive: 'Put simply, he was worried that if he made another public statement on apartheid he might be dropped from future commentary, and also other broadcasts. He had not forgotten his suspension from *Any Questions?* Never far beneath the surface was an insecurity that few discerned.' The immediate upshot, recalled his son Tim, was 'a large postbag', in which 'most were in favour but some were against', with 'the most unpleasant letter' coming from Peter May. Swanton, meanwhile, continued to despair of the whole situation. 'Pre-eminently, of course, 1970 is due to be known as the year of the South African confrontation,' he wrote on 22 April in his preview of the season, 'and the grim prospect necessarily overshadows all else.'

There was little doubt about where much of the cricketing world stood – certainly that large *Telegraph*-reading, Conservative-supporting part of the cricketing world, especially once the Labour prime minister, Harold Wilson, had said on television on 16 April that people should be free to protest against the tour. By late April it was a perceptibly hardening mood, encouraged by the formation of the 1970 Cricket Fund (Jack Bannister, Alec Bedser and Colin Cowdrey among those on the administering committee; Douglas Bader, Rachael Heyhoe, the Duke of Norfolk, Brian Close and two bishops among the patrons) seeking to raise £200,000 to enable the tour to proceed in the face of increased costs and reduced, all-ticket gates. 'Those like myself who support the tour, have been too timid so far to speak up for what they believe,' D. N. Arnold of Oxted, Surrey declared in the *Telegraph* on the 27th. 'I support the tour. I shall be watching many games, and I shall contribute to any "Save the Tour" fund, and woe betide anyone who tries to use violence on me.' With the latest opinion poll showing two-thirds of people in favour of the tour, a letter on 6 May from John Baker White of Street End, Kent, was revealing, as he disclosed how, at a recent meeting of Kent members to consider a resolution that the county's players should not take part in any matches against the South Africans, only eight out of some 400 present had voted in favour, four had abstained and all the others had voted against it. Two days later, with the South Africans due to arrive at the start of June, MCC let it be known that applications had been 'pouring in' from members offering themselves as stewards.

On the evening of Thursday 14 May, the House of Commons held a three-hour emergency debate on the issue, despite MCC stating in advance that the debate was 'not cricket' and would not alter plans for the tour 'one jot'. Swanton listened to it from the visitors' gallery. Back on 24

April he had in passing described himself in the *Telegraph* as 'one who has long doubted the wisdom of the tour taking place and who has not long arrived, narrowly, at the view on a balance of evils'; but this was the defining moment in terms of adopting that position in full-frontal mode, and in his autobiography he recalled how he was particularly influenced by the anti-tour speech of the liberal-minded Tory politician Sir Edward Boyle, 'a passionate supporter of Sussex whom I had known since Pusey House days'. Swanton's piece in the *Telegraph* next morning, 15 May, proved a telling intervention:

One can well understand the temptation of cricket authority, pressurised as it is being, to react defiantly to threat and virtual blackmail. One can appreciate the attitude that says: 'If we give in here, where does it end?' One can sympathise wholly with the view that the atmosphere has been further embittered by the 'free to demonstrate against' speech for which many in the cricket world may never forgive the Prime Minister. One can understand, not least, the widely held view of sporting people who want to see a fine team pitting themselves against England, and are indignant at the prospect of being deprived ...

The Cricket Council, however, I believe must rise above the misrepresentation of motive, the vilification even of the less scrupulous of their opponents and must weigh the balance of evils. If they do this in the light of the facts as they are, and of the likelihood of violence and of the division of the sporting world into colour camps, I sincerely trust they will have the moral courage to call the thing off.

Swanton fully conceded that on his part this had involved a change of mind:

> After many misgivings, I felt before the situation had reached its present pass that perhaps the risks were worth taking. I believe now they are not, and that the consequences might well do irrevocable harm to cricket.
>
> Most of the players likely to be concerned, and many responsible administrators, are now of this opinion. There would be no joy in the tour for them, and certainly not for the South Africans. Nor could the games be a conclusive test. Note the cricket considerations again, as distinct from the political.
>
> If I be accused of vacillation, I would say that the person who sees this agonising issue in absolutely clearcut 100 per cent terms is surely either extremely clever or very stupid. And I would presume to remind readers that for the last year and more, in *The Daily Telegraph* and also in the South African press and in *The Cricketer*, I have pressed for a multi-racial tour party, sufficient to make two sides, to come over together.

'What an infinitely melancholy thought,' he ended, 'that if such an initiative had been taken we might have been looking forward to the tour with pleasure and in comparative peace of mind!'

The major development over the weekend was Dexter stating in a radio interview that he was now opposed to the tour, citing 'real problems for race relations' in Britain and saying that 'the growing opinion of a lot of sensible people and a lot of responsible bodies seems to me to sway the argument against the tour taking place'. Arlott on Monday the 18th, after several weeks of relative silence on the issue, sought to gauge the state of play: 'Mr Swanton's – and Mr Dexter's – conversion to opposition are, surely, significant. These are substantial straws in the wind: it must be difficult for anyone who has examined the problem and its potentialities to believe that the advantage of the tour can possibly outweigh its dangers.' Next day, the *Telegraph* printed a letter from L. V. Hale of Ilford, Essex, condemning the paper's cricket correspondent for 'taking the line of least resistance': 'Let cricket take the belting Mr Swanton prophesies for it. If the majority of cricket followers are prepared to take a chance on that, why should we take notice of a few?'

Also on the 19th, the Cricket Council announced that the tour was still happening, but that this would be the last England–South Africa Test series until South African cricket became multi-racial. 'I think it is a marvellous decision and wonderful for the game,' acclaimed Denis Compton, while the title of the *Telegraph*'s editorial was 'Victory for Liberty': 'It cannot have been an easy decision to take: just a few cricketers ranged against the Prime Minister and a horde of violent and non-violent agitators, with only the vast quiet majority to back them up.' On another page, Swanton's reaction was altogether different:

We know the worst: the South African tour is irrevocably on. Conflict and travail lie ahead, and all that remains in doubt is the degree thereof ...

Some will characterise the Council attitude as courageous, others as the outcome of purblind obstinacy ...

Sad as I am at their decision, I would only presume to criticise it in that they have given the appearance of affording undue weight to the political – or civic – implications of the decision, rather than answering the one relevant question: What is best for *cricket*?

Giving in to minorities threatening violence is abhorrent to all self-respecting people. But there was far more to the issue than this. And as for majorities and minorities, in terms of intelligent and knowledgeable support and opposition, who shall say that the balance against did not outweigh the balance for?

A special concern of this sixty-three-year-old was the younger generation. 'With the glamorous counter-attraction of the [football] World Cup to take the imagination of sporting youth,' he added, 'it would be particularly unfortunate if the rising generation came to identify cricket, of all games, with venom and violence.'

Two days later, on Thursday the 21st, the Home Secretary, James Callaghan, unequivocally demanded – on the grounds of civil order as well as race relations in Britain and relations with other Commonwealth countries – that the Cricket Council withdraw its invitation to South Africa. 'The Cricket Council should still stand firm, and with a clear conscience,' urged the *Telegraph* on Friday morning. 'The object of many of the demonstrators is not the cancellation of a tour or even the end of apartheid but nothing less than the overthrow of our society.' In the course of the day, however, the news emerged that the Cricket Council had decided – reluctantly – that it had no alternative but to comply. Swanton himself was at the Glamorgan

v. Hampshire match in Cardiff, where he combined lengthy TV commentary stints (in the absence of fellow commentator Wooller, who had been called to Lord's for the Cricket Council meeting) with writing his match report as well as, more importantly, his comment piece on the cancellation of the tour. 'From the viewpoint of cricket this must be for the better, enjoyable and exciting though the Tests might have been in different circumstances,' he declared with relief. 'Our cricket fields will not now be a political battleground. The barbed wire can come down, and cricketers and administrators can sleep more peacefully at night.'

By that Friday evening he was in London, appearing with Helen Suzman and Peter Hain on BBC1's *24 Hours*, fronted by David Dimbleby. 'I said why I was relieved by the decision, and how much I hoped eventually to see a multi-racial side here,' Swanton would recall. 'I looked full into the eye of the camera, and said I thought that lovers of cricket might never forget Mr Wilson's recent remark on television that opponents of the tour should feel "free to demonstrate" against it.' Full into the camera indeed ... A general election was due in less than a month's time; over the past week, he had – in terms of his loyal readership's core beliefs and prejudices – gone disturbingly rogue; and this was his chance, understandably taken, to reassure the base.

7

1970–77: A Coarser Game

Cricket during the 1970s became coarser, more brutal, and more exciting. It became, despite some differences, the game we know today. Viewed in retrospect, the early years of the decade seem like the lull before the storm. But even then, appearances could deceive.

Swanton's decade could only improve after its intensely difficult start. 'It's hard really to know which of the extremes is the more pathetic, the violent young demonstrators of the left or the elderly skinheads of the right,' he reflected a few weeks after the cancellation of South Africa's 1970 tour. The Duke of Norfolk was not exactly a skinhead, but his aggrieved letter to Swanton – 'If people cannot support the game, I cannot support them' – undeniably 'cut' its recipient. 'Me not support cricket?' he replied. 'It has given me my livelihood, and I have given it most of my life. As to "support", for the last five years I've given something like half of my time to keep *The Cricketer* going almost for nothing – I get a few hundred a year – because I believe the game should continue to have an independent paper.' 'The anger all round here is enormous,' the Duke responded ungraciously as well as unyieldingly; but eventually the controversy died down and Swanton was able to resume normal Swantonian service. This, of course, included his end-of-play Test summaries – Henry Blofeld in 1972 was struck by how he 'insisted on a glass of whisky and water being ready beside his microphone and he would not be pleased if the ice was missing'. That same year, a young Australian (whose first cricket book he had ever bought had been *Elusive Victory*) got to know Swanton through becoming his deputy editor on the *Cricketer*. 'Although he never was a father, he could be fatherly,' recalled David Frith. 'It was agreed that I could call him "Jim". I did all the editorial work. He dished out orders. No sweep shot to be featured in the magazine ... His missives zoomed in from Sandwich by first-class post, or via sepulchral phone-calls ... For me the most amusing expression, frequently used, was "Now look heah!" It was his way of asserting himself, an attempted rib-crusher ...'

It was also in 1972 that Swanton published his autobiography, *Sort of a Cricket Person*. Calling him 'the most influential cricket writer of the post-war period', and 'active in the game's corridors of power', Arlott reviewed it in the *Guardian* with a perhaps surprising degree of warmth (especially given that some years earlier at Lord's, watching Swanton being appallingly rude to his secretary, he had expostulated to a young Frank Keating, 'Have nothing to do with that man; that man is a bully.'):

> The narrative is lucid. Jim Swanton has always been an unaffected writer, reporting fact, stating opinion, and if he does not traffic in imagery he is always admirably clear. His style is at its best in the chapter entitled 'One

Man's War', a passage of admirably controlled and surely communicated feeling. It is matched in sincerity and modesty by the opening 'The Universal Thread' where he attributes his success – being alive to do the thing he wants to do above all, which is write about cricket – to 'common-or-garden luck'. It is, too, a generous book, recording gratitude as well as achievement; sometimes regretful but without rancour; he has mellowed since the days when he sees himself as 'brash'.

A more critical paragraph followed, in which Arlott complained about the book's excessive name-dropping ('too few of those 1,100 in the index are people the author knows – as distinct from having met – to belong in a true autobiography'), before he returned to the positive:

> Mr Swanton is best as himself, especially in his unstated, but constantly implicit, dilemma. Many people regard him as a member of the cricket establishment – and he has often been active in its support – but in fact it never admitted him. Possibly it could not rely upon his unquestioning conformity. Certainly, he is one of the few who ever stood [in 1968] as a candidate for the undemocratically self-perpetuating committee of the MCC. He was defeated but not diminished. He has sometimes disagreed with the hierarchy but, at the pinch, he has always laboured for the benefit of the game as he sees it. He is not exploiting hind-sight when he recalls his efforts to prevent errors – as they subsequently proved – of appointment or selection.

Arlott also noted appreciatively how Swanton had come down on the side of the angels in relation to the 1970 tour, thereby failing (not only in the Duke of Norfolk's eyes) a loyalty test. 'He was innocently surprised,' added Arlott, 'when at a subsequent election night party someone commented on his enthusiasm for Conservative successes [taking Edward Heath to No. 10] with "Oh, we thought you'd gone over to the enemy."' The review's closing sentences had a particular resonance: 'The week-long, year-round routine of cricket makes it the most devouring of games for everyone concerned. To live nearly fifty years in it with undiminished conviction, relish and gratitude a man must be a special sort of a Cricket Person; and his book shows Mr Swanton to be exactly that.'

Arlott himself in these years was in the commentary box as much as the press box, though it was probably by the early 1970s that he was starting to scale down his frequency of twenty-minute spots on *TMS*: two before lunch, one after, and then he started to focus on his daily report for the *Guardian*. That still gave him time to introduce wine into the commentary box – something that Brian Johnston initially deplored as unprofessional, though later coming to see the virtue of a glass of dry white at midday. What about quality? 'Although a genius, he didn't always employ his talent to the full – he was up and down; brilliant many times, he could also be rather poor,' recalled Robert Hudson, who had moved from commentating to run the BBC's outside broadcasting. Or anyway, 'nearly poor'. Some colleagues thought Arlott's commentary slowed down in the post-prandial spot. Perhaps also he was thinking about two things at once – his verbal broadcast and his written match report. It is worth quoting, though, what Hudson added after his 'nearly poor' verdict on some (probably not many) of Arlott's stints: 'I do remember one occasion when a match was so exciting, and his commentary so scintillating, that it produced a round of applause on the air from his fellow commentators.' Blofeld joined the team in 1972, a season after Arlott's irresistible comparison of Asif Masood's crouching run-up to 'Groucho Marx chasing a pretty waitress'. 'In my first years,' remembered Blofeld, 'I often handed over to Arlott, and I would stay in the box to listen to him. After five minutes I would leave, wondering why I even bothered to try.' The doyen's 'ringing Hampshire tones', he went on, 'grew richer and richer over the years as his vocal cords were increasingly marinated in ever more spectacular bottles of claret'. And: 'His pace of delivery never changed much; he merely sharpened his words a fraction when a wicket or some other drama occurred.'

A celebrated story comes perhaps from about this time, nicely told by Patrick Collins, a devoted admirer:

Although he was a kind man, he didn't suffer foolishness. I asked him about a fellow commentator who once set out to emulate Arlott by injecting colour into a county match with some absurdly florid language. Unfortunately, it was always the same phrase. For instance, he'd say: 'The bowler trudges back to his mark as the sun sets slowly in the West.' Later: 'And that single takes Somerset to 153 for 2, as the field changes, and the sun sets slowly in the West.' And later still: 'The Essex attack continues to struggle, and the sun sets slowly in the West. Now, over to John Arlott.' And Arlott took the microphone and announced: 'The sun is still setting slowly in the West.

And if it should start to set anywhere else, I'll be the first to let you know.'

'Years later,' added Collins, 'John confessed that he was slightly ashamed of his mischievous outburst. But only slightly.'

The book-writing urge was becoming less strong, but Arlott took advantage of a two-week postal strike to write in white heat a biography of Fred Trueman. Published in 1971, and reckoned by its author to be his best book, *Fred* became almost instantly celebrated for its virtuoso set-piece description of Trueman's compelling action at his youthful fastest: 'He was a cocked trigger, left arm pointed high, head steady, eyes glaring at the batsman as that great stride widened: the arm slashed down and as the ball was fired down the pitch, his body was thrown hungrily after it, the right toe raking the ground closely beside the wicket as he swept on ...' Two years later, in 1973, Arlott set eyes for the first time on a future hero. The setting was Taunton; Ian Botham, not yet in Somerset's first team, carried his luncheon basket (heavy with wine bottles) up a rickety staircase to the commentary box; and Arlott by 10.30 was giving the young man a drink and starting to teach him about the mysteries of the grape. But it was at home in Alresford, giving a dinner party, that Arlott was in his absolute pomp. 'We all listened, spellbound, and the bottles kept coming,' remembered Blofeld about one such occasion. 'It wasn't easy to get a word in oneself, but it was all so amusing that it didn't matter, although those who were regular visitors to his dining-room probably had to suffer a certain repetition.'

Arlott continued to see himself as an anti-establishment man. 'Cricket, like much of industry – and cricket is part of the entertainment industry – ought now to extend its government,' he declared in the *Guardian* in 1971. 'It ought to follow a system of including in effective numbers those for whom the game is their livelihood – players, umpires, coaches, groundsmen – instead of the present method, which is in effect of governing with an upper chamber alone: the power of the Lords may have been reduced but not that of Lord's.' There also remained a persistent, gnawing, driving insecurity. 'I lived under real fear of the sack until around 1975,' he observed in 1980 about his relationship with the BBC. 'And if there was a letter from the *Guardian* in the post I always opened it first in case it was the sack.' Even towards the end of the 1970s he still once a year took out for lunch the whole of the paper's sports department, secretaries and all: an act of benevolence, certainly, but also an insurance policy.

As in every decade, the question of who should captain England was seldom off the agenda. In July 1970, three years after the Close affair, it involved (in Arlott's words at the time) 'all the issues – like North against South, amateur against professional, Yorkshire against the Rest, loyalty against expediency, and short-term against long-term wisdom – which Lord's ought by now to have learned from experience to avoid at all reasonable cost'. The choice for the coming tour to Australia lay between Colin Cowdrey, captain until a ruptured Achilles tendon early in the 1969 season, and his replacement, Ray Illingworth. The former had already been vice-captain on three previous tours there, but never captain; the latter – described by Arlott in 1965 as 'a true Yorkshire cricketer, technically studious, intelligent and, at heart, ready to battle out a cricket match against any opponent' – had shown himself to be, by general consent, an effective leader as well as capable all-rounder, especially batsman. The two men were chalk and cheese (Tonbridge School on the one hand, Wesley Street School, Farsley, on the other). 'I have the highest respect for the young player of today – fitter and keener than ever before,' Cowdrey wrote shortly before the 1970 season. 'I beg him to remember that, in his search for technical ideals in an ultra-professional world, cricket is still a game to be enjoyed and that the crowd's fun is wrapped up in *his*.' For Illingworth by contrast, 'foon' was at best an irrelevance.

That July, ahead of the imminent decision, Swanton predictably favoured Cowdrey, essentially on non-cricketing, ambassadorial grounds – 'I expect that most readers with a sporting interest will have an inkling of the qualities needed in a man leading his country abroad without my needing to elaborate them' – while Arlott expressed sadness that 'the situation between two good cricketers and captains has been brought to a point which those who follow the game can only see as contention'. In the event, the selectors plumped for the man in post. 'The appointment of Illingworth is a completely professional one,' wrote Arlott, while Swanton confessed to 'mixed feelings': 'Whether the right choice has been made in preferring a man who has been, frankly, a failure on two tours [before he became captain] to one who has succeeded on nine only history will show.' Even so, 'I do not doubt for a moment Illingworth's capacity to carry out his function to the credit of English cricket'.

Arlott as usual stayed at home that winter, but nothing could deter Swanton. Although England regained the Ashes – lost back in 1958–9 – he experienced two moments of serious disappointment. The first came with the decision, wholly welcome in his eyes, to play an additional Test, following the complete washout of the Melbourne Test that had been due to begin on New Year's Eve. 'I wish I could say in honesty that it has been greeted if not with enthusiasm at least with understanding by the touring team as a whole,' he noted, reporting on a team meeting (attended by all except D'Oliveira, Alan Knott and vice-captain Cowdrey) that had led to a request for an extra fee. Swanton did not mention the captain by name, but he hardly needed to. Then in mid-February, during the decisive seventh Test at Sydney, occurred the memorable episode late on the second day: bumpers from John Snow; a warning by umpire Rowan (no neutral umpires then); Illingworth expostulating bitterly; visible discord on the long-leg boundary between an unrepentant Snow and angry, well-oiled spectators; Illingworth apparently cocking his thumb in the direction of the dressing room; cans starting to be thrown; and Illingworth, without consulting the umpires, taking his men off the field. Swanton's analysis for the *Telegraph* was fiercely critical. Through his 'openly questioning' the umpire's decision to warn his fast bowler, Illingworth had 'shown a singularly bad example to cricketers everywhere as well as putting a superfluous strain on cricket relations between England and Australia'; his walk-off decision had been 'precipitate'; and altogether, 'with a modicum of tact and self-discipline all round the situation would never have arisen'.

Swanton returned to the charge shortly after the match – 'It is admirable that what has been palpably the better side should have won the Ashes, but it could have been done just as certainly, if not more so, without a surly, unlikeable attitude by a few members of the team' – while two months later, back in England, there would be a piquant coda. Robin Day was presenting *It's Your Line* on Radio 4 and his guest was Illingworth (about to be honoured with a celebration banquet at Lord's), when up popped Swanton on the telephone. Near the end, after an inconclusive discussion about whether he had been remote from the cricketers, staying at different hotels and so on, they properly crossed swords:

DAY: Just before you go, I'd like to know whether Ray would like to ask you a question, because it's rare that we get a critic of your standing and a cricketer of his standing.

ILLINGWORTH: Well, there is one piece I would like to … you wrote a summing up on the tour, Jim, and you did write that there'd been a lowering of standards on and off the field, and I wasn't very impressed with that for the amount I did see you on the tour.

SWANTON: I said there was a lowering of standards. Yes, I did say that, Ray, with very great reluctance. It's no pleasure to anybody like myself who loves to see England win and nothing else, to see certain of the things that went on. I thought I'd never hope to see an England captain threatening or seeming to threaten by wagging his finger at an Australian umpire with twenty or thirty thousand Australians looking on. If the game is going to come to this sort of pass where the umpire is going to be openly challenged on the field, I think that the end of cricket in the Test Match sense is really pretty near …

DAY: Now Ray Illingworth, do you want to add to your explanation of why you did that?

ILLINGWORTH: Well now, Jim knows why. Does he think the umpire was right on that occasion?

SWANTON: Did I think the umpire was right? Well, I think that the umpire must always be right, and he must always be respected by the players. I know all about tensions and that sort of thing, but I've been watching Test Matches for longer than I care to remember. I've seen some two hundred odd of them, and I've never before seen a captain resort to that.

ILLINGWORTH: No, it's probably very true, but you've never ... captain's spoken his mind before.

SWANTON: We've had a great many captains who've spoken their minds very well, Ray. Don't imagine that because you're a Yorkshireman and tough, you're the only person who can speak your mind.

ILLINGWORTH: Oh no, I don't imagine that at all.

SWANTON: I think that there were a great many of them before that.

ILLINGWORTH: Well, we shall see.

SWANTON: Douglas Jardine for a start.

ILLINGWORTH: Ah, well, I don't go back that far, Jim.

SWANTON: No, well there you are – I have the advantage of you.

ILLINGWORTH: Yes, you're quite right there.

And there indeed the exchange ended. 'You haven't convinced one another,' commented Day, adding hopefully that 'perhaps the matter will come up again'.

Illingworth retained the Ashes in 1972 (Arlott and Swanton both very damning about the blatantly prepared-for-Underwood wicket at Headingley), but by 1973 was under pressure. Tony Lewis had won plaudits during the winter for his captaincy in India and Pakistan (Illingworth having chosen not to go), so that by the time of the Test trial at Hove in late May – Lewis's tour team against Illingworth's 'The Rest' – a sniff of regime change was in the air. Lewis's duck on the first morning ('Illingworth showed no pleasure,' reported Arlott), followed by an inconclusive second innings (not out 8 ahead of a declaration) and a victory for The Rest by four wickets, saw off this particular pretender. Lewis himself thirty years later would give the inside story of that fateful Wednesday morning. At eight o'clock a phone call from Arlott: 'Meet me in Turnbull's, the wine merchant, at 8.45. I will be waiting for you with Mr Turnbull in the cellar.' There, Lewis cautiously sipped half a glass of sparkling Vouvray, with Arlott assuring him that it was 'the only time in the day to drink it, nine o'clock, so as to approach the day with equanimity'. Equanimity indeed:

> Two and a half hours later, the second ball I faced pitched on the seam and left me off the pitch. Bob Woolmer bowled it and Alan Knott caught it, standing up, off the faintest flick from the thumb of my right glove. Back in the dressing room, nursing my nought, the attendant announced that Mr John Arlott was at the door in the hope of seeing Mr Lewis. I went down the steps to the concrete concourse at the back of the pavilion where John was distraught. Mopping his forehead with a red handkerchief, he shook his head with apologies. 'No! No! It was my fault, all my fault. Taking you to Mr Turnbull before a Test trial. Gawd, I'm sorry. I've cost you your

England place.' Nothing I said in favour of the Woolmer delivery could console him.

'Not even a telephone call some days later,' adds Lewis, 'when I had been selected [though not as captain] for the First Test at Trent Bridge could persuade him that he was not a crucial part of my potential downfall at Hove. Every inch of cricket was for John a heart-wringing drama.'

Arlott himself was a staunch Illingworth man, noting darkly before the Test trial that 'there are those who, perpetuating in their own minds the officially abolished amateur-professional distinction, will continue to lobby for Illingworth to be superseded', whereas in reality Lewis 'has not yet done quite enough to establish himself'. England in due course beat New Zealand 2–0, but then came badly unstuck against the West Indies, culminating in an ignominious thrashing at Lord's (Illingworth 1 for 114 with the ball, 0 and 13 with the bat). Although Arlott continued to make the case for his captaincy – 'the team has not been strong for a long time, but its weakness has been artfully concealed' – the selectors now decided to sack him, appointing instead Kent's Mike Denness, wholly untried at Test level against the then major countries. Arlott detected an element of a PR job ('he is a keen, well-drilled, neatly turned-out, good-mannered cricketer'), but the noisiest broadside came from Michael Parkinson in the *Sunday Times*, calling the decision 'barmy' and declaring that, if Illingworth had to be replaced, then it should have been another Yorkshireman, Geoffrey Boycott, taking charge. Swanton was appalled. Recalling in the *Cricketer* that Parkinson six years earlier had been equally cross about the sacking of Close, he described the Barnsley man as 'that caricature of a Yorkshireman who is guaranteed to glorify anything and anyone who comes from his own small corner of the world and to denigrate almost all else'; noted that 'I never remember seeing Parkinson at any match or cricket function I have ever attended'; denied that he was a 'bona fide cricket writer'; and concluded scornfully that the case he had put forward was mere 'piffle'.

By now the reach of the one-day format had advanced significantly further. 'Sponsors, it seems, are queuing up to give the occasion the incentive it needs to sharpen the appetites of players and public,' Swanton wrote from Melbourne ahead of the hastily arranged pioneer one-day international on 5 January 1971 between England and Australia. Afterwards, he reported on how it had 'turned out wonderfully well ... a day of sustained interest with the arts of the game in full display ... 46,000 sat sprinkled thickly round the great bowl enjoying the sunshine and lapping it all up ...' Some six weeks later, a Test and County Cricket Board (TCCB) subcommittee proposed from 1972 an additional one-day competition in the English domestic calendar: a 'league cup' to be played in the first half of the season, with a zonal dimension. 'The attraction of one-day limited-over play has endured far beyond its novelty,' reflected Arlott. 'It is now the soundest economic aspect of the county game ... Most sections of the first-class game will probably support it [the proposal] for fear worse should befall.' Swanton was similarly pragmatic. 'County cricket must be viable to live,' he wrote after the plan had been confirmed in March, 'and when there comes a year like 1970 with the most wonderful summer in memory, yet at the end of it every single county club showed a loss, the writing on the wall cannot be gainsaid.' Moreover, whatever his regrets about the inevitable 'overshadowing' of the county championship, 'at least the summer cannot lack variety'.

That said, neither man felt any great enthusiasm for the short-form Sunday version of the one-day game, as embodied in the John Player League. Swanton seldom covered or wrote about it, while for Arlott it was only the money that induced him to remain a commentator on the TV coverage. 'He would take the first twenty overs of each innings of the "forty-over bash", so as to be on the road homewards soon after five o'clock,' notes Rayvern Allen. 'In most games the predictable pattern of play quickly lost its interest, and sometimes he would fall asleep while on air.' C. P. Snow would have sympathised. 'For myself,' he wrote in the *Cricketer*'s April 1971 Jubilee issue, 'I wouldn't walk across the road to watch it.'

The continuing one-day revolution undoubtedly caused some serious heart-searchings. 'It puts the accent on stopping a man scoring rather than getting him out,' Swanton that summer told an Australian cricket journalist who had asked for his views about one-day cricket. 'With this limitation it provides skilful and attractive play. The important thing is to maintain a balance between the two types.' Soon after the season's end, Arlott pondered on how the different types of cricket (even within the one-day game) were leading to 'a lack of uniformity of approach disturbing in batting which is often a reflex action', but did not gainsay one-day cricket as such: 'Cricket would not be true to itself if it did not accept the general demand for instant and popular entertainment. When a Gillette semi-final at Old Trafford [the legendary longest-day thriller between Lancashire and Gloucestershire] draws more spectators than a full Test match on the same ground the economic argument is established beyond question.' And sponsorship? Swanton had always been broadly relaxed, while Arlott that autumn welcomed the news that the new league cup was to be sponsored by Benson & Hedges, paying £80,000 for the privilege, even as the venerable but largely unwatched county championship failed to attract a commercial backer. 'So the turn-round of English cricket, financial, technical and, to some degree, social – is almost complete,' he declared in the *Guardian*. 'It may not yet be completely solvent but it is far more nearly so, from all sources, than appeared even remotely possible four years ago.'

In fact, Arlott by July 1972 did have a proposal for the county championship, hopefully one that would see it 'find a backer, or even a series of separate sponsors for each county': namely, to convert it from its present twenty-match three-day structure ('an ill-favoured hybrid') into 'a programme of 16 four-day games with each county playing every other once, home and away in alternate seasons'. That would be filed in the pending tray, but next month, after the end of the Ashes Tests, international one-day cricket truly became a reality with a three-match series between England and Australia, sponsored to the tune of £30,000 by the Prudential. 'The good things much more than outweighed the less good,' reported Swanton on the first encounter at Trent Bridge; at Lord's for the second match, he highlighted 'the continuous applause coming from an almost full ground'; and at the Edgbaston finale, the 18,000 crowd got 'very good value for money'. Even so, both men entered reservations. 'This version is essentially an occasional variant,' insisted Swanton, while Arlott reflected that 'it would be a pity if the entertaining and rewarding tail were to wag the dog so hard as to shake it off.'

Soon afterwards, as the season ended, Arlott reflected more generally on instant cricket. 'It is disquieting,' he noted, 'that some batsmen of Test quality who have not come to terms with the 40-overs game have been left out of their county sides for those matches – like any number of spin bowlers and some specialist wicket-keepers. This means that the two games are being accepted as different.' Nevertheless: 'It is a general truth that a team successful in the county championship is likely to do well in over-limit play. There is no substitute for true cricketing ability.' And: 'The tail enders may have to slog but the batsmen who play the crucial innings are those raised in the three-day game with its accompanying technique, standards of judgement and above all flexibility and improvisation in stroke making.' What would the future bring? 'Over-limit cricket will undoubtedly change the pattern and style of the English first-class game: how much, and whether ultimately for good or ill, no one can yet foresee with certainty.' And he concluded: 'Two facts are certain: the over-limit game has drawn, excited, and satisfied larger crowds than the three-day game could do in these times: but it cannot continue to exist on a satisfying level of performance without players – especially batsmen – who have learned the game in greater depth than the new shape permits.'

There was as yet no direct correlation made between the rapid growth of one-day cricket and declining standards of on-field behaviour. As almost always for Swanton – the main exception being his more flexible ethics when it came to captaining or managing his Arabs matches – the upholding of those standards mattered at least as much as the quality of the cricket itself. 'Of all pastimes there is about this one a special tradition of courtesy and good manners,' he reflected at the start of 1971, just as the English tour of Australia was about to turn sour, culminating in the Sydney blow-up. Not long after Illingworth's men returned home, the Cricket Council issued a statement – applauded by Swanton – recording 'their grave concern about incidents involving dissent from umpires' decisions by word or deed', and warning 'all players that such conduct, which is contrary to the spirit and tradition of the game and brings it into disrepute, will not be tolerated'.

Later that summer came Snow's notorious shoulder charge of Sunil Gavaskar at Lord's, sending the diminutive Indian flying. 'As Gavaskar scrambled to his feet,' Swanton noted, 'Snow compounded his offence, in the eyes of those old-fashioned people who have regard for the traditional chivalry of cricket, by picking up his bat and throwing it to him.' The upshot at the lunch interval was an enforced apology by Snow and an acceptance by India that the incident would be forgotten. 'But of course it cannot be,' commented Swanton, 'especially with the background of the lack of self-discipline that so marred the tour in Australia. So the melancholy tale continues.' Arlott for his part only reluctantly included the incident in his *Guardian* report, apparently under some pressure from his sports editor John Samuel. Moreover, a few days later, when Snow was dropped for the next Test for disciplinary reasons, he observed that the incident was apparently 'to be dragged on indefinitely so that what seemed no more than a storm in a tea-cup is to be allowed to boil over, to the damage of the English cricket team'; and he added that the Bognor vicar's son was 'not by any means the first, and he is unlikely to be the last, fast bowler to burst out in anger or violence in word or action on a cricket field', given that 'fast bowlers are fundamentally aggressive people, otherwise they would not be fast bowlers'.

Two years later at Edgbaston saw what was – amidst stiff competition – possibly the most ill-natured Test of the 1970s. 'One way and another, I found it rather a disgusting sort of morning,' reported Swanton after the first day. He was unhappy that only thirty overs had been bowled by England in the first two hours, a rate that 'left plenty of room for improvement'; and that across the day as a whole, as West Indies batted through for 190 for 5, it had been 'a weariness to the flesh'. The Friday was apparently unexceptional, though unreported by both men was the angry reaction – then and over the next two hours – of the West Indian fielders to the umpire, Arthur Fagg, ruling a caught-behind appeal in Boycott's favour. That evening, Fagg threatened to pull out entirely, while next morning, in symbolic protest, he refused to stand for the first over. That Saturday morning, an acrimonious first session unfolded: twenty-six overs in two hours, accompanied by a barrage of short bouncers from Keith Boyce and Bernard Julien, plus constant running down the pitch. 'An unhappy fall from grace' was the title of Arlott's report, as he itemised the 'little pleasure for players or spectators', the disappearance of 'competitive fellowship' and the 'grim restriction' of the day's play (as the match began to head towards a sterile draw). As for the case of Fagg, he argued that there would be 'much sympathy' for the umpire's 'feeling that some protest was necessary against recent increase in criticism and demonstrations against umpires' decisions'. By contrast, Swanton was critical of Fagg for having failed 'to register his protest officially with the authorities concerned, as regulations prescribe, rather than vent his grievances in the Press and then sour the atmosphere further by threatening to withdraw from the match'. Swanton acknowledged that he had had letters 'now and then from people who suggest I lay too much store by what they consider old-fashioned standards of sportsmanship', but was unabashed: 'The truth, of course, is that it is perfectly possible to play the game with all the vigour in the world, and yet with fairness and chivalry. It is not only possible; in the present permissive atmosphere on the part of crowds [a nod to the frequent pitch invasions at the previous Test at The Oval], of so much inherent disrespect for authority, it is the only way disruption and disorder can be avoided.'

The following English season, 1974, was Swanton's twenty-ninth and last for for the *Telegraph*. 'The itinerant cricket writer returns to all the familiar heralds of the new season, the gay club fixture-cards, the various Annual Reports from that of MCC right down the scale, and the modern chatty newsletters which keep everyone "in the picture",' he noted in cheerful mood in his April preview, adding gratefully that 'in the first-class game most clubs seem to be announcing a profit (thanks, of course, to TV and sponsorship money)'. Even so, it would not have been a magisterial Swanton overview without a grumble or two.

'Of all the modern heresies, I have found the systematic demotion of spin the most depressing.' And in the context of what he saw as a foolish modern fad for concentrating pre-season on physical fitness rather than the harder matter of improving technique: 'Alec Bedser tells me scornfully that on a visit to The Oval the other day he found the Surrey XI playing *football*. Coaches seem to prefer their cricketers in tracksuits rather than flannels ...'

Sadly, a cold, wet summer lay ahead, but it still had its moments for the correspondent and his followers. Take a fortnight or so in June. On the 12th, Swanton lamenting after the poorly attended England v. India Test at Old Trafford that 'it really looks as though the addiction to one-day cricket at this ancient home of the game has killed the appetite for Test Matches'; next day, a report from Canterbury of a B&H quarter-final (Kent v. Leicestershire) beginning with the assertion that 'even by the standards of Gillette and Benson & Hedges cricket this game for sustained excitement and uncertainty earned the highest possible rating'; two days later, a moderately understanding take on Boycott's omitting himself from the forthcoming Test at Lord's ('a complicated, introverted fellow ... one way and another I expect the selectors may be glad there is only one of him'); on the morning of the Lord's Test, trusting that the 'ghastly din' that had been made by India's supporters at the end of the recent MCC game would not be repeated; and during the match itself, complaining about Indian delays in the field ('when Chandra hurt his thumb a five-minute coffee-house preceded his going off'), taking pleasure in their spin attack ('relished especially by the over-Forties'), and bestowing a kindly word after the visitors had been routed for 42 ('as

I left the Nursery the whole Indian team were at the nets practising hard for Edgbaston next week – may they have better luck there!').

There was no Varsity match this year for Swanton, as it clashed with that Test; but in mid-July he did cover Eton v. Harrow at Lord's, a fixture that despite a thinnish crowd ('to be measured in four figures, if not perhaps with much to spare') was, he declared defiantly, 'not dead yet'. A week later saw the B&H Final, in which Swanton was disappointed by 'the modern situation of accurate out-cricket, cannily directed by Illingworth and Edrich, exerting a stranglehold despite conditions that should have been all in favour of run-making'; at the end of the month he was at Canterbury for 'a magnificent match' (Kent v. Leicestershire) in the Gillette; and August saw a raw deal for Pakistan on a rain-affected Lord's wicket ('these accidents take all the savour from success'), another Gillette thriller ('breath-taking') at Canterbury which featured Botham yorking Cowdrey with his first ball ('his arm is high, his wrist loose, and his whole delivery rhythmic and easy, pace orthodox medium'), and at The Oval his final home Test for the paper. Swanton's preview quoted a reader wanting the England team to stop hugging each other after the fall of a wicket, on which he commented: 'Can one imagine Len Hutton throwing his arms around Cyril Washbrook or Bill Edrich? The very idea raises a smile. Other times, other ways: I know, but if our Test side could restrain themselves just a little the older generation at least would be duly grateful.' The match itself was the dullest of draws, largely because of a pitch he called a 'dead stretch', which 'even at the end did not show the slightest signs of wear'. Should the captains have made a match of it through bold, enterprising declarations? Despite the overall spirit of 'weariness and frustration' during proceedings, Swanton thought not: 'The fact is, whether people approve or not, Test matches are not contested in this cavalier spirit, nor ever were they.'

September was, of course, the domestic curtain call: a resolution of the county championship, with rain-thwarted Hampshire very ('grotesquely' according to Arlott) unlucky to be pipped by Worcestershire, with the southern county not helped at Bournemouth by umpires who, in Swanton's judgement, 'might well' have made a start at a critical juncture; and then on Monday the 9th, after no play on the Saturday, the Gillette final at Lord's, 'a grimly tense battle' in which Kent beat Lancashire by four wickets. 'As to the noise there were contrasting views, ranging from those who thought that the red-bedecked cluster [supporting Lancashire] in front of the Tavern bar "made the day" to certain crusty reactionaries more inclined to mutter about mindless oafs,' Swanton reported. 'Denness was roundly booed on arrival, the applause being all but drowned. But I was assured it was all friendly stuff. What the older generation chiefly resent, I think, is the unceasing assault on the ears.'

The season was over, and soon the focus would be on the winter tour to Australia, to be Swanton's eighth and last as the *Telegraph*'s main man. A month or so before the English party under Denness flew out, news broke that Boycott had decided to pass. Arlott wrote with characteristic sympathy about the 'deep doubt' besetting a 'lonely' man vainly in search of 'batting infallibility': 'His unremitting practice, study of opponents, persistence in batting for batting's sake, and his obsession with technique, are all facets of a man seeking perfection in a realm where, axiomatically, perfection cannot exist.' Swanton's language was harsher – Boycott, in his words, had 'cried off' – but he managed a degree of sympathy, calling him 'a singular fellow, a problem, maybe, for the trained psychiatrist', and concluding that 'it is a personal tragedy that he seems to have developed this persecution complex'. Would Boycott's absence make a crucial difference to the outcome? On that, both men were tacitly agreed that it would all depend upon what fast bowling the Australians had in their armoury.

On a Brisbane pitch of uneven bounce – a pitch curated by the city's mayor, Clem Jones – a terrible beauty was born. Willis started an ultimately one-sided bouncer war on 29 November 1974, the first day of the first Test, before next afternoon the virtually unknown Jeff Thomson, backed up by the more experienced Dennis Lillee, started to make nonsense of Swanton's pre-match prediction that England began as 'the proper favourites'. Soon he was writing that England 'have not been confronted by such speed at both ends since Hall and Griffith were at their peak'; though on the rest day, with the match still in the balance, he speculated whether Thomson, albeit clearly more than 'a wild tearaway with little or no control', might yet 'prove to be a mere flash in the pan': 'Fast bowlers need a particular dedication to fitness, a tough constitution as well as a stout heart. Whether Thomson has all the attributes we shall soon see.' Swanton and the rest of the English press corps did indeed, as on the final day Thomson (6 for 46) destroyed the

England batting, backed up by two wickets from Lillee. 'I can imagine followers at home wondering whether the fast bowling offended the law in persistent shortness,' reflected Swanton. 'The answer is that Lillee was warned for intimidation when bowling at the tail-enders, and I would say that both he and Thomson were near the knuckle.' England then lost again on a fast wicket at Perth – Thomson once more doing the most damage – before they managed a creditable Christmas draw at Melbourne. England's star with both bat and ball was Tony Greig, admired by Swanton for his fearlessness but not his conduct. 'I cannot think of a single English cricketer of any generation who would ever have thought of letting loose his feelings to the extent of pointing the way back to the pavilion to a batsman who had been dismissed,' he noted after the match. 'This is the competitive spirit run riot to a degree, the latest symptom of a decline in the courtesies which have generally dignified Test warfare, however fierce.'

Sydney, starting on 4 January, settled the series. Australia by the end of the third day were in total command; but next day, rest day, that was far from Swanton's main concern. 'Time now to call "no ball" to the intimidators' was the title of his *Telegraph* piece. 'The atmosphere has been something after the manner of the bull-ring,' he reported. 'Most of the high feeling has been aroused by the fast bowling and the over-use of the short-pitched ball which Dennis Lillee, at least, has been foolish enough to say he bowls to hurt and thus intimidate.' After observing that in all his Test-watching experience – that most familiar of Swantonian tropes – he had never seen 'such fast bowling' as by Thomson and Lillee as on the second day, he went on:

If this bowling were pitched to a good length it would be difficult enough, but with the incessant din and cries of the crowd inciting them, both bowlers had recourse to a great deal of short stuff which, on a pitch hardened and quickened by the sun, flew at various heights from the hips to the head and over …

I have an idea that too many of the players on both sides, whether or not they have consciously formed such a philosophy, would say that they are prepared to push the law – any law – to the uttermost, and that it is up to the umpires to penalise them.

This, of course, is a concept of cricket that is quite foreign to my generation and to those that have gone before. If it gains general hold, the virtues of this complicated and beautiful game will soon be a thing of the past.

Edrich sent to hospital by Lillee, Fletcher deflecting a Thomson rocket onto his forehead, not a helmet in sight – England predictably folded on the final day, as Australia regained the Ashes.

By early February, when Arlott (who had been faithfully watching the TV highlights) wrote a major overview for the *Guardian*, the hosts were 4–0 up. 'The dominance of a series by fast bowlers is not new; neither is intimidation by short-pitched bowling,' he emphasised. 'It is the instinctive weapon of the fast bowler, used since cricket began; and neither England nor any other country is in a moral position to condemn it. Every one of them has used the weapon when it has commanded it.' Instead, what disturbed Arlott was England's 'lack of truly great players' – what he called 'the most dire famine the game has known'. His explanation was economic. Whereas 'until a dozen or so years ago, cricket offered a professional a more rewarding living than any other sport except top-level golf or boxing', by this time 'the number – and the greater financial inducements – of other professional sports' effectively deprived the game of 'potentially great cricketers'. Accordingly, 'the outstanding athlete who turns determinedly to cricket now is almost certainly one who is emotionally dedicated to the game'; and, concluding in thoroughly gloomy vein, 'it is most unlikely that there will ever be enough of them to restore the English game's shortfall'.

The following week at Melbourne – with Thomson wholly absent, Lillee mainly absent – saw England's consolation victory. Back home the Duke of Norfolk was being buried, and the Conservative Party was falling into Margaret Thatcher's hands, but for Swanton there was an understandably high consciousness that this was his swansong as the *Daily Telegraph*'s cricket correspondent. 'Better late than never!' he exalted during the match itself about England's progress, while as the final Australian wicket fell he was having his health proposed in the dining room of the Melbourne Cricket Ground Trust. The match was a valedictory occasion for Colin Cowdrey, too; touchingly enough, the two men exchanged compliments. 'As popular a cricketer as has ever visited Australia' was how Swanton ended his last report, while the batsman sent the scribe a note signed 'Yours, very humbly, Colin': 'I know you will be writing again from time to time, so it is no time for solemn farewells – suffice it to say that I noted the end of the official E.W.S. era – a sad occasion – but we thank you, Sir!'

Swanton's first summer of official retirement (including from his end-of-play radio summaries) coincided with cricket's first World Cup. During its vivid and memorable final at Lord's in June 1975, between West Indies and Australia, the BBC's managing director Ian Trethowan paid a visit to the commentary box, prompting Arlott to pull out all the stops in a virtuoso passage matching the brilliance of Clive Lloyd's batting:

> Gilmour comes in, bowls – (*crowd roar*) and Lloyd hits him high away over mid-wicket for four, a stroke of a man knocking a thistle-top off with a walking stick. No trouble at all, and it takes Lloyd to 99. Lloyd 99, and a hundred and eighty-nine for three. (*Whistles, shouts*) Umpire Bird having a wonderful time, signalling everything in the world, including stop to traffic coming on from behind. But he's let Gilmour in now, and he comes in, bowls (*crowd roar*) and Lloyd hits him into the covers – there's his hundred – only half fielded there on the cover boundary, and the century's up and the whole ground seething with leaping West Indian delight …

'All that anyone could have hoped of it' was Arlott's written verdict on the contest, adding of the virtual absence of short-pitched bowling that 'nothing in a completely heartening day was more happy than that'. A month later, however, his perspective was very different, as Leicestershire comfortably beat Middlesex in a dour, low-scoring B&H final virtually determined by Norman McVicker's destructive morning spell. 'In entertainment terms, it demonstrated the essentially superficial quality of the one-day game,' he reflected.

Though Australia retained the Ashes, England over the rest of the series certainly did become a more fighting and competitive unit, due not least to the resolute batting of the grey-haired, bespectacled, thirty-three-year-old debutant, David Steele. But it was for two episodes that had nothing to do with the cricket itself that these matches would most remain in the collective memory. At Lord's on the fourth afternoon, as England's second innings drifted on in the heat, it was Trevor Bailey in the commentary box who first noticed that a 'freaker' (normally called a streaker) had invaded the playing area and was heading for the middle. Arlott at once with some relish took up descriptive proceedings: 'And a freaker, we've got a freaker down the wicket now. Not very shapely, and it's masculine ... And I would think it's seen the last of its cricket for the day. The police are mustered, so are the cameramen, and Greg Chappell. And now he's had his load, he's being embraced by a blond policeman, and this may be his last public appearance, but what a splendid one ...' A fortnight later, at the end of Headingley's fourth day, the outcome seemed deliciously uncertain: Australia, with seven wickets left, needing 225 more runs to win. That night the pitch was vandalised – on the basis that 'GEORGE DAVIS IS INNOCENT OK', the slogan for a campaign claiming that Davis, a north London criminal, had been wrongfully convicted for armed robbery. Next day there was no possibility of play, even if the weather had been better. Arlott in the commentary box took the hardest of lines, arguing that the possibility of an injustice having been done to a man behind bars did not in itself justify the illegal, high-handed ruining of pleasure for millions. There were, in short, limits to this ex-policeman's tolerance.

The following spring, in March 1976, his beloved wife died: of a brain haemorrhage, at the age of only forty-four. 'Valerie was fierce in argument for the underdog and against social injustice,' noted the obituary by Mary Samuel in the *Guardian*. 'She did not always agree with John on matters; but put her point of view firmly and her differences with affection and tolerance.' Barely a year later, Arlott married for a third time. His new wife was Pat Hoare, whom he had met at Lord's (where she was working) in the late 1940s, and with whom he had stayed in touch. Essentially a pragmatic union – with Arlott motivated in significant part by concern for the welfare of his teenage son Robert – it gradually evolved into something warmer. Nothing, though, made up for the loss of Valerie, arguably an even harder blow than the death of his son Jim in 1965. 'The second loss increased his tendency to lugubriosity,' recalled Mike Brearley after Arlott's death. 'The pleasures of life, of friendship, family, cricket, wine, food, poetry, were real enough, but even the best moments were tinged with an awareness of their eventual ending. So a claret or an innings became "desperately good" and those protruding eyes would fill with tears.' In 1976 itself, as in 1965, he sought to assuage grief by plunging himself back into his work. That summer a young American and future cricket writer, Mike Marqusee, fell in love with the game, not least through listening to Arlott on the radio. 'While I can no longer swallow his belief that the cricket world reflected his own idealism and generosity, I am grateful still that through his rigour and his sympathy, his mastery of light and shade, he helped me to see and enjoy the epic nature of Test cricket,' Marqusee would write many years later in his searing critique of English cricket, *Anyone*

But England. 'On first acquaintance, it is almost impossible for a newcomer to the game to get hold of the ever-shifting rhythms of a five-day struggle. Arlott's commentary helped me see the whole, not just the parts.'

That season, a year and a half after their ordeal down under, England faced the West Indies, themselves recently humiliated in Australia. Clive Lloyd's strategy was clear from the outset – pace – and his formidable armoury comprised Andy Roberts, Michael Holding, Vanburn Holder and Wayne Daniel, a quartet accurately described by *Wisden* as 'four hostile and genuinely fast bowlers'. Between them they took 84 of the 91 English wickets during the series, only three wickets going to the slow bowlers. Played in the hottest of summers in living memory, it was the series in which cricket's terms of trade changed decisively.

The key match, after two draws, was the third Test at Old Trafford. Briefly, England had a sniff, dismissing West Indies for 211, before collapsing for an abject 71 – during which (*Wisden* again) 'some balls lifted at frightening speed', while Greig and Underwood 'both had narrow escapes from what could have been serious injury'. Gordon Greenidge and Vivian Richards then batted imperiously, before Lloyd declared lateish on Saturday. He set England 552 in just over thirteen and a quarter hours, but more immediately the prospect of eighty minutes' batting before the temporary haven of rest day on Sunday. England's openers were John Edrich and Brian Close, aged thirty-nine and forty-five respectively. Together – somehow – they survived. 'Holding was warned by umpire Alley for intimidatory bowling after a series of short-pitched balls to Close,' reported Arlott in Monday's *Guardian*. 'There is no doubt that his bouncers are deliberate: they are also fearsome …' And: 'Close and Edrich made no secret of their purpose, which was simply to remain at the wicket. They did that with unflinching bravery. In the 80 minutes to the end of the day, they faced 17 overs – three of them from the off-spinner, Padmore – and scored 21 runs. Close made one and accepted a cluster of bruises. Edrich's two far separate boundaries were greeted with such cheers as might have greeted the winning of the match.' It was an unforgettable passage of play, with a brutality and sense of raw danger about it to which, sadly, Arlott's description only partially did justice.

That Monday, England succumbed, finishing a rain-affected day at 125 for 9 (and quickly losing the last wicket on Tuesday morning). 'Once again it was a day of heavy artillery,' noted Arlott, before devoting a paragraph of his report to the larger question:

> The bouncer is a matter of principle. If a cricket ball is propelled at high speed about a batsman's head, it may prove fatal. That issue is not one to be decided on degree. If one bouncer is enough to kill, the true decision for the cricket authorities is whether to admit intimidatory bowling as part of the game or ban it altogether.

On that, he was unwilling at this point to offer an opinion. What about Swanton? From his vantage point at home in Sandwich, he despatched a letter to the *Telegraph* arguing that 'on the evidence of television' the West Indian fast bowling on the Saturday evening had, in its deliberate intimidation, been 'disgraceful' – to such an extent that it was time for umpires at last to start invoking the full extent of Law 46, allowing them to suspend a bowler for the rest of the innings. 'In times past (except in the Bodyline episode) captains could generally be relied upon to see that the players in their charge obeyed the spirit of the game,' he added. 'Now they are often unable or unwilling to intervene, with proper effect. So much the worse for the poor umpires, and for the game itself.'

Arlott did not disagree that the situation was serious. 'There is little hope that positive action will be taken,' he predicted later in July ahead of the ICC's annual meeting. Accusing that body of 'complete evasion of responsibility' to date, he went on: 'The evidence is that, failing some precise and generally visible standard of measurement as distinct from assessment of motive, umpires are not prepared to impose strict control. This is the nettle the cricket administrators ought to grasp before they are forced to do so by a fatality for which they must be prepared to accept responsibility.' The ICC did in fact take some action – umpires told to regard as potentially dangerous and intimidatory any ball pitching short and passing above shoulder height; captains told to instruct their players that fast, short-pitched balls should at no time be directed at non-recognised batsmen – but few imagined that the issue had been resolved.

Eight months later, in March 1977, Arlott flew out for the Centenary Test in Melbourne: the first (and in the event last) time since 1955 that he would see England play overseas. Fortified in some ways – his beloved county championship had at last found a sponsor (Cadbury Schweppes), Pat had accepted his marriage proposal, he had brought along his own supply of vintage Bordeaux – he also travelled with misgivings to a less than favourite country. 'The period of the Centenary Test coincides with the Royal visit, so newspapers, radio, newsreels and television are on a quite staggering safari,' he wrote grumpily enough ahead of the match itself. 'It is difficult to leave the coolness of an air-conditioned room [in the Hilton] for the turgid heat outside without being televised. Indeed it can happen to you – as yesterday it did to me – in the "privacy" of your air-conditioned room with the invasion of a crew who switch off the air conditioning … and leave, with a curt nod, a cloud of smoke, a thicket of cigarette ends and a grey layer of ash.' Still, a compelling contest produced a wonderful last day, when *TMS* for the first time stayed on air all night. 'Their hopes are mounting,' Arlott told sleepy listeners at home, with England chasing 463 and Derek Randall playing the innings of a lifetime. In the end Australia got home by forty-five runs – the exact same margin as a hundred years earlier – and the euphoric feeling immediately after the match was that all was well in the cricket world.

Swanton shared that elation ('cricket's command performance came off with a vengeance'), though he was not present, thereby missing his first Anglo-Australian Test in almost forty years. Instead, he was in Barbados, completing the draft of a further slice of autobiography, predictably to be called *Follow On* and essentially a more discursive ramble round his life. As usual there were harsh words for 'the worst of the cricketers of today' – 'with their long, greasy hair, grubby flannels and the apparent contempt for club colours which reaches the point of a strange, inverted snobbery' – whereas, by contrast, he noted of England's current captain, Greig, that 'he has courage and strength, both moral and physical, right out of the ordinary'. What, more generally, of the future? In the book's final paragraph, Swanton sought – as ever – to take the long view:

> I concluded the last edition of *A History of Cricket* by saying that the key to the health and prosperity of the game lay in the hearts and minds of the players. This maybe is not an original sentiment, and it may even be considered a banal one. Yet I end by repeating it, for no game holds up such a clear mirror to character as cricket, and this is the property which has been the secret of its appeal and fascination from Hambledon right through to the present.

8

1977–80: The Packer Style

'The announcement of the formation of a freelance international cricket circus is the most historic event in the history of the modern game,' declared Arlott on 10 May 1977. The impresario responsible for this extravagant-sounding but in the event fully justified assertion was Kerry Packer, an Australian media magnate who, three years earlier, had inherited a sprawling media empire which included commercial TV stations in Sydney and Melbourne. Like his fellow countryman Rupert Murdoch, who had also inherited a media business, Packer was impatient with – indeed, contemptuous of – traditions and institutions that did not suit his business plans.

His TV stations were a problem that by the mid-1970s needed drastic action: audiences were falling away, costs were rising and politicians were insisting on more Australian content. The solution was sport. Packer's first ploy – to buy the rights to Australia's Golf Open in 1975 – proved that live sport was good commercial TV. That made cricket his top priority. Gideon Haigh has neatly defined the game's virtues from Packer's bottom-line perspective: 'Cricket lasted longer, with even less motion, and naturally embroidered ad slots.'

Once Packer had discovered that the Australian Cricket Board of Control was not interested in collaboration over Test match TV coverage (traditionally the preserve of public television), he decided that – in order to force the cricket establishment's hand over TV rights – he would temporarily fill the country's small screens with his own series of one-day matches and four- or five-day 'Supertests', known in due course as World Series Cricket. The leading Australian players, the West Indies Test team and the best South Africans were recruited on three-year contracts at what were, for professional cricketers, unheard-of sums: at least as much, some said, as they would earn in a whole Test career. England's captain Tony Greig, who thought the concept irresistible, was engaged to captain the World XI; and he persuaded his colleagues Snow, Knott and Underwood to join him.

Packer's May 1977 *démarche* could hardly have been a more dramatic move. 'The course of the battle cannot be foreseen,' wrote Arlott. 'Indeed, it may not be clear for a long time.' And he concluded: 'Essentially it is a struggle between a deeply entrenched establishment and players who scent the kind of financial reward for their ability and crowd attraction that they and their predecessors have long been denied.'

Within days, Greig (who had been working closely with Packer, even during the Centenary Test) was stripped of the England captaincy for the forthcoming Ashes series – 'as,' Arlott noted, 'every logical-minded observer must have expected'. Yet he was torn. Every fibre in Arlott's body loathed the circus aspect and the challenge it presented to the game's cherished character and rhythms. But, equally, he was aware that Packer's expansive chequebook had potentially letter to Greig, accusing him of having lent himself 'to something which – if what I read is true – looks like blowing the whole fabric of Test cricket sky high', and beseeching him to 'see this miserable business in perspective and pull out in time to save your own reputation – and that of others who would probably follow your lead'. The letter ended with a sentence that perhaps only Swanton could have written to a current England captain: 'See things straight, Tony, before it's too late.' That boat had sailed, as soon became clear, so Swanton's next major intervention was inevitably in the *Telegraph*. Packer, he declared in June, had 'burst into cricket like a bull in a china shop'; for all his air of 'almost injured innocence' in a recent TV appearance with David Frost, the underlying reality was that Packer was 'threatening the fabric of established cricket for the short-term benefit of a few players and his own television companies'; and 'with any luck', his 'estimate of Australian sporting tastes' – including their appetite for circus-style, razzmatazz cricket – would prove 'wide of the mark'. As for the breakdown of the talks, Swanton responded with a *Cricketer* article naturally entitled '… And the devil take K Packer!' He praised the ICC's 'united front of utter reasonableness'; asserted that it was now all too transparently clear that Packer's players 'one and all, and not least his truculent spokesman, Tony Greig', were 'mere pawns in a local commercial dogfight'; and declared that 'since the news of the business first broke, Packer has united the cricket world against him to a degree which gives confidence that his takeover bid will come a cropper', so that 'in the end this piratical promoter will be seen to have bitten off more than he can chew'. What about the players (by now upwards of fifty) who had gone over to Packer? 'One cannot imagine the generations before them, though they were in relative terms far worse off, defecting in such numbers from Test cricket – and certainly not in such secrecy.'

Swanton fired off another lengthy missive ('I apologise for seeking your space again') to the *Telegraph* during August. Against a background of the ICC seeking to ban Packer players from also playing in Test cricket, and a High Court hearing due to begin in London in late September, he asked, 'If the Packers of this world are to be allowed to come along and, with impunity, skim the cream off the top of the milk, what price Test cricket and the financial viability of the counties?' 'No one,' he added, 'should have any illusion: it is the future of international and first-class cricket that is at stake.' And the last two paras (as he would have called them) saw the septuagenarian in fighting form:

I happen to think that, irrespective of legal judgements, Packer's take-over will fail in the end; for the obvious artificiality of his exhibitions, whatever stunts are got up to with yellow balls in football stadia, will not entertain his hard-headed fellow-countrymen, except maybe as an occasional diversion.

Happily the present Test series [against Australia] has taken the best possible course, for every wholesale defeat devalues Packer's Australian purchases the more. For this reason, since I saw Armstrong's great side at The Oval in 1921 I have never wanted England to win more keenly than this summer. And how handsomely they have obliged! May I finally, with due and humble respect, make a plea that the phrase 'super-Test', whether in inverted commas or not, be banned from the *Daily Telegraph* vocabulary? A Test by definition is a match played under the home country's Cricket Board. These affairs will be super-nothing.

For Arlott by this time 'the ultimate solution' was clear. 'As soon as the national bodies find enough support to pay their players as well as will Packer, his will seem a camp of has-beens,' he wrote after the ICC's banning move. In early August the TCCB sought to supplement that move, proposing that all Packer players should likewise be banned from English county cricket. The Cricketers' Association duly met at Edgbaston on 5 September to determine its attitude. Arlott, still president, was in the chair, and the CA's secretary, Jack Bannister, would recall how at this and subsequent meetings Arlott managed, amidst much acrimony, to 'keep the lid on and, at the same time, steer it into quite a reasonable debate' – an achievement, reckoned Bannister, that owed much to the fact that 'he'd got the respect of all the players'. At this meeting, some 180 county cricketers attended, sixteen (including Greig) spoke, and a motion supporting the proposed TCCB ban at county level was carried by ninety-one votes to seventy-seven. In truth, that fairly narrow margin may not have accurately reflected the membership's overall mood: the strongly pro-Packer Sussex had more than twice as many players present as the average county representation; while Hampshire's players, overwhelmingly pro-ban, were unable to vote, being engaged at Scarborough against T. N. Pearce's XI for the Fenner Trophy (and for their pains being told by Pearce that it was the worst festival match he had seen in his twenty-five years' connection with Scarborough). 'Considering the depth of feeling on both sides,' Arlott told the press, 'the meeting was extremely good humoured.'

The CA also voted (139–36) for negotiations between the ICC and Packer to be reopened. That was certainly Arlott's fervent wish. 'Everyone with the good of cricket at heart must wish that somehow, and on however flimsy lines, the two sides could keep talking,' he wrote in the *Guardian* ten days after the meeting, ten days before the court case. There followed a finely weighted passage:

> If it is a question of right and wrong there can be little argument. If the Packer operation had been launched in the long-term interests of the players the judgement would be different. The fact that it was projected by Mr Packer solely for his own short-term financial advantage gives it no moral arguments over the establishment who, perhaps inflexibly, but for no personal gain, have sought to maintain the status quo. There can be no question that the Packer project has led to increased rewards, not only for the players who have signed for him, but for those who have not. That, though, was not its purpose. If the establishment had taken such steps earlier, the Packer situation could never have arisen; certainly not on such a scale as it has now assumed. There lies the moral weakness of their case.

Arlott then itemised ways in which English cricket's various sponsors had been raising their financial game since the breaking of the Packer storm. Even so, he insisted, this 'glimpse, or more, of prosperity' was still 'inadequate': 'It needs an increase to make it clearly more attractive to the players on the high plateau: and, secondly, and in human terms more importantly, to the everyday county players, many of whom will never reach Test level, and others who might do so but could be discouraged to the extent of leaving the game for better rewards elsewhere.'

For Swanton, awaiting in November – like the rest of the cricket world – Mr Justice Slade's judgement, it was a piquant case of my enemy's enemy. 'Michael Parkinson comes down strong on the establishment side, as also do Ray Illingworth and Geoff Boycott,' he noted. 'One way and another I haven't felt so warm towards Yorkshiremen for a long while!' The judge's unwelcome ruling later that month – that to deprive a professional cricketer of the opportunity of making his living was unjust – no doubt cemented that improbable alliance. 'The judgement will amaze the cricket Establishment,' wrote Arlott immediately afterwards about a decision that he reckoned was 'the most important piece of cricket history made since the introduction of Test cricket a century and eight months ago'.

What next? Reviewing the saga so far, it was clear to Arlott that Packer held most of the high cards. 'He demanded exclusive television rights to Test matches; in Australia, and probably elsewhere. That was a concession the authorities found impossible to grant. Yet it is difficult to see how they can now deny it to him ...' Accordingly: 'The price of the official body's freedom to organise and play Test matches without simultaneous competition for players, spectators, and television revenue, may be the complete surrender to Mr Packer of television rights to as much cricket as he chooses to demand. The authorities could drive themselves

Cricketer's first issue of 1978, that 'there may well be a sort of Australian cricket public looking for the sadistic pleasure of watching Dennis Amiss in a crash-helmet, among others, weaving about and avoiding the bouncers from which it has been stated that even tail enders will not be immune'.

'Packer peace hope' was the *Guardian*'s headline on 14 April 1978, as Richard Yallop reported on the latest CA meeting at Edgbaston: some 280 county cricketers present; two Packer emissaries talking of ICC/WSC 'co-existence', prompting Arlott to tell Yallop that they had not come with specific terms to put before the ICC, but, rather, in the spirit that some form of co-operation must be possible; and the CA agreeing to allow a series of motions criticising, even stigmatising, Packer players to lie upon the table while a fresh peace initiative was attempted. Simultaneously, however, the county cricketers made their feelings sufficiently known by passing a motion (by a thumping 219–50 majority) deploring the presence of Packer players in both Test and domestic competition. Three days later, the very different headline was 'Packer's action turns doves into hawks', this time above a thoroughly disenchanted Arlott piece about how 'the printer's ink was not dry on the report of the meeting before the illusion of goodwill was shattered' – namely with the news not only that Packer was starting proceedings against four Australian state cricket associations (over use of their grounds), but that he was intending to broaden his operations beyond Australia. 'This must,' declared Arlott, 'appear as a contemptuous rejection of the peace overture of the Cricketers' Association and an invitation to open warfare between the two camps.' With palpable dismay, he looked forward to a coming English season 'of bitterness and strife within dressing rooms and between players of the same and competing counties'. 'Many cricketers in England will be playing with and against others whom they have proposed to ban from the game,' he reiterated two days later. 'The poison has been injected; English cricket will not find it easy to work it out of its system.'

For Arlott, perhaps more than anyone, it was an unbearable prospect, and soon afterwards he and Bannister went to Lord's with a letter that they wanted the ICC to send to all member countries, urging those countries to talk to Packer and try to resolve the stalemate. 'I don't trust them,' Arlott muttered to Bannister as they were about to enter the Pavilion's Committee Room. 'I don't trust them. Never have.' 'Them' in this case were David Clark (chairman of the ICC) and Jack Bailey (MCC and ICC secretary). Initially, there was indeed resistance – Clark and Bailey objecting to any exercise of what they called 'player-power' – but ultimately the letter was sent, though only to limited effect. At one point in the meeting there was an adjournment, and after 'them' had left the room Arlott observed to Bannister that no drink had been offered, and that even if it had they 'probably haven't got a bloody corkscrew'; so he reached into his battered, faded brown briefcase, taking out a corkscrew and a bottle of Beaujolais.

Bannister also told Rayvern Allen the story of another memorable encounter during the Packer affair, likewise in London but harder to date. Those present in the Harlequin Suite at the Dorchester were Arlott, Warwickshire's David Brown (chairman of the CA), Bannister himself – and the man whom Swanton sometimes privately called 'the anti-Christ':

We're sitting and talking, and there was an onyx table and a cigarette lighter, and Packer's on about litigation and it doesn't bother him and he doesn't get emotionally involved with these cases anyway. And John suddenly said, 'Well, forgive me for saying so, but I think you are emotionally involved in this particular cause, and that's the problem.' There was a slight gear-shift and Packer replied, 'I'm not emotionally involved – I don't get involved in my causes, I don't ...' 'Well, I think you do.' 'Well, I assure you I don't.' The decibels were rising, and John continued, 'I really think that's the problem between us.'

'Next thing,' related Bannister, 'it was like Packer had got a little moustache and it was Adolf Hitler. His hand came down on the table really hard, the cigarette lighter jumped up in the air. "I am not emotionally involved," he hissed. "I never have been and I never will be." He absolutely blew his top.'

In any case, positions remained largely entrenched during the second half of 1978. 'It simply is not possible to divide the outstanding cricketers of the world between two conflicting camps,' Arlott wrote in early July, lamenting that seemingly no one had responded to the CA's suggestion for another summit between the foes. 'It is hard – if not impossible – to recall a state of affairs when the media, at least in Britain, was so unanimously on the side of the Establishment as about the Packer venture. That does not alter the fact that the overwhelming weight of top-class cricketing talent is now contracted to him ...' Later that month, the ICC rejected WSC's proposal of a virtually round-the-year (September to June) programme of WSC one-day matches punctuating official Tests; while in early August the TCCB, following negotiations with the CA, announced a basic wage target of £4,000 for capped county cricketers. 'An unenforced minimum wage', noted Arlott, 'is, of course, simply an unresolved pledge; it pays lip service but not cash.' Those were details that only marginally concerned Swanton, but the bigger impasse certainly did. 'It is ridiculous to talk of a projected WSC programme covering all the Test-playing countries for ten months of the year as offering a chink of light,' he told Reg Hayter, in a conversation published by the *Cricketer*. What about Keith Miller's recent assertion that WSC had 'ruined a great game'? 'I don't think that has happened yet,' Swanton reflected. 'But the damage and dislocation are plain for all to see. The harmony and fellowship of the cricket field have been disrupted, to the financial benefit of a few cricketers certainly, but basically to satisfy the vanity and power-lust of one man.'

WSC began in November its second season – including coloured clothing and three more Australian/World XI 'Tests', with Greig this time managing four runs in three innings – while the English tourists under Brearley thrashed 5–1 a radically understrength Australia side. The affair was not over yet, but by the end of 1978 it had found its first book-length historian: Henry Blofeld. Arlott's review praised a 'cogent, readable' account and ended by quoting Blofeld's own speculative conclusion about Packer's possible master plan for the world's richest market: 'In a few years the situation could arise where a form of popularised, bastardised cricket, full of instant appeal, is played to mass television audiences in the United States and maybe Australia, while the traditional game continues as it does today ...' That passed without comment, as did Blofeld's final, Panglossian thought: 'People who have never shown the smallest interest in cricket have become fascinated by the Packer affair, and when cricket appears on television or on radio or in the papers their subconscious now makes them pay attention. Eventually they may even go to watch. And that can only be good.'

Anti-Packer feeling among many of England's county cricketers continued to run high. In March 1979, ahead of the CA's AGM on 5 April, Arlott noted that motions had been tabled which 'call for such action against Packer-contracted players as could wreck the World Cup due to be played in England this year' – motions reflecting 'the known attitude of the majority of CA members', as opposed to 'the official ruling that Packer-signed men might take part in the World Cup'. At the meeting itself, as usual at Edgbaston, anti-Packer proposals submitted by Mike Brearley and Keith Fletcher were indeed carried – thereby reserving the right of CA members not to play with or against any county club that had signed any new WSC players – but crucially, Arlott emphasised to the press, they would be considered null and void if a peace settlement were reached. That at last was now in prospect; and prior to the meeting Charles Palmer, chairman of the ICC and president of MCC, had explicitly asked the players not to do anything that would 'rock the boat'. Indeed, at the meeting itself, the motion carried with the largest majority (166–28) was that proposed by Mike Smith, calling for 'amiable co-existence' between traditional cricket and WSC.

Arlott was profoundly relieved. 'The aim of the association has always been for co-existence,' he told the *Guardian*'s Paul Fitzpatrick. 'There was every intent not to rock the boat, not to disrupt the World Cup and to give both sides the chance to complete negotiations. I think both sides would like to see a settlement. I am satisfied of that.' He also expressed pleasure that good progress had been made on the most bread-and-butter front, with all but three counties having established the minimum wages recommended by the CA. On this matter, he declared, the counties had 'co-operated handsomely'. In his own writing, moreover, Arlott continued to push the cause of peace. 'Both sides ought to fear a war of financial attrition,' he warned two days after the meeting. And he noted that 'this is something the Packer organisation with its wide diversification of investment might be able to endure better than official cricket with its heavy reliance on the product of Test cricket'.

The good faith placed by the county cricketers in Palmer's assurances proved justified, as within a few weeks it became clear to all observers that peace was in the imminent offing. 'At last we have something to be thankful for,' Swanton wrote in May for the *Cricketer*'s June issue. Yet in a solemn passage, after noting 'friendships broken [including to a significant degree his with Richie Benaud, whose wife Daphne had once been Swanton's secretary] and trust eroded', he could not but dwell on the heavy price:

Most worrying of all is the strain on the self-control and general attitude of the best players now that money becomes more and more the dominant factor. The average first-class cricketer is still at heart a sound enough fellow, as the responsible attitude of the Cricketers' Association over recent months has exemplified. But he has never been in more need of wise and firm direction if, in the environment of the eighties, the game's old values are to be kept alive and cherished.

Peace was announced on 30 May, but Swanton continued to fret, summing up his emotions in a piece for the July *Cricketer*. 'Good! But at what price? So much cash. So much opportunity to put it to good use. But will the ACB [Australian Cricket Board] continue to control the game? How successfully will they be able to resist television exploitation, tied financially so tight to their "Promoter"?' And he expressed satisfaction with how in England the game's various sponsors – 'notably' Gillette, Prudential, Cornhill, Cadbury Schweppes, Benson & Hedges, John Player – 'have all invested their money, and continue to do so, with no thought of interfering with the cricket'.

Relief remained Arlott's overwhelming emotion. 'Bitternesses,' he wrote on 31 May, 'have developed between players who had long shared the same dressing rooms; and, alarmingly or ridiculously – families have been split on the issue.' He was also realistic: 'Let there be no mistake about it; Packer has won what he wanted. He has paid dearly for it: but in his field of operations such expense is unimportant if it achieves the desired end.' Specifically, 'for ten years to come Mr Packer's organisation will promote the interests of Australian cricket and cricketers in the spheres of television and publicity'; while in terms of the actual cricket in Australia, there would be a major shift towards a heavily incentivised one-day format, complete with 'such

WSC originations as the thirty-yard field limitation circles, floodlit matches and coloured clothing'. During the rest of the summer, Arlott continued to mull over the implications of it all. 'The players have made pronounced financial gains which can only be attributed, directly or indirectly, to the Packer operation,' he fully acknowledged in the July issue of *Wisden Cricket Monthly* (newly founded by David Frith, non-establishment, non-Swantonian, with Arlott on its editorial board and indeed in some sense its presiding spirit). In the next issue he argued that the Australian authorities had had no alternative but to come to terms, pointing out that all over the world traditional long-form domestic cricket was struggling to survive:

> England has good reason to be grateful to Schweppes who, in sponsoring the County Championship, undertook the least glamorous of our competitions. Yet, for the cricketers there is no better cricket in the world than that within the three-day county frame. The fact remains that it is not to the popular taste of the second half of the twentieth century. The point has been reached at which even the contributions of sponsors and Test revenue combined can barely maintain domestic play solvent. Hence to turn to professional promoters and marketing experts to make the largest possible amount from the commodity available was simply logical.

Finally, in September, his end-of-season review included a passage in its way as solemn as Swanton's. 'Whether the whole shape of the game is to be distorted to produce the profits expected, indeed demanded, by the alliance between the Australian Board and its recently greatest enemy remains to be known,' he wrote in the *Guardian*. 'To retain old grudges and continue the feuds, which originated in the fundamental gift, is primarily to damage the health, perhaps even the natural life, of the game itself.'

Would in fact 'the whole shape of the game' be 'distorted'? An early indication – deeply troubling to traditionalists – came with the hastily arranged English tour of Australia the following winter. By October 1979, writing to the *Telegraph*, Swanton could only contemplate with dismay the fixture list facing Brearley's men:

It has been patently cobbled up by the television promoters in what they regard as the most exciting deal for their customers. There is to be a plethora of one-day internationals with fast bowlers propelling white balls in-the-dark against a black sight screen no doubt monopolizing the stage.

England's fixtures consist of eight one-day internationals [including against West Indies], four of them finished under floodlights, a mere three three-day, two four-day matches and the three Tests. In 93 days in Australia there are 20 internal flights and only 17 days' first-class cricket outside the Tests.

One can well believe that eight defeats by England inside two years have left Australia burning for revenge. Well, let them achieve it under the traditional arrangements if they can, either in England in 1981 or down under in 1982–83. The Cricket Council and the advice of the TCCB will be making their decision about The Ashes any moment now. I hope they stand firm …

The game, alas, is for the moment in the grip of Australian commercial interests to whom the old standards of conduct and the game's special charisma mean little or nothing.

Money is all.

The English authorities did indeed stand firm on the question of the Ashes – they would not be at stake – but more broadly it was undeniable that this Australian summer of 1979–80 represented a shape-changer, unmistakably pointing the way ahead. Arlott as usual sat out the tour, one conducted in an almost uniquely unpleasant atmosphere; but in early January he was moved to write a strong piece condemning the ACB for their decision to include the misbehaving Lillee (aluminium bat, plus open mocking of Brearley) and Ian Chappell (throwing away his bat in protest at an umpire's decision) for the second Test. 'In the urge to please their new masters [i.e. Packer and his organisation] by mustering a winning team, the Board are apparently prepared to sacrifice the last shreds of dignity,' he declared in the *Guardian*. And he finished with some grave thoughts that, if written anonymously, might as easily have been attributed to 'the Archbishop of Lord's':

It may be argued that, in play under floodlights – a logical development of the one-day game – with its concomitant use of a white ball and black pads, cricket moved with the times, to present itself in 'pop' form to a major paying audience. On the other hand, these offences by the players and the pusillanimous reaction of 'authority' reflect disdain for the disciplines upon which all human activities should be based. Such behaviour, on both sides, discredits not only the parties responsible but, far more important, cricket itself.

———

No longer 'the reigning chief scribe', no longer the maker of *de haut en bas* end-of-play summaries, Swanton during the second half of the 1970s was nevertheless almost as busy as ever. Much time and energy were expended in his role as a member of the MCC Committee: a position he secured in 1975, after the humiliation in 1968 of coming bottom of the poll – a reminder that, whether at Lord's or in the City's square mile, even highly respectable working journalists are never quite accepted as 'one of us'. Swanton was not admitted to the inner circle dictating MCC's losing strategy against Packer. Before joining the Committee, he had been on the Club Facilities subcommittee, where he was an enthusiastic advocate of a new indoor cricket school. Now Swanton was chosen as the spokesman for the school's steering committee. By 1977 the school was nearly finished, and MCC minutes record that Swanton was anxious to get his old pal Don Bradman to open it. After he had declined, Swanton wondered if Prince Philip or Prince Charles might be available – but they were busy, too. When the school formally opened on 28 November 1977, the honour went to Gubby Allen, the grandee closest to hand.

His writing – often looking back, arguably through somewhat rose-tinted spectacles – seldom stopped, his 'Off the Cuff' column for the *Cricketer* giving him a monthly platform. At his crustiest, he could still be pretty crusty, typified by his March 1979 lament for the lost art of batting against spin – 'one came away from Sydney wondering which was the weaker, England's pawky, fast-footed efforts against Higgs [leg-spinner Jim Higgs] or the Australians' palsied jabbing against Miller and Emburey'; and he concluded about the feeble batting in general (David Gower the sole recipient of 'unqualified admiration') that 'the root trouble lies in the faulty grip and abbreviated pick-up of the bat'. Yet, as ever, Swanton could also be positive about the current crop of cricketers. Later that year he wrote enthusiastically about Essex's county championship triumph – 'not least among their virtues is the saving grace of humour, from the laconic variety of the captain [Keith Fletcher] and John Lever to the almost (so I am informed by those close to the scene) goonish capers of Ray East' – while a distinct favourite was Mike Brearley, whom in 1978 he described as 'England's natural captain just as long as his skills keep him in the first XXII – or, if you like, XXXIII'. And with evident satisfaction he quoted Brearley's rebuff to the man whom (on a mild, non-apocalyptic sort of day) Swanton called 'the pirate': 'Money apart, Kerry Packer is not my style. England is my home. I prefer the chugging British coaster with a cargo of pig-iron to a monstrous supertanker hurriedly constructed. Temperamentally I am for reform not for revolution.'

By this time, Swanton's *Follow On* had appeared, aimed astutely enough at the Christmas books market for 1977. 'I have never quite understood why John Arlott has such a stranglehold on the "voice of cricket" title,' Tim Rice mused in his admiring foreword. 'I am second to no man in my admiration for Mr Arlott's magic vocal delivery, but I have always believed that in cricket there is many another larynx deserving of the awed respect accorded to the Arlott vocal cords. Jim Swanton's is one, and as more and more of the voices of sport become totally indistinguishable from one another, hysterical and nasal, lacking class and region, a voice such as Jim's [still sometimes heard on *TMS*, for instance in lunchtime features] becomes even purer gold.' As with *Sort of a Cricket Person*, Arlott himself reviewed it in the *Guardian*; and this time, 'beyond name-dropping', he was struck by 'some prodigious title-sprinkling':

An empress, a queen, five kings and two princes head the list in the 1,200-strong index; peers of the realm are common (at a rough count, 38). The curious searcher will discover such strict sequences as 'Ponsonby-Fane, Sir S., Pope John XXIII, Porbander, Maharajah of, Portal of Hungerford, Lord'; or, again, 'Berry, Hon. Michael (*see* Hartwell, Lord), Besier, R., Birkenhead, 1st Lord, Birkett, Lord, Black Prince, the' (and he does not mean the pub, either).

Those of wide outlook will be delighted to come upon Enid Blyton, Drs Vorster and Verwoerd, Mr Karamanlis, Dame Clara Butt, Madame Bollinger, and the Mackinnon of Mackinnon. There is a quorum of Bishops, and one Archbishop, but they are, collectively if surprisingly, outshone by St Thomas à Becket.

Arlott also noted how 'at the end of this informed, gossipy, friendly, amiably egocentric, slightly papal and satisfying read, close the book and there, on the back of the dust wrapper, is a half-length portrait of Jim Swanton in a dinner-jacket holding – title towards camera – a copy of his earlier autobiography'. That distinctly barbed observation was almost the end of the review, but not quite, for Arlott went on: 'He has, though, already had his modest last word. "Only I know how much more I have received from the game than I have given to it."'

These were the years, through the caprice of which tapes were preserved and which (the overwhelming majority) were wiped, that featured some of Arlott's most celebrated passages of commentary. For instance, 'Thomson ... comes in, bowls to Boycott, Boycott pushes that ... there must be a run-out here, oh how tragic, how tragic, how tragic, how tragic ...' in July 1977. And he went on: 'We welcome World Service with the news that Randall has just this minute been sacrificially run out and England are 52 for 3 ... Let's leave the applause for Randall from a Trent Bridge crowd as he comes in, very crestfallen and very unlucky. (*Applause.*) Almost with tears in his eyes, he looks very disconsolate ...' Next summer – in the same series against Pakistan that Botham ran in 'like a shire horse, cresting the breeze' – Gower was facing his first ball in Test cricket: 'Liaqat comes in, bowls to Gower, and Gower turns (*shout from crowd*) and he hits it for a four behind square leg. Oh, what a princely entry!'

During the 1979 World Cup, addressing *TMS*'s scorer Bill Frindall, he gently guyed the remorseless mathematical requirements of high-pressure one-day cricket: 'What I really want to know, Bill, is if Australia bowl their overs at the same rate as England did, and Brearley and Boycott survive the opening spell, and that the number of no-balls is limited to ten in the innings, and assuming my car does 33.8 miles per gallon and my home is 67.3 miles from the ground [Lord's], what time does my wife have to put the casserole in?' Then later that summer, at the Lord's Test against India, came the Saturday morning aftermath of the previous day's spectacular storm. 'This mammoth uncovering is going on – you might almost call it an unveiling,' began Arlott's virtuoso, unscripted set piece:

The old 'taking off the covers' – which was only running a couple of trolleys of corrugated iron off the pitch – was nothing compared to this. This is a real Cecil B. de Mille job, with – four, five, six, seven, eight wheeled covers, huge tarpaulins – eight of them – and a whole team of removers. They seem to be in two shifts. Those in the red jerkins removing the covers and those in the white jerkins admiring them – which is not quite a fair division of toil, but it does give an impression of labour to spare out there.

And so it went on for the next five or ten minutes, culminating – with Arlott still going strong – in the umpires at last being able to see for themselves and inspect the pitch. 'Groundsman Jim Fairbrother standing beside it as if he didn't want to intrude on their private conversation, and Dickie Bird there looking very worried, stroking his chin, hands on hips, one in the pocket. Poor old Dickie. All the troubles in the world, always, hasn't he?'

It was not invariably so cherishable. 'It would be his first session of commentary of the day that would be the one most likely to be below par,' recalled his producer, Peter Baxter, about Arlott by the late 1970s. 'He would have arrived out of breath and in desperate need of his first cup of cooled black coffee.' Tony Lewis, who was in the *TMS* commentary box during these years, was generally full of admiration. Arlott was 'like a computer full of recollections and reminiscences'; he 'never dealt in second-hand phrases or lazy clichés'; 'the tale he was telling appeared to come from his heart and soul'; and the effect was accentuated by 'the dramatic intake of breath and by seconds of silence'. How did he compare with his best-known colleague? Arlott, noted Lewis, 'scowled whenever Johnners [Brian Johnston] failed to treat the endeavours of a professional on the field with the appropriate gravitas'; but 'as he got older he became more lugubrious, and a jape from Johnners was just what the listener needed'. Lewis himself, after several years of comments between-overs, made his ball-by-ball debut in 1979. 'Not good,' pronounced Arlott in private to him after his first self-conscious stint. 'You have never called the bat "the willow" in your life. Your language is so artificial. You're commentating as you think commentators ought to, and the verbs you used were so long ... Look, don't broadcast, just talk to people.'

Even by this stage, Arlott still richly appreciated watching youthful talent come to bloom. 'Gower played a range of strokes, from the glance through the hook and the drive to the cut,' he wrote during the Lord's Test against Pakistan in 1978. 'It was all so much more than arithmetical: free and natural, it seemed like an echo of the days before batsmen merely accumulated ...' The young Botham struck, if anything, a still deeper chord. 'Fundamentally he has natural rhythm, perfect balance, and sense of timing; they are applied with an immense competitive urge and backed by unusual strength,' he observed later that summer about the twenty-two-year-old's bowling. 'Magnificently built, with strong legs, wide hips, deep chest, wide shoulders, and heavily muscled arms, he has all the physical attributes a cricketer needs.' As for his 'naturally gifted' batting, 'the main source of his stroke-power lies in an instinctive sense of timing, reinforced by sheer force … he has such a splendid, long swing that even his mishits travel so fast that they are difficult to stop or catch.'

His strong and usually empathetic feelings were not just for the young. Take three contrasting openers. Arlott stoutly supported Brearley as England captain ('the strictest objective judges will agree that his tactics, approach, and handling of men are finer than those of any other Englishman within memory,' he plausibly claimed in August 1979), while sharing his agonies as a Test batsman. 'He seems to worry rather than to play naturally (which is easier to recommend than to do),' he reflected in the same piece. 'He is constantly edging outside the off stump; so are others, but not quite so frequently as Brearley. Some expert observers feel his footwork is sometimes inhibited by anxiety.' Arlott was likewise sympathetic when Yorkshire the previous autumn announced its decision to remove Boycott from the captaincy on the day after his mother's death. 'He is fighting two battles: with an intensely deep personal suffering and with the media which he has never trusted,' commented Arlott (who had seen the news 'in a single English headline squeezed between Italian on a kiosk in Siena'):

He is their meat; but he has never understood them or felt with them. And they have brought him more agony than is generally realised. Many who work within the media will say, as a conditioned response, that it is his fault; in truth, it is his misfortune, the misfortune of a painfully honest man who has never, in his heart, come to terms with the standards prevailing outside Fitzwilliam, his home village.

The third opener was the uniquely gifted Barry Richards, whose autobiography appeared earlier in 1978 and revealed a man for whom county cricket had become 'a chore', and who declared that 'when I walk off a county ground for the last time – whenever that may be – it will be with an enormous sense of relief'. Arlott was appalled. 'It is,' he wrote in his *Guardian* review, 'simply hard – indeed, tragic – to believe. Milton wrote, in a different context, of the talent "lodg'd with me useless": but talent without joy is also – and wastefully – useless.'

Gower, Botham, Brearley, Boycott, Richards – these were all major names, but it was at the more journeyman level that Arlott kept his warmest ties, not least through his continuing close involvement with the Cricketers' Association. Patrick Symes was a novice freelance reporter when he got to know 'a wheezing and perspiring' Arlott on a hot afternoon in the mid-1970s in 'the tiny six-seater press box' at Dean Park, Bournemouth, even going to Arlott's 'big old Mercedes' to fetch a bottle of wine for him. Symes tells a pleasing story from July 1977. Hampshire were playing Nottinghamshire at the May's Bounty ground in Basingstoke, just next to Arlott's primary school back in the early 1920s. 'On the eve of the final day [with the visitors chasing 351 to win], Arlott entertained some of the Nottinghamshire side to dinner at his home, the Old Sun in nearby Alresford. The next morning some of the Notts boys were in a sorry state and one of them, Bob White, was so ill he was unable to bat. Mike Taylor took 7 for 23 and it was all over by lunch, Arlott's "subterfuge" helping Hampshire to victory by 233 runs.'

As would almost certainly have been the case even if Packer had not happened, cricket in the late 1970s continued to evolve into a spectacle – off the field as well as on – that both Arlott and Swanton found increasingly disturbing, as did many other seasoned observers. The *locus classicus* was the bouncer. 'In modern times, the act of deliberate intimidation to make the batsmen fearful of getting severe injury has become almost systematic, with all countries, excepting India, exploiting this evil deed,' reflected *Wisden*'s editor, Norman Preston, in his overview of the 1978 season. 'I wonder whether present-day sponsorship, which offers huge sums of money to the victors, has not encouraged players to *win at any price*.' And he went on:

> Matters came to a head in June, in the England v Pakistan Test at Edgbaston, when Bob Willis injured Iqbal Qasim, a late-order batsman who had gone in as night-watchman. An experimental note agreed at the International Cricket Conference in 1976 reads: 'Captains must instruct their players that the fast short-pitched ball should *at no time* be directed at non-recognised batsmen.' Willis contravened this edict …

The television picture of Qasim being led from the pitch bleeding freely made a considerable impact, prompting later in June a full-scale treatment by Arlott of the whole issue. 'External critics must accept two facts,' he declared in defence of the existence of the bouncer as part of any self-respecting quick bowler's armoury. 'The physical threat implicit in fast bowling has always been an integral part of the game, and the eventual legislation will be framed by elder cricketers, who are invariably traditionalists and not idealistic humanitarians.' Quite so: but as he also unequivocally explained to any non-cricketing readers, 'the present problem is the proliferation of the bouncer', arguably explained by 'the perfection – for batsmen – of modern pitches'. There followed the article's most arresting passage: 'Whatever the cause, it has now assumed such menacing proportions that it must be checked before someone is killed or, as has lately been suggested in the Packer series context, cricket can be sold for its danger, violence and promise of blood.'

Arlott also noted an important accompanying development. 'It must seem odd,' he observed, 'that a batsman who wears leg guards, thigh pad, box, batting gloves and a chest protector should not guard his head which is both vulnerable and vital. Significantly, as soon as Brearley donned his steel skull-protector, there was an immediate and widely-spreading move to design and wear helmets.' Swanton was predictably unimpressed. 'It is the urgent task of cricket authority in 1978 to try and ensure that the added degree of fierce contention which greater monetary rewards have brought with them finds less outlet than it has been doing of late in the form of physical threat to the batsmen,' he declared later that summer in his 'Helmet Heresy' piece for the *Cricketer*. 'If Test and first-class cricket were decently conducted by all captains and umpires, the batting helmet would be superfluous as it is incongruous and ugly.' Not that he was against helmets for batsmen as a matter of absolute principle – whereas, he was adamant, 'I would forbid the use of helmets by fielders, and the sooner the better.' Arlott's overall position was one of reluctant acceptance. 'There were protests, especially from those who do not have to face modern pace bowlers,' he noted in his *Guardian* review of the 1978 season. 'In fact, though, helmets are the logical consequence of the intensification of attack by short-pitched bowling. As financial rewards increase so, too, will the practice of intimidation.' He and Swanton at least agreed about that. 'It is,' added Arlott, 'morally impossible to legislate against batsmen wearing protective gear; that would assume responsibility for any death that might occur for lack of protection.'

Neither man was much enamoured of behavioural trends, though each had a different focus. For Swanton, what he most loathed by this time was on the playing side of the boundary rope, and in July 1979, in the context of the TCCB seeking to get the counties to discourage needless exhibitionism, he unburdened himself:

Perhaps we of the old brigade take too seriously the frantic overflow of emotion whenever the fielding side takes a wicket. Up they go to the bowler or fielder or both, jumping, back-slapping, rumpling the hair, and only narrowly, it seems, stopping short of a fervent embrace ... The whole charade is all of a piece with the excessive appealing – excessive both in volume and in frequency, by fielders often in no position to form an opinion ... Do we 'protest too much'? If we do, it must be because we believe cricket is a game that can reflect personality and individual idiosyncrasy in so many more subtle ways. It is such a large part of its charm that its participants can portray so many of the human virtues: courage, unselfishness, daring, patience, humour – and, not least, self-control.

Arlott, by contrast, was usually reluctant – in public anyway – to criticise current professionals for how they conducted themselves on the field of play. Instead, he concentrated on what he saw as the most malign legacy of the one-day revolution – namely, as he put it in his 1978 review, a 'hooliganism among spectators' that was 'approaching the intolerable':

Frequently the rowdy element of the crowd can be seen already drunk before they enter the ground. They are undoubtedly a reflection of football if not an overflow from it; their reactions are those of the soccer terraces. [Arlott himself, thoroughly disenchanted, had a few years earlier stopped reporting on football.] They are not to be seen at three-day matches, and only occasionally – and then usually on Saturdays – at Test matches. They are most often present in substantial numbers, and at their most aggressive, on the grounds of the more successful one-day sides, Lancashire, Leicestershire, and perhaps surprisingly, certainly in part in rebuttal of the football link, at Kent and Somerset.

In his piece a year later on Brearley's self-harmingly 'introverted' batting in Tests, he identified something arguably more disturbing than outright rowdiness – something that struck at the very heart of cricket's best self. 'He has reason to feel stressed, for he has had cruelly little sympathy from crowds,' reflected Arlott. 'Others in other sports suffer from modern crowd-attitudes. It is not simply the effect of distance that recalls spectators – especially at cricket – between the two wars as far more inclined to applaud or even to sympathise than to jeer in the current fashion.'

Cricket and society: that intimate, inextricable relationship had over the years become one of Arlott's most insistent themes. 'It has long been said, facilely, that cricket is unprogressive, reactionary, class conscious, resistant to change', and that 'so are the English', he noted in September 1979, before going on to suggest that in the bigger national picture the true composition and character of the game was altogether more complex. A lengthy, heartfelt passage ended with just a hint of Hegel's Owl of Minerva spreading its wings at the fall of dusk:

> Not long ago the English cricket establishment were in favour of going ahead with the visit of a South African team; and they persisted in their attitude despite the protests from a wide section of the community. That is not fully explained by the fact that the English are the most right-wing people in Europe. It can, though, be attributed to the fact that the cricket establishment is almost entirely composed of right-wing conservatives.
>
> The game in this country, however, is not completely of that political persuasion; it includes village people, the league cricketers of the industrial areas and, to an increasing degree, the immigrant population from India, Pakistan and West Indies.

So, while the senior committee men may make decisions about the laws, fixture lists and the allocation of Test Matches from their room at Lord's, a grass roots section of the community plays, and controls for itself, by far the largest proportion of the cricket of the country. The ordinary evening, Saturday, Sunday, public parks and village green players are little beholden to the distant committees and authorities.

The English people retain certain national characteristics of mind and quality. On the whole, though, they have been diluted and changed as much as any; and their game – at least their senior and traditional one – has changed in sympathy ...

———

'The constant travel and pace of work, along with his gradual disillusionment at the way market forces were dictating the future of cricket, made him long for a less pressured existence,' is how David Rayvern Allen convincingly depicts Arlott in the late 1970s. 'Incredibly, he still managed to fit in everything he wanted to do without the appearance of hurry, but the price was rising. The tax was on his body, the toll was on his health.' Arlott himself, at the point in 1980 of his retirement from broadcasting and full-time journalism, told Ian Wooldridge that he wanted retirement to be 'my choice, not someone else's', before adding that he had reached the stage 'where I simply don't enjoy talking all day on the radio, writing my piece for the *Guardian*, driving 240 miles home and then getting up next morning to do it all over again'.

He seems to have reached the decision during the 1979 season. It was a decision possibly prompted or strengthened by an intensely embarrassing cock-up at Edgbaston in June when, just over a fortnight after the end of the Prudential World Cup, he mistakenly referred in his report to the first Prudential – not Cornhill – Test, with the mistake finding its way on to the front page of the *Guardian*. (In return for their money, sponsors required an advertisement in the form of published credits in Test match reports, and were cross if they did not get one.) Quite likely, Arlott had another concern. 'I used to be working at new things to say on radio,' he explained at The Oval later that summer to Tony Lewis. 'The perfect descriptions, or near-perfect, which would prompt listeners to write to me and tell me what a fine moment of inspiration I'd had. 'T'wasn't that. It was hard work. I can't do it any longer. I'm not as I was. Haven't thought of something new to say for ages.' Perhaps he exaggerated – some half an hour later, after Alan Butcher had played and missed, he described him as 'looking sheepishly at Kapil Dev just like a small boy who has been caught stealing jam' – but the chances are that the concern was genuine. Or as he put it to Simon Hoggart on the eve of the 1980 season, in the first of a summer of seemingly innumerable media profiles, 'As you get older, your techniques get better, but you begin to run out of fresh ideas. It's time to give other people a chance.' Hoggart took the opportunity to find out whether his perspective on the cricket establishment had mellowed. 'They are completely reactionary, totally reactionary,' insisted Arlott. 'And yet they refuse to admit it.'

Around this time, Arlott wrote for *Wisden Cricket Monthly* a closely printed, double-page article, 'Into the unknown', looking ahead to his valedictory season. 'Cricket is a personal matter: as different in its significances and qualities as the people who follow it,' he declared. 'In a lifetime we look forward to many seasons, their import-ance varying with our age and experience. To look forward knowingly to one's last summer in the game, though, is a personally unique experience in which the demanding and the generous are intermingled.' Much of the piece was a typically well-informed assessment of what lay ahead in the first summer of the new decade, including an analysis of the 'most disappointingly arrested' development of many of England's 'most promising' batsmen:

> The one-day game provides lively and concentrated entertainment; and it has lifted the standard of our outcricket to heights of excellence barely envisaged 20 years ago. On the other hand, it strikes at the foundations of the craft of batsmanship fostered by three-day county cricket, for which there is no true sub-stitute. Perhaps the risk was consciously taken; it would be difficult now to put back the clock; and impossible for the game to exist without the sponsorship attracted by the over-limit form.

The writer could not but acknowledge that his 'own personal taste' was for 'county cricket in three-day matches', albeit 'the three-day pattern' was not 'what it was' prior to 1969. 'The John Player competition stimulated both interest and finance but it took away the county cricketer's away-match Sunday,' explained Arlott. 'There were generally five or six of them in the summer. Everyone got up late and, over the newspapers and talk of the previous day's doings in their own match and those reported, breakfast was a leisurely, long drawn-out affair; in retrospect, generally regarded tolerantly by hotel staffs.' Even so, he still looked ahead keenly in 1980 to a final summer of county championship cricket 'at such places as Taunton, Hove, Bath, Worcester, Cheltenham, Southampton, Bournemouth':

There, among quiet and ruminative crowds; where one can hear the batsmen calling; the bowler's grunt of effort; the smack of ball into hand or glove; feel the thud of the chasing fieldsman's feet; a man as close indeed to the game and the players in a way that never occurs in any other country or any other major spectator sport – at a football match, for instance, the spectator feels cut off – not even at a Test match nor on such grounds as Lord's, which are remote in feeling.

In such a setting, the outsider shares the atmosphere of cricket. The sounds, too, are as evocative as they are peculiar to this facet of the English scene; the murmur of conversation; the hush as the bowler moves in at a crucial stage; the appreciative clapping prompted by a pleasing stroke; the sharp half-gasp, half-killer-shout that greets the fall of a wicket; the sigh at a dropped catch. The initiate can identify them all with his eyes shut.

At Bournemouth, the batsmen walk out from the dressing-rooms over the spike-splintered floor boards, through the drinkers in the members' bar to the crease; and, after play, repair to the marquees on the boundary edge; at Hove, Taunton, Bath and Southampton, they walk down between the seats from which their friends and relations can wish them luck; or, on the way back, commiserate with them *sotto voce*.

'For this year,' Arlott concluded, 'that will be the main hunger; for the rest of my life the abiding nostalgia.'

The long goodbye began at Lord's, an 'amiably appreciative quorum' watching 'typical April stuff' between MCC and Essex, 'the players easing themselves into the season with due consideration for strainable muscles'; in early May at Ilford, a 'meagre crowd' saw 'a finely contested day', with virus-hit Essex holding out against Somerset even after Botham had dismissed Hardie with 'a short-pitched ball which rocketed like a partridge'; at Arundel, the setting 'ringed by the great cedars', the West Indian tourists tuned up against Lavinia Duchess of Norfolk's XI, for whom D'Oliveira's 'characteristic' half-century expressed one last time 'his delight in the freedom, which came so late in his life, to play cricket against men of all races', a sight that made the occasion 'all more than a diversion'. In late May he was at Bournemouth for Somerset's B&H visit (gold award to Vic Marks, 'an unspectacular, thinking, grafting cricketer, whose worth has not yet been fully appreciated'); in mid-June at Lord's for Viv Richards's 'princely' century against England; Lord's again in July for a tight B&H final ('a relief and a pleasure to have a day's cricket free of bad light or rain'); late that month a serious complaint during the third Test at The Oval about the 'niggardly' over-rate of the tourists ('never until this current West Indies series has an entire team strategy, as distinct from short-term tactics, been based on slowing the tempo of the match'); and at Hove in late August, his last three-day county match as a journalist. Between Sussex and Middlesex, with the latter closing in on the title, it was not a happy affair, culminating on the final day in John Barclay's refusal to make a declaration that might have given Middlesex a sniff but could also have brought Sussex a win. 'The only possible explanation of the decision to deprive them of that opportunity,' surmised Arlott, 'is that the earlier disagreements between Imran Khan and Brearley were allowed to poison the match in which cricket in general, and the paying spectators in particular, were cynically shrugged aside'. Of Barclay's 'self-defeating gesture' to bat on pointlessly, he added: 'Thus are bred the inter-county grudges which have so unnecessarily and small-mindedly damaged much of our post-war cricket.' And his last championship report ended miserably, as he described how Le Roux 'slogged Sussex to the season's highest total in the sluggish death throes of a callously murdered cricket match'.

That unpleasantness was on Tuesday 26 August. A glance at the fixtures list revealed that Arlott would be bowing out almost a fortnight later, and so indeed it turned out: on Saturday 6 September when he commentated and reported on Middlesex's Gillette Cup triumph over Surrey at Lord's (Brearley's 'closely-executed strategy' as 'the conclusive factor'); followed on Sunday the 7th at Edgbaston by a final John Player League commentary stint. Those were Arlott's chronological farewells. But in the eyes of the cricket world, the *real* farewell had already happened: at the Centenary Test between England and Australia, starting at Lord's on Thursday 28 August.

'Arlott ascends to the top of the Lord's pavilion for the first of his last broadcasts, stops and mops his brow, heaves back his shoulders and wades straight in,' observed Scyld Berry on that first morning. Off air, Arlott told him of his conviction that cricket broadcasting had a bright future. 'The harsher reality becomes,' paraphrased Berry, 'the more unemployed there are, the higher the rate of inflation, the deeper the Soviet Union penetrates into the Free World – the more people will want to escape into another world. "It's an escape," says Arlott. "It's no coincidence that there is a high brick wall surrounding Lord's."' The play itself was unspectacular – 'the crowd spent a subdued day, short of event or excitement,' noted Arlott in his match report – with Australia losing only two wickets; but at least there was an almost full day's cricket, unlike the Friday, when bad light followed by torrential rain ended play at 12.45. Star of what play there was was Kim Hughes – with Arlott in his report detecting 'the stamp of a thoroughbred' in addition to 'a generosity which will win him affection as well as respect' – but the larger story was of 'this grimmest of English summers' ensuring that a very special occasion, attended by battalions of former Test cricketers, was 'being honoured more in the bars and at the dining tables than on the pitch'. 'Who shall say alas?' went on Arlott. 'The bottle, the grill and the oven are more predictably hospitable than English climate or English turf.' Bottles indeed were present that afternoon, as Peter West took advantage of the rain to conduct a lengthy interview with Arlott – a sight that provoked one viewer, Ronald Ian Jeffrey of York, to write to the *Radio Times* claiming that it had been 'highly reprehensible' of West 'to ply John Arlott with drink in front of the cameras'.

The third day, Saturday the 30th, was wretched for almost all concerned, not least Arlott. By early afternoon there was still no play, and the conversational mood in the commentary box was increasingly animated:

> What I hate [Arlott declared on air to a colleague] is this sun blazing down and people waiting for cricket and getting none, and I think you're over-polite. I think they're not quiet and contented and patient, I think they're becoming impatient, and I think they've every right to be impatient. And I think what they're facing is the worst type of bureaucracy, which is doing the thing by the letter of the law instead of the spirit of the law. What we want to see is some cricket out there. And even if they tell the fieldsmen not to go on the mud, surely these people playing an historic match, celebrating a hundred years of Test cricket in this country, with a Saturday crowd here, ought to say, 'Well, we'll go out there even if we do slip up.'

Some play did take place later in the afternoon, before bad light intervened; and, with levels of frustration continuing to run high, there occurred the notorious incident in which, on the Pavilion steps, umpire Bird was jostled by members and his fellow umpire David Constant had his throat seized. Declaring that English cricket had 'donned a dirty mask', Arlott in the *Guardian* on Monday morning ('Unacceptable face of Lord's') used both barrels: 'The traditionalists of the game have long, and justifiably, pointed the finger of disgust at football followers. The offenders on Saturday, however, were not underprivileged roughnecks from the slums of some great city, but the people in the MCC members' seats in the front of the Pavilion.' And he quoted the Australian captain Greg Chappell (who had sought to protect Constant): 'It was the worst performance I have seen by members any-where in the world.'

The last two days of an ill-fated match were played in mocking sunshine. 'Good morning everyone, I've got the feeling I've been here before' was how Arlott greeted his listeners on Monday, as his *Guardian* colleague Frank Keating watched and listened admiringly. Soon, he (in Keating's words) 'started to unroll the leisurely strokes': 'Lillee in his nightshirt of a shirt ... Lillee erect as a guardsman and that saturnine expression so remarkably like the drawings of Spofforth the Demon ... Umpire Constant in his panama hat and new moustache and a definite oriental look ... the ball races away and Gower's going to feel thrice the young man for that ...' Undoubted star of the fourth day was Lillee ('not merely fast and resourceful, but highly astute,' noted Arlott in his report), while on the final day 'a fair – by objective standards a generous – declaration' by Chappell just for a moment seemed likely to prompt a thrilling and redemptive run chase, before Boycott decided to 'renew his own personal credit with a century of quite monumental rectitude'. The result, concluded Arlott mildly enough in his final Test report, was an 'honourable' draw for England, as after 'the muddles, traumas and problems of the first few days', the historic occasion 'ended in good humour and celebration'.

Unmentioned in his report was not only the crowd's slow handclapping towards the end, but his own farewell on that Tuesday 2 September. Fairly early in the afternoon session – with the last vestiges of a chase disappearing by the over, and after Arlott had declined the MCC Committee's invi-tation to join them for lunch ('Why now?' he said to Tony

319

Lewis. 'They never asked me before …') – he took to the microphone for his final stint of the match. Its understated end would become legendary: 'Bright again going round the wicket to the right-handed Boycott, and Boycott pushes this away between silly point and slip, it's picked up by Mallett at short third man, that's the end of the over, it's 69 for 2, nine runs off the over, 28 Boycott, 15 Gower – 69 for 2, and after Trevor Bailey it'll be Christopher Martin-Jenkins.' There have been different versions of what happened next, among them Keating's, who was again present:

> The little frail commentary box perched high over London – Mosey, Johnston, Frindall, Baxter, Bailey and all of them – burst into touching applause. The old boy got up and, hearing it, said 'someone's got a fifty'. He looked for a necessary drink and smoothed down over his paunch a gay blue-black striped Van Heusen …
>
> He went off to do non-stop interviews with everyone from *Today* to *Nationwide* to Anna Ford's little lot and was doing that business when the Lord's announcer said: 'That over of Bright's represents Mr Arlott's last Test match broadcast.' And the crowd went on clapping – more than a century, really and truly a double-century job.
>
> And so continued the green-capped fielders, all looking up to the perch we were in above the pavilion. And Geoffrey Boycott, who takes his gloves off only at the end of an over or the end of an innings, took off his batting gloves and joined in the applause …

Keating did not record, perhaps did not hear, what Arlott apparently said to Don Mosey as he left the box: 'That's stuffed Johnston. He won't be able to retire for at least three years now.' Malicious or jocular? The jury, as Johnston's son Barry rightly reflects, remains out. Soon afterwards – whether before or after the immediate round of interviews is unclear – he bumped into Lewis as he came down the wooden steps at the back of the box. 'I thought,' remarked Lewis about the mundane end to the commentary session, 'you would have reflected for a moment and said something more romantic than that.' To which Arlott replied: 'What's more romantic than the clean break?'

Romantic or unromantic, there was still time for the cricket world's last act of homage. It came at the end of the match, as Arlott (due to present the Man of the Match award) stood on the lower balcony of the Pavilion and, after being introduced over the public address system, listened to wave after wave after wave of clapping from the several thousand gathered on the playing area. 'You'll have to stop applauding, otherwise I won't be able to speak,' he finally said, visibly overcome. For those clapping (including one of the authors), it would be an imperishable memory – an out-pouring of affection to a man, to a game, to an irrecoverable time in their lives.

9

1980–2000: Into That Good Night

The Arlott family had enjoyed their holidays on Alderney, one of the Channel Islands, and he decided it would be the right place for retirement. In 1980, he sold a large part of his collections of cricket books and wine, and bought a substantial house, called Balmoral. Arlott, more of an oenophile than a monarchist, promptly changed that to The Vines. Once settled, he enjoyed a short walk each morning to a spot from which he watched the breaking waves, spied France across the water and cleared out heavily congested bronchial tubes.

The most satisfying account of this late stage in Arlott's life is contained in Mike Brearley's series of television interviews in 1984 for Channel 4, subsequently turned into a book. Their conversations in Alderney were discursive, free-association affairs, each lasting two hours or more on three successive mornings (with Beaujolais for elevenses), when Arlott was at his best. In these, he claimed that since his move he had, in some ways, never worked so hard in his life. Nobody on Alderney interrupted him; and because he no longer lived on the mainland, people thought twice about telephoning. 'I am working at the things I like doing.

Sometimes when I get really tied up with something, my wife says, "Come in for your dinner. Why don't you stop?" But I would sooner carry on than have my dinner, sometimes.'

Brearley's presence was a good excuse for rumination on his dramatic return to the England captaincy in the legendary Headingley Test of 1981, when England dumbfounded the Australian tourists by winning a game – and turning the series – after following on. Arlott confessed he could not bear to watch it. He had desperately wanted to be present at one of the most heroic Test series, ever; it would have been, he added, 'the greatest of all series to broadcast'. But as he explained, he no longer wanted to go to cricket matches: 'I feel I am useless. To go to a cricket match, and not be doing anything, makes me feel almost deprived.'

Before that Headingley Test, England had not won a single one of Ian Botham's twelve Tests as captain. At Lord's, in the previous Test, a duck in both his innings (a miserable four balls faced) was the end of it. There was even talk of dropping him altogether. Writing in the *Guardian*, Arlott sympathised with Botham: it had been asking too much to expect him to cope simultaneously with four varieties of stress – batting, bowling, close fielding and captaincy. That had been beyond even Gary Sobers, the greatest of all-rounders. 'There has never been,' Arlott further pointed out, 'a consistently successful all-round captain in Test cricket; certainly not one 24 years old.' Even captains like Hutton and May, who did not bowl, had found captaincy such a strain that they had left the game early. The selectors, he argued, 'should have recognised that Ian Botham was – and is – essentially an instinctive and not an intellectual crick-eter'; and he insisted that Botham – for whom he had a soft spot, as a man as well as a cricketer – was too good to leave out. 'It is difficult to believe that he cannot be rehabilitated as a player at Test level. To do so, though, he must be allowed complete freedom from all stresses apart from playing … He deserves, and English cricket needs him, to have that opportunity.' Granted it at Headingley, Botham took six wickets in Australia's first innings, scored a leonine 149 not out in England's second, and with help from Brearley's sympathetic captaincy proved Arlott to be entirely correct.

Having given up broadcasting, Arlott now had the time he needed to complete a biography of England's greatest twentieth-century batsman, Jack Hobbs. He had been in love with the idea of the man since adolescence or even earlier, and working in Fleet Street after the war he was able to extend this to a delight in Hobbs's company. When Hobbs was managing his sports shop on Fleet Street, the great man would sit at a table at the end of the room, happy to chat with young boys whose fathers were buying them a bat. (The older author's first bat came from there.) Arlott was in the habit of phoning Hobbs, who would ask solicitously how he was; and when he replied that he was very well, Hobbs would say, 'Couldn't you feel a bit better?' That was code for Arlott to join him for champagne in the cellar of the next-door restaurant. Before long, in the early 1950s, the arrangement was formalised on Hobbs's birthday, 16 December. Regular guests were enrolled in what became called The Master's Club. Many years after the deaths of both men, the birthday is still celebrated each December at The Oval, with the same menu of Hobbs's favourites: soup, roast lamb and apple pie. Arlott claimed the roast was beef, and *Wisden* once printed a correction stating that the first course was pâté, but precise facts are elusive in convivial surroundings.

Hobbs was knighted in 1953, though only after Sir Walter Monckton, a cricket-loving Tory grandee, had persuaded him that, since the knighthood honoured English professional cricketers as a whole, it was his duty to accept it. Arlott told Brearley that he could write a book only about a good man, and that books about good men did not sell very well; but this time he was not principally interested in the money. Instead, he was determined to show that Hobbs's greatness was in himself: 'Sometimes I used to think that he was nearer perfection than anybody else that ever played.' The outcome was a slim and evocative volume published the year after he moved to Alderney.

In it, on the first page, Arlott quotes Plum Warner as providing the best definition of Hobbs's art: 'Jack Hobbs is a professional who bats exactly like an amateur.' This was a gentleman-cricketer's way of saying that Hobbs batted with the style and verve of a man who did not rely on cricket for his living, as well as the concentration and dedicated accumulation (the first 100 runs, anyway) of one who did. Hobbs was, reckoned Arlott, a complete batsman in every way, despite – or maybe because of – never having had an hour's coaching in his life. He was also content in his own skin, devoid of social ambition, and had an amateur's sense of humour. For example, when on that vital first day at The Oval in 1926, in front of the young and enthralled Arlott, the Australian leg-spinner Arthur Mailey bowled Hobbs with a high full toss, the batsman simply laughed out loud. Wally Hammond, who had made the transition from professional to amateur in order to captain England, once asked

Hobbs if he would have liked to have been an amateur. 'I just wanted to be a professional cricketer, that made me quite happy and, if I had my time all over again, I would want to do the same thing,' he replied. Hobbs was unselfish, but not without self-interest. His marriage was very strong, and in 1924 he informed MCC that unless they waived their rule about wives not being allowed to travel with the players, he would not go to Australia. MCC judged that Hobbs's presence was more important than their rule, and that winter Mrs Hobbs duly accompanied him.

Arlott delighted in the speed at which Hobbs scored his runs; in 1914, for instance, innings of 220 in 202 minutes and 141 at a run a minute. But that was history; run-scoring since Hobbs's day had lost much of its ebullience. This was partly because the productivity of bowlers had steadily declined, too. Both he and Swanton grumbled for years about bowlers dawdling through their overs. Arlott in November 1980 contrasted the 72 overs bowled by the four West Indies fast bowlers at Old Trafford earlier that year with the 162 overs bowled in a day at the Lord's Test in 1950 (the general rate then was 132 in a day). He argued that a slow over-rate had precisely the same effect as bad weather, short-changing the spectators. Or as he would nicely put it a few years later in a different context (that of what he still saw as inadequate pay for county professionals), 'there is little recompense in observing that it is, after all, only a game'.

Arlott's admirers, however, were not short-changed in his last decade. Until the mid-1980s he continued to write extensively for the *Guardian*, as much on wine as on cricket; his column, usually historical in nature, remained a cherished feature of each issue of *Wisden Cricket Monthly*; while as for books, there appeared, in addition to the Hobbs biography and *John Arlott's 100 Greatest Batsmen*, no fewer than four collections of his written work (mainly on cricket), plus a couple more specifically on wine. Rumours of a coming autobiography were current when in February 1984 he celebrated his seventieth birthday at home in Alderney. The *Guardian* sent Frank Keating for a celebratory interview – Keating finding the 'old spaniel soft-boiled eyes shining bright' – while the BBC despatched Tony Lewis. He was met at the tiny Alderney airport by Arlott and a couple of bottles of white Burgundy, to be consumed before starting off for The Vines. Recording interviews with Arlott was by this stage a drawn-out business, as Brearley would also find. But he was considered worth the time because he was a genuinely iconic figure among cricket-lovers, even, indeed, a national treasure: remembered for the riches of his language, and for the instantly recognisable voice.

Those rumours about an autobiography were ultimately proved accurate. Titled *Basingstoke Boy*, it was published in 1990, the year before his death. Arlott never willingly rejected a commission, and publishers had offered generous advances. Unusually, he had taken his time before contracting to produce the first of two volumes, covering his life until 1958. Instead of a conventional account in the first person, Arlott's was in the third. He explained in the introduction that too many autobiographies suffered from the intrusive 'I'. Indeed, he told Brearley it had appeared in his copy only twice in the previous ten years, on each occasion inserted by a disobedient sub-editor. Arlott was aware that some literary-minded friends thought his third-person strategy at best unwise, with the danger of seeming horribly self-conscious. Those friends were right. Moreover, though *Basingstoke Boy* contains some charming vignettes from his youth, far too many pages are given over to routine accounts of Test series much more vividly described in his earlier books. There is also no satisfying explanation of the dramatic transition in a mere eighteen months in 1944–5 from well-read policeman to a place among the London intelligentsia: no admission of a driving ambition, or of carefully building a network of influential friends. The reader is left with the unreflective assertion that he had been very lucky to be in the right place at the right time.

The autobiography included, near the end, a touching paragraph about his third wife. He explained that he leaned increasingly on Pat, who, besides her domestic duties, had typed the manuscript. 'Through this autobiography, their relationship has grown through affection to understanding; his reliance upon her is great.' But, sadly, the last chapters of the book read for the most part perfunctorily, as if written under pressure from an impatient publisher belatedly imposing a strict deadline. His loyal biographer Rayvern Allen, in his entry on Arlott in the *Oxford Dictionary of National Biography* (*ODNB*), suggests that it had been 'started too late, when his energy had been depleted by the afflictions of ill-health'. Reviewing Tim Arlott's memoir in 1994, Swanton said much the same thing, remarking sympathetically that, by 1990, 'life was an almost intolerable burden for him'. (Swanton himself, at the time of Arlott's retirement in 1980, had successfully proposed Arlott for honorary life membership of MCC – a generous gesture that he had accepted, whether or not with misgivings we do not know.)

It was with a degree of exaggeration, but still telling what he saw as the essential truth of life in the Grub Street tradition of Dr Johnson, that Arlott told Brearley during their televised conversations that – 'except for poems in the early days' – he had never written anything that he was not sure he would be paid for. 'That', he explained, 'is why I have never written a novel, and that I suppose is the biggest failure of my life.' In truth, he had neither the literary compulsion, nor the financial imperative, to write the novel. In its absence, *Basingstoke Boy* may be a candidate for the biggest failure of his professional life.

Ian Botham, who had a family cottage on Alderney, was a regular visitor during the 1980s. In his own autobiography, he recounts their routine morning telephone conversation:

'What time are you coming round?'
'What time would you like me, John?'
'As soon as possible, and bring your thirst with you.'

Botham's first task was to sort out the morning's delivery of wine and take it to the cellar. There, he would 'fill a little wicker basket' with the 'six bottles' which Arlott had 'chosen to drink that day'.

The last chapter of Tim Arlott's loving, sympathetic and at times almost brutally frank memoir of his father is called 'Decline and the Fall'. The drink had become part of his personality. For as long as it did not affect his work, friends were tolerant, disastrous though it was for his health. By the 1980s he was suffering badly from bronchitis, and needed a nebuliser to supply him with more oxygen. His internal organs took a beating, but his liver kept on processing a remarkable amount of alcohol. Cancer of the bowel was diagnosed in 1985; fortunately, the operation was a success. A year later, Arlott had a stroke. 'The basic faculties returned,' notes his son, 'but more subtle aspects of the brain were lost – he was never able again to dial a telephone number with ease, and retreated further into a demanding, obsessive world of worrying about his health.'

Arlott visited Forest Mere, a health hydro in Hampshire, presumably on the basis that this would help him to cut down his drinking. In practice, it did no such thing. Rayvern Allen was a co-conspirator in flouting the rules (which prohibited any alcohol), later recalling how passing reception with two or three bottles of wine in an attaché case felt like going through the green customs channel with undeclared goods. Arlott then asked him if he wouldn't mind removing the empty bottles from the wardrobe as he left. His doctor, a friend of the family, was shocked to observe him at mealtimes, head down, saying hardly anything. He recommended antidepressants, but there were already too many ingredients in his cocktail of drugs. It was becoming a life without pleasure.

Ian Botham had tried to persuade Arlott to stop going down to his cellar to select the day's wines. One day in January 1990, the advice was ignored. As he was climbing the steps, he fell backwards, knocked himself out, broke some ribs and would have choked on his own blood if a neighbour had not intervened. Instead, he was taken to Southampton General Hospital. Visiting him there, Tim was in tears and apologised for having been 'such a bugger' to him in recent years, adding, 'it's been hard watching you fall to pieces'. Smiling, Arlott replied, 'What do you think it's been like for me?' Arlott was able to go home; but the following year, he developed a chest infection that proved fatal. He died at home on 14 December 1991, aged seventy-seven.

Arlott told Brearley that he had been brought up to go to church and be a practising Christian, but that he had doubted his faith after his son's death. Graeme Wright, a sympathetic listener and one-time *Wisden* editor, believes that Arlott saw the loss of his son as a form of Old Testament retribution for having left his son's mother. Rayvern Allen, during a late-night conversation not long before Arlott died, asked him whether he thought there was a God? 'I say my prayers without question, if that's any answer.' 'What,' probed his biographer, 'do you really think?' 'I do, yes,' Arlott admitted. 'Have you always thought that?' 'Yes.' Arlott went on to say that he believed in the afterlife, but had become frightened of meeting his maker. He did not go gentle into that good night.

After the funeral, he was buried at St Anne's church in Alderney. Botham and Brearley were present. A memorial service was held in Alresford the following month. Tony Lewis's moving, well-judged address emphasised Arlott's love of cricketers: 'As a commentator, by placing himself inside the cricketer's head, he could hear the heart beat, understand the hopes and fears and the financial frailties of the average county professional, the worries and the hard-learned skills.' Lewis then directly quoted Arlott – 'They call it a team game, but it is in fact the loneliest game of them all' – before going on: 'John could write about the truly great player, like Barry Richards appealing "both to the savage and the artist in us", but somehow he felt more for the loyal professional like [Hampshire's] Mervyn Burden, whose humour was never extinguished by failure and whom John simply called "salt of the cricketing earth".'

Arlott himself would have been content with his lengthy obituary in the next edition of the cricketer's bible, to which for many years he had contributed a comprehensive, generous and perceptive round-up of the previous year's cricket books and other publications. 'Of all John Arlott's talents,' declared the 1992 edition of *Wisden Cricketers' Almanack* (which also included Brearley's notably insightful, sympathetic tribute), 'it is his unique gift for cricket commentary which will bring him lasting fame. And nothing became him more than the manner in which he quietly slipped away from the scene at the end of his final commentary at Lord's while the crowd stood and, along with the players of England and Australia, applauded.' He was, *Wisden* concluded, 'a humble and generous man'.

The publication of Tim Arlott's memoir in 1994 led to a regrettable postscript. The *Daily Mail* persuaded his widow, Pat, to question Tim's motive and made much of her accusation that in order to make money he had ruthlessly exploited his father's fatal illness. It was a tawdry example of a newspaper posing as a moral arbiter. Arlott's unhappiness as he aged is part of his story, and Tim Arlott was bold enough to describe his decline unvarnished, in effect anticipating the trend to frankness in future similar family memoirs. Swanton wondered, in a review in the *Cricketer*, whether the sorry detail could not have been better left to the imagination. Tim Arlott, a journalist himself, belongs to a different generation, which does not assume that discretion is required in describing a father's death. This particular father had lived for the moment during an immensely rewarding working life; but 'the moment' ended several years before his death. John Arlott's luck had run out at last.

––––––

Since Jim Swanton's occupation enabled him to evade retirement, he never contemplated it. In his late eighties, he was still chairman of the *Cricketer* magazine and its leading book reviewer, as well as contributing quite often to the *Daily Telegraph*; he remained a man to be reckoned with at Canterbury's St Lawrence ground; and the voice, not quite so booming as in its prime, could still be heard at Lord's. By 1993, well into his mid-eighties, he no longer stood so firmly on his dignity, and he was willing to let his hair down in a Q&A feature in the *Cricketer* about his life and times. This was the stuff of colour magazines, though not the *Sunday Times*, which, he said, he did not read. Swanton's 'Lifelines' were less august than his image as cricket's exacting grand inquisitor might have suggested. He revealed his favourite actors (Peggy Ashcroft, Penelope Keith, John Gielgud), and his favourite TV programmes (*The Two Ronnies*; *Yes Minister*; *Mastermind*). His favourite drama series was *The Jewel in the Crown*, and he loved Handel and Haydn. He drove Jaguars, and had catholic taste in drink: 'Beer for lunch after golf, rum punch after a swim in the Caribbean. I like a whisky and soda in the evening; a glass of white burgundy or claret with my dinner. Champagne? As a celebration before lunch.' His most improbable confession was that if he had not been a 'games writer' (meaning sports journalist), he would have liked to play the harp.

Swanton's pet hate, he also revealed, was 'anyone who cheapens or blackens the game of cricket', and he still obstinately believed that the game would be improved by uncovered pitches. He then expressed a romanticism which had normally been well hidden. Invariably, it was inspired by MCC. His wildest dream, he said, was to be in the Committee Room watching English spin bowlers winning a Test match against Australia or West Indies. In further semi-mystical mode, he invested the Lord's Pavilion as 'a sanctified place'. But his most heartfelt contribution was his fundamental complaint about cricket after Packer. 'Its spirit is in mortal danger,' he warned, 'chiefly because commercialism has been allowed to run riot.'

During these post-1980 years, Swanton's main, non-daydreaming role at Lord's involved MCC's Arts and Library committee, of which he became chairman in 1982. That October, he solemnly – and justifiably – informed the main Committee of the inadequacy of the accommodation for the club's library, which he said should be the best of its kind in the world. Swanton's desire to locate it on the top floor of the Pavilion was, however, regularly frustrated. When the new library opened in September 1985, it was instead cheek by jowl with the squash courts. This was shortly after his term on the main Committee ended. Though he was hoping for something better, such as the presidency of MCC, the new library is Swanton's monument at Lord's – sadly separated from the commanding portrait by Andrew Festing, commissioned by MCC in 1992.

Having so visibly joined the Lord's establishment (not that he was ever a great distance from it), he would not have been surprised by a publisher's suggestion in the early 1980s that G. O. B. ('Gubby') Allen, a long-time Test selector and the kingpin at Lord's first as president and then treasurer, would be a suitable subject for a biography by him. Initially he thought his association and his friendship meant that he was too close; but he overcame his doubts, and *Gubby Allen: Man of Cricket* appeared in 1985. Allen had been chairman of selectors in the 1950s, and provided Swanton with intriguing insights on the process. He had, for example, backed the controversial choice of Frank Tyson over Fred Trueman in 1954, not because Trueman had been accused (including by Swanton) of behaving badly on the recent tour of the West Indies, but because Tyson was stronger and faster than other bowlers who could do more with the ball on English wickets. Allen knew that the shine did not last long in Australia; and though Trueman was no slouch, he believed that Tyson's exceptional speed would make the crucial difference. How right he was.

Swanton had a long history with Allen. He had pressed for his inclusion in the touring party to Australia in 1932–3, and had agreed with Allen's distaste for Bodyline. After the war, Allen dedicated himself to the accumulation of power at Lord's. He remained a wealthy bachelor, living in a house whose back gate opened onto the ground and was situated a convenient few dozen yards from the Committee Room, where he sat to watch the cricket. There, he took pleasure in his view of the tops of the trees in St John's Wood churchyard, and was influential enough to prevent the public seats at the Nursery End being built up to a height that would have obscured that view. He did not have enough power, however, to sabotage Swanton's indoor school project, which proceeded despite his opposition. This in no way diminished Swanton's admiration for Allen, including his analysis of the state of cricket when he retired as treasurer in 1976. 'What we have now got,' Allen declared that year at MCC's annual meeting, 'is a general pattern: "seamers" bowling endlessly at a funereal over-rate, off-spinners and an occasional left-armer pushing the ball through flat, to batsmen pushing endlessly forward. Containment is the theme. Efficient it is, backed by brilliant fielding, but variety and a sense of urgency, once amongst the charms of our game, are no longer there.'

At the end of an impressively solid, thoroughly researched piece of work, Swanton summed up his subject neatly by quoting from Joseph Addison's adaptation of Martial: 'In all thy humours, whether grave or mellow, / Thou'rt such a touchy, testy, pleasant fellow;/ Hast so much wit, and mirth, and spleen about thee, / There is no living with thee nor without thee.' He noted in passing that this crisp characterisation had also been applied to E.W.S. himself, by that best-read of cricket commentators and writers, Alan Gibson.

Preparing the book, Swanton had revived his correspondence with Don Bradman. The Australian used the Allen biography as a pretext to return to the attack on Jardine and Larwood for their role in Bodyline. Bradman also denied that Allen had taken the lead in banishing chuckers from Test cricket, claiming that instead it was he himself who had been the key figure. Later, in the 1990s, the Don was not at all pleased by the introduction of match referees into the Test arena, declaring to Swanton that their appointment diminished the role of captains, whose job it was to control the players, and that back in the day he had had his own way of dealing with dissenters – a method that had avoided publicity or fines. Swanton's admiration for Bradman prevented him from being frank, but his own criticism of contemporary cricket suggested that control could not be left to captains who did not have Bradman's way of handling troublemakers.

Each was keen to let the other know that, despite the ailments of old age, they were still active. 'I've gone in the legs and still potter round our great links, but by buggy,' Swanton wrote in 1995. Significant birthdays, however, were treated differently. Whereas Bradman complained that his eightieth had set off such an avalanche of publicity that he and his wife had gone to the seaside to dodge phones and callers, Swanton in July 1997 itemised, for Bradman's benefit, his 'protracted 90th birthday celebrations – five in all!': 'First my Arab club in the Long Room at Lord's, then a Kent dinner at Canterbury, and another at Royal St George's: a Reception by Town and Parish at the Guildhall, Sandwich and finally, an MCC Committee dinner.' Swanton continued to take his religious duties seriously, and was actively involved in funding the restoration of the tower at St Clement's church in Sandwich, where he worshipped, as well as writing for the Canterbury diocese a twenty-nine-page sketch on the history of the Anglican Church.

Although he merited the status of an old fogey, he voted in 1997 for the admission of women to MCC (as 'an encouragement for the spread of the game'), and did so again the following year when the motion finally succeeded. If that was a sign of broad-mindedness, even in his nineties, so, too, in his autumnal years did external perceptions of him begin to soften. Back in 1956, the *Daily Telegraph* had printed a letter from a reader, L. T. Sainsbury, which was more widely circulated. 'Sir,' it read, 'Don't you think that the time has arrived for your cricket correspondent to be quietly disposed of, stuffed and placed in the Long Room with the curved bats, the sparrow, and other freaks of the noble game?' Two decades later, in 1978, Sainsbury wrote to Swanton to explain that he had emigrated to New Zealand shortly after writing that letter. Having come across it recently, he realised it could be taken as offensive; and so he wanted to assure Swanton that, on the contrary, he had enjoyed for many years his authoritative reports, comments and books. The exchange was slim but early evidence of a collective change of heart about Swanton, including by 'Arlott Men'. In his entry on Swanton for the *ODNB*, written after Swanton's death, John Woodcock noted that 'inevitably, Swanton had his critics, not to say his enemies' – but that, as he aged, 'the more benevolent and patriarchal he became, the fewer they were'. Swanton's one-time amanuensis also wrote: 'His snobbery was by now so familiar that it had become a joke, usually spread fondly. Indeed, he started to turn the joke on himself. But there was no relaxation of the standards in what he described as "our once-glorious and beautiful game".'

This old man's lament recalled Packer's takeover bid for Test cricket. Swanton came to believe that, in all of cricket's history, it had been the most serious assault on the game's accepted values. Long experience had made a pessimist of Jim Swanton. Shortly before his death – of heart failure at Canterbury's Chaucer Hospital on 22 January 2000, fourteen months after his wife's death – he was interviewed by his biographer, the versatile and indefatigable Rayvern Allen. He concluded by asking his ninety-two-year-old subject what were his hopes and fears for the future? Swanton's reply was unequivocal: 'I think it's going to be a great struggle to keep cricket anything like the game that we've known and loved because now television has got it by the throat, and we need the money.' Also criticising slow scoring-rates and the absence of spin bowlers, Swanton clung to the remembrance of earlier pleasures. 'There was a wonderful feeling, a fellowship of cricket ... People think I'm rather wet and soft and so on, but there was a wonderful feeling about the game then, which I fear we can never recapture.'

A month or so earlier, Frank Keating, a quintessential *Guardian* and Arlott man, had joined Swanton in a televised discussion about the future of cricket. This was to be his last broadcast (transmitted by Sky on Millennium Eve), and it converted Keating into an uncritical admirer. His account of the occasion was published in *Wisden Cricket Monthly* after Swanton's death. Titled 'In a Class of His Own', the piece was a joyous celebration of the man and his life. 'You can read two sentences of Neville Cardus,' reflected Keating, 'and have a confident stab at telling how old he was when he wrote them; same with Arlott. But Swanton's style was Swanton's style from womb to tomb: from Woolley to Hussain.' Keating admitted that Swanton might have 'looked and acted pompous', and 'even cultivated it' – but, he stressed, 'never in his craft'.

In January 2000, several fine obituaries and appreciations appeared in the newspapers; but one that did not appear as intended was that by Michael Henderson, who at the time of Swanton's death occupied his old post at the *Daily Telegraph*. He duly contributed a piece to the paper, but it was spiked. Instead, brief extracts were published in the *Observer*. 'The first thing to acknowledge about Jim Swanton was that, in all honesty, he did not belong to the first rank of cricket writers' was its bracing opening sentence. Henderson went on to describe Swanton as 'a malign influence at Kent'; as 'a snob'; and as a man with 'an abundance of flaws' who, years before his death, had been rendered 'increasingly marginal' by changes in the game such as Packer and one-day cricket.

A far more benevolent appreciation appeared in the *Guardian*. 'It is hard now to convey the influence he wielded in his prime,' observed Matthew Engel. 'Perhaps only a thundering *Times* leader in the mid-19th century carried as much weight at Westminster as Swanton's pronouncements did at Lord's. But he was doubly influential; he was so deeply involved in the inner counsels of the MCC that what he said in private mattered as much as what he said in print.' Perceptively, Engel remarked on the extraordinary degree of flexibility he had shown during his long professional life. 'Though self-deprecation was not his strongest suit, Swanton would call himself a dinosaur. In fact, he was the reverse. His genius was that, whether he liked change or not (and usually he didn't), he adapted to it, understood it, and was able to comment pertinently on it. He kept this up for 70 years. It was a breath-taking performance, and he will be remembered with awe.'

At Swanton's funeral at St Clement's, the address was delivered by a former Archbishop of Canterbury, no less. Lord (Robert) Runcie had been a friend from Pusey House years, and knew him well enough to say, to knowing looks and prolonged laughter from the congregation, 'Not a man plagued by self-doubt'. The irony was fond. 'He was a big man who loved the grand occasion, and there were those who said that when he passed the throne of St Augustine in Canterbury Cathedral, he cast a wistful glance towards it. But in Sandwich we learn the truth of Chesterton's "Nothing is real unless it is local".' Runcie's emphasis was on Swanton's commitment to the Anglican Church: 'I can testify that he took more trouble over choosing a new rector than he would for the selection of an English cricket side.' And Runcie, himself mortally ill, concluded with a flattering assertion which could only have come from a churchman: 'He had long since left behind the tantrums and the sulks; but he never lost that child-like quality which Our Lord assures us will be needed for heaven. It explains his faith, his enthusiasm, the loyalties and energy that lay behind the authority, lucidity and measured words.'

Swanton would surely have thoroughly approved. He might – but perhaps only might – have also relished a coda six weeks later, as a congregation of some 1,200 gathered at Canterbury Cathedral for his memorial service. John Woodcock read Psalm 139 ('your enemies take your name in vain'); Lord (Bill) Deedes gave the address; and at the end, as they stood up after a not-ungruelling hour and a half that had been planned in Churchillian detail by the man himself, someone with bitter-sweet memories of touring in the 1950s, Doug Insole, turned to another, Geoffrey Howard, and said, 'Well, that's it. Swanton's revenge. Made us all sit quiet and listen.'

Over the years there have been many great, well-publicised rivalries – to take British political history alone, Gladstone and Disraeli; Heath and Thatcher; even Blair and Brown – and undoubtedly there was a rivalrous element in the

Arlott/Swanton relationship. Normally, in the fullness of time, only one rival gets the opportunity to pronounce the last word on the other. But in this case, happily for posterity, it was different.

'John Arlott was known as "the voice of Cricket",' began Swanton's addendum in December 1991 to the *Daily Telegraph*'s formal obituary. 'It was a garland that no one begrudged him. His broadcasting had a flavour all its own, both in the imaginative, strictly individual way he painted the picture and the broad Hampshire tones in which he put it across.' Noting with a surprising degree of intimacy that 'John' had 'cultivated from the first the friendship of the players', Swanton described how 'his work thus developed a warm humanity, well laced with humour, the whole effect enhanced by that rich, well lubricated rumble'. A solitary para in a seven-para piece contained an explicitly critical note: 'Only a small minority perhaps minded that he sometimes went a bit astray on the technical and tactical side. In any case this mattered less when famous players joined the commentary team for talks between overs and summaries at intervals and close of play.' Swanton then reverted to the positive – though perhaps there was just a whiff of condescension in his pigeonholing of Arlott as 'essentially a reporter with a keen eye and a ripe vocabulary' – before he drew himself up to deliver the final very handsome verdict: 'Words never failed him. As a master of his craft he was in the class of Richard Dimbleby, Alistair Cooke and Howard Marshall.'

Just over eight years later, in January 2000, Swanton's own death triggered the publication in the *Guardian* of a full-length obituary (preceding Engel's appreciation) by its long-gone cricket correspondent. Presumably written in the 1980s, it was a Parthian shot that mixed praise with faint – and sometimes not so faint – damns. 'It is probable that he was the most thorough, reliable, and accurate cricket correspondent of his period,' stated Arlott. 'He was not an imaginative recorder of play in the manner of Neville Cardus and he had no striking turn of phrase. But he was a sound, professional journalist who wrote lucidly and without affectation. His judgement and values were sound and he always maintained a historical and moral perspective.' What about the man? 'Fastidious about his clothing and his car, Swanton was essentially a serious man with little sense of humour. In his early professional days he was often autocratic, fussy and even pompous … He was, at bottom, shy and most anxious to be liked.' Arlott's concluding words, published more than half a century after the 'Bullingdon' squib, were carefully chosen: 'Swanton was loyal; he could be generous; and, beyond his autobiographical title, he was very much indeed a cricket person.'

He could be generous … In truth, comparing their pieces, the greater generosity had indeed come from Swanton. Because towards the end of his life he was the more comfortable of the two in his own skin? Because – perhaps going back to their respective class origins – he was less insecure? Because temperamentally he was not a holder of grudges? Or just possibly because Arlott had an essential artistry, whereas Swanton did not – and, in Shakespearean phrase, nice customs curtsey to great kings.

Postscript

In September 2017 – more than a quarter of a century after Arlott's death; approaching two decades after Swanton's – the *News Bulletin* of the Cricket Society led with a *cri de cœur* from its editor, John Symons. 'Lately,' he began, 'we have received some letters wondering whether cricket has lost the general interest of the public, or if decisions have been taken, specifically by media outlets, to decrease or discontinue their coverage of the game … Those letters reflect a more general worry among followers of cricket about the lack of actual cricket being played, the fact that grounds lie empty and unused during the peak summer months, and Test and T20 cricket now dominating the scene to the detriment of the first-class game.' Symons feared that 'a schism might be on the horizon': between those, being 'ushered to the fringes', with a love of the game's history and a respect for its traditions, and those who control the purse strings. For the moneymen, he went on, 'the new, exciting, thrill-a-minute, yet-another-"maximum" style of cricket' is 'the only game in town'. And Symons concluded: 'I, like our correspondents, am seriously concerned that the game as we know it is slipping away from us and there seems to be nothing that we can do about it.'

There were certainly good reasons not to be cheerful. To itemise just a further three: top cricketers increasingly prioritising the T20 jackpot, especially the IPL, over Test cricket; fewer than 280,000 adults in the UK regularly playing cricket – down by almost half since the 1990s, albeit potentially counteracted by the heartening growth of colts cricket at the clubs; and, despite the best efforts of Chance to Shine, cricket in most state schools continuing to recede. 'The summer game, squeezed out of view this year by football's European Championship, as well as the rituals of Wimbledon and the Open, is drifting towards insignificance', plausibly argued Michael Henderson in the *New Statesman* in June 2016. 'How often do you now see children playing it in parks, or families improvising games on the beach? As for street cricket, with stumps chalked on walls, it has not been spotted in years.'

Admittedly, this doleful recital is interrupted by Test matches, which still often live up to their billing, such as West Indies' momentous, wholly unexpected win over England at Headingley in the summer of 2017. Tests fill Lord's, The Oval and Trent Bridge, and do good business at Edgbaston, Old Trafford and Headingley. So they do in Australia; not so good, it is true, in South Africa and India. Ashes series check declining interest in the game; that began in 2005, and has survived for more than a decade. Arlott and Swanton would have been intrigued and delighted by turn. Although neither would have been enthusiastic about reporting T20 and many one-day games, even they would have responded to the odd match, such as West Indies winning a World T20 tournament in 2016 with four consecutive sixes in the final over; and they would surely have welcomed the injection of substantial revenue from T20 games into the coffers of county clubs. Both, moreover, would have appreciated the on-field exploits of Ben Stokes and Joe Root, and the consistency of Jimmy Anderson and Stuart Broad.

None the less it is inevitable that older followers of the game will tend to pine for a lost golden age. In such a mood, the cricket historian of choice is undoubtedly Stephen Chalke, who in 1997 wrote his first book, *Runs in the Memory: County Cricket in the 1950s*, and thereby initiated a remarkable innings of his own, as publisher as well as author. His approach is essentially that of the pioneering, sympathetic and fairly uncritical oral historian; he quotes at length from the largely (but not entirely) roseate-hued memories of long-retired players; and the intensely nostalgic picture he evokes is of a warmly competitive, warmly collegiate, warmly humorous way of life, cherished by participants and spectators alike. A particular favourite in his extensive canon is *One More Run* (2000): an engaging, book-length account of Gloucestershire's match against Yorkshire at Cheltenham in August 1957, owing much to the colourful, thoroughly seasoned recollections of Bryan ('Bomber') Wells, the home side's spinner with the one-pace run-up who once bowled a complete over as the bells of Worcester Cathedral chimed twelve. 'Lord MacLaurin's got no idea,' Wells observes to Chalke about the then chairman – Tesco-style unsentimental and modernising – of the ECB. 'There have always been doddery old men at cricket. They can spend their leisure hours watching it, passing their lives away. You get keen young men and women, but in time they will become old and they'll see a different game.' And the book finished with another, seemingly timeless, Wellsian observation: 'It's the funniest, loveliest game under the sun if you just let people get on with it.'

As with almost any 'golden age', a degree of scepticism is surely in order. The year 1957 may have been one of a justly memorialised encounter at Cheltenham, but it was also the year of the Altham Report, with its stark evidence of county cricket's rapidly declining popular appeal since those immediate post-war years of mass spectatorship amidst relatively few competing attractions. Between Altham in February and Cheltenham in August came, moreover, the Edgbaston scandal and the James critique. In the former, during the final two days of the West Indies Test, England's finest two amateur batsmen, Peter May and Colin Cowdrey, cynically deployed a huge amount of pad play, tacitly supported by the home umpires, in order to counter Sonny Ramadhin. 'I could have wept for him,' recalled his fellow spinner Johnny Wardle, the English twelfth man. 'If he appealed 50 times, at least 30 were plumb out lbw even from the pavilion. It was a great partnership in its way, but an utter scandal really.' Pad play was an intrinsic part of what undeniably by this time was cricket's over-defensive, slow-scoring malaise, with three runs an over generally reckoned to be a quick scoring rate, and two and a half perfectly respectable. Later in June 1957, C. L. R. James launched in the *Cricketer* an assault on 'the long forward-defensive push, the negative bowling' as 'the techniques of specialized performers (professional or amateur) in a security-minded age', and memorably called those cricketers 'functionaries in the Welfare State'. From the opposite, non-Marxist end of the political spectrum, another discerning observer would presumably have agreed. 'Is it too much to ask that cricketers, who enjoy tortuously, the domestic one-day revolution came to pass, accompanied by the first wave of sponsorship: Gillette Cup in 1963, John Player League in 1969, Benson & Hedges Cup in 1972. The systematic opening up to county teams of overseas players was no less driven by money, to enable the game to project itself to a new audience. As for the ubiquitous box in the corner, the natural order of things was that television coverage (like radio coverage) belonged, as by right, to the BBC. Perhaps gates at county matches suffered during televised Tests, but English cricket still enjoyed for many years the best of both worlds: no interference from the broadcasters, but an ever-growing source of income from the sale of TV rights. From the late 1970s, all that changed with Packer – at first only in Australia, but with unmistakable implications for the rest of the cricketing world. The servant was poised to become, if not the master, then at the least a potent factor in all major decisions. Cricket had been recognised as a sector of the entertainment industry.

Our account has traced, in some detail, the real-time responses of Arlott and Swanton to all these developments through the sixties and seventies, as English cricket – in many ways a byword for entrenched, unimaginative conservatism – started gradually to align itself with society as a whole. Of the two, it was Arlott rather than Swanton who continued until the mid-1970s to be the more resistant to change (leaving politics and class aside); whereas once Packer came along, it was unequivocally Swanton who sought to lead the unsuccessful resistance, never deviating from his entirely justified belief that what was at stake was a potentially fateful crossing of cricket's Rubicon. Even so, by the time of the first fully Packerised (non-circus) season, involving England's intensely difficult tour to Australia in 1979–80, Arlott was at one with Swanton in fearing that the very *nature* of cricket – its soul – was in danger of changing irreversibly for the worse, almost irrespective of one-day or three-day or five-day format. 'Money doesn't talk, it swears,' Bob Dylan had sung in 1965; a decade and a half later, cricket found itself horribly exposed to that uncomfortable truth.

One moment above all stands out in the story of English cricket since then. In September 2005, after five compelling, larger-than-life matches, England regained the Ashes – sixteen years and seven dismally one-sided series after losing them. It was, by universal consent, the greatest series in anyone's living memory. Yet at that very point, with national enthusiasm for the summer game greater than at any time since at least Botham's Ashes in 1981, cricket disappeared from terrestrial television, as the ECB (chairman of marketing: the entrepreneur Giles Clarke) decided instead to take Sky's millions. The folly of that decision – admittedly made before the Ashes series, but with profoundly damaging consequences for years to come – is almost impossible to exaggerate, notwithstanding the in many ways excellent (if hardly cheap at as much as £480 a year in 2017) coverage provided by Sky. 'Most children these days would struggle to recognise many of England's top-order batsmen if they walked past them on the street,' observed Ed Aarons in the *Guardian* in June 2017. 'That was not the case for previous generations, when even in the dire days of the 1990s players like Robin Smith and Graeme Hick were almost household names.' Cricket, in fact, had begun to disappear from the national conversation.

We now have a game increasingly dominated by T20, the short – very short – form: often highly skilful, occasionally thrilling, yet brash, loud and ultimately ephemeral. Arlott and Swanton would have been sceptical of one-day cricket in its present model. Both savoured the development of a narrative in a game of cricket; one that lasted long enough to absorb fluctuating fortunes, changing the direction the game was taking. Nor, almost certainly, would they have appreciated the proliferation of international tournaments. These are organised by the ICC principally to generate – and justify – growing TV revenue; yet the more frequent they are, the less they mean to all involved, including the audience. It would be easy to devise a list of much else that Arlott and Swanton would probably not relish – perhaps not least the chaotic, higgledy-piggledy shape (or, rather, lack of it) of the fixture list each summer. Could they have adapted? Arlott, surely not; Swanton, the great adapter, perhaps. By and large, they were fortunate to live their lives in their own lifetimes.

We began work on this book as 'Arlott men', and we remain so at the end. The great biography of Arlott has still to be written, and, if it ever is, it will identify three major influences on the making of what Anthony Powell would have called his 'personal myth'. The first was the early nineteenth-century man of letters William Hazlitt. In Arlott's own words, his writings were 'the greatest influence', above all for their 'perfect length, structure and shape'; while, as Tony Lewis has pointed out, Hazlitt was a role model for Arlott not just as a supreme essayist, but also as 'a poor man, a prolific professional writer, a journalist, drama reviewer, art critic, and champion of the radical cause in politics', as well as championing the self-taught. The second profound influence was Hardy's *Jude the Obscure*. Arlott once remarked to Lewis that it was the book that had always rested most heavily on his mind; and Lewis himself is sure that, at times at least, Arlott strongly identified with the tragic central character – 'his wish to pour more and more learning into his life, to catch up with what he had missed as a youngster, and to drive his body and his brain with a grinding purpose'. The third influence, inescapably, was Neville Cardus. 'He was,' wrote Arlott after Cardus's death in 1975, 'the first writer to evoke cricket; to create a mythology out of the folk hero players; essentially to put the feeling of ordinary cricket watchers into words. They warmed to him and created for him a following which never faded.'

That in large part was also Arlott's own achievement – an achievement that owed much not just to his gifts and his dedication (formidable though both were), but also to the fact that he had such a compelling personality. He was a man for whom cricket prompted powerful emotions, yet it was very far from being his whole life. He will be remembered less for his writing – which ultimately, for all his truly impressive body of work, did not quite fulfil his early promise – than for his broadcasting, at which he was from the start a natural and remained one to the end. For more than three decades, that familiar, distinctive, generous voice was, for many millions, one of life's enduring satisfactions. The *Guardian*, the day after that celebrated farewell commentary stint at Lord's in September 1980, called it right: 'There can rarely have been in the history of the game any man outside the ranks of its greatest players who has given such pleasure, commanded such universal affection, or made himself so much a part of cricket's history.'

Arlott men can never quite be Swanton men, but the experience of writing this book has enhanced our admiration for Swanton. There was a measure of truth no doubt in Arlott's cruel rhetorical question (said only in private), 'Can you imagine what it must be like to write as much as Swanton did over so many years without leaving one memorable sentence?'; and some truth also in John Warr's witty description of his writing style as 'somewhere between the Ten Commandments and Enid Blyton'. The larger truth, though, is that over a period of almost three-quarters of a century he was consistently readable, consistently reliable, and he consistently produced a weight of reportage and comment that is unlikely to survive as literature but will remain an indispensable historical source. It is also impossible not to respect greatly two other aspects of Swanton: his almost invariable privileging of cricket's best interests (as he saw them) over narrow partisanship; and his principled stand on race and apartheid, at a time when all too many of his natural followers saw things very differently. Looking at his life and work in the round, the shame is that fatal Swantonian mixture of pomposity and snobbishness – ameliorated somewhat as he got older, but never entirely lost. The stories (apocryphal or otherwise) are legion: the reply on *Desert Island Discs* ('It all depends upon the character of the governor-general') when asked how he would cope with being cast away; the claim that he was so snobbish that he would not even travel with his chauffeur; and so on. Swanton loved cricket dearly – yet because of his stature, because of his manner, because of a widespread perception that he was an unreconstructed establishment man with a down on the non-public-school professionals, he inadvertently damaged the cause of a game that badly needed to rid itself of its class shackles, and still does.

We end with Arlott. Back in 1949, that *annus mirabilis* of his writing life, he co-authored with Wilfred Wooller and Maurice Edelston a book called (in telling order) *Wickets, Tries and Goals*. His contribution finished with an optimistic statement of faith: 'English cricket is among the enduring, self-renewing games of the world.' But almost three-quarters of a century later, the capitulation to television – and commercial forces generally – has imperilled the soul of English cricket. Can it be renewed? Or has the pass already been sold? The encouragement of a torrent of sixes in the shortest one-day game is designed to increase crowds and TV revenue, and may well do that. The unintended consequence will be the slow sacrifice of the longer and more subtle drama of Test and county cricket. This move with the times – a crude version of cricket's self-renewal – is not one that either Arlott or Swanton would have endorsed. Approaching the third decade of the twenty-first century, does the traditional game have a future? Faced by that disturbing question, they might not be optimistic.

Sources

The principal sources are the written works of John Arlott and Jim Swanton. Both wrote autobiographies:

Arlott, John, *Basingstoke Boy: The Autobiography*, Willow
    Books, 1990
Swanton, E. W., *Sort of a Cricket Person*, Collins, 1972
Swanton, E. W., *Follow On*, Collins, 1977.

There is also much that is autobiographical in *Arlott in Conversation with Mike Brearley*, Hodder & Stoughton, 1986.

They were prolific authors. When friends of John Major wanted to give him the works of Swanton as a present, they discovered there were twenty-four of them. This is not a full bibliography of either author, but a list of their books we mainly used.

JOHN ARLOTT:

*Indian Summer: An Account of the Cricket Tour in England,
    1946*, Longmans, Green, 1947
Gone to the Cricket [the South Africa tour of 1947], Longmans,
    Green, 1948
*Gone to the Test Match: Primarily an Account of the Test Series
    of 1948*, Longmans, Green, 1949

Concerning Cricket: Studies of the Play and Players, Longmans, Green, 1949

Gone with the Cricketers, Longmans, Green, 1950

Days at the Cricket [the West Indies tour of 1950], Longmans, Green, 1951

The Echoing Green: Cricket Studies, Longmans, Green, 1952

Test Match Diary, 1953: A Personal Day-by-day Account of the Test Series England–Australia, James Barrie, 1953

Australian Test Journal: A Diary of the Test Matches Australia v. England, 1954–55, Phoenix Sports Books, 1955

John Arlott's Cricket Journal, Heinemann, 1958

John Arlott's Cricket Journal: 2, Heinemann, 1959

Cricket on Trial: John Arlott's Cricket Journal 3, Heinemann, 1960

The Australian Challenge: John Arlott's Cricket Journal 4, Heinemann, 1961

Vintage Summer: 1947, Eyre & Spottiswoode, 1967

Fred: Portrait of a Fast Bowler, Eyre & Spottiswoode, 1971

Jack Hobbs: Profile of the Master, John Murray/ Davis-Poynter, 1981

E. W. SWANTON:

A History of Cricket (with H. S. Altham), George Allen & Unwin, 2nd edn, 1938

Elusive Victory: With F. R. Brown's M.C.C. Team, 1950–51: An Eyewitness Account, Hodder & Stoughton, 1951

Cricket and the Clock: A Post-War Commentary, Hodder & Stoughton, 1952

West Indian Adventure: With Hutton's M.C.C. Team, 1953–54, Museum Press, 1954

Report from South Africa: With P.B.H. May's M.C.C. Team, 1956–57, Robert Hale, 1957

West Indies Revisited: The M.C.C. Tour, 1959–60,
  Heinemann, 1960
Cricket from All Angles, Michael Joseph, 1968
Swanton in Australia with MCC 1946–1975, Collins, 1975
Gubby Allen: Man of Cricket, Hutchinson/Stanley Paul, 1985
The *Daily Telegraph* published in book form Swanton's reports
  of the Ashes series of 1953, 1954–5, 1956 and 1962–3.

Arlott and Swanton were fortunate in their lifetimes with
the two resourceful editors of their writings (and, in Arlott's
case, broadcasts), George Plumptre and David Rayvern Allen,
both of whom produced capacious, well-judged, book-length –
and immensely helpful to us – gatherings of original material
that otherwise would have been inaccessible to the general
reader.

EDITED BY PLUMPTRE:

Swanton:
As I Said at the Time: A Lifetime of Cricket, Collins, 1983
The Essential E. W. Swanton: The 1980s Observed, Collins
  Willow, 1990

EDITED BY RAYVERN ALLEN:

Arlott:
A Word from Arlott, Pelham Books, 1983
Arlott on Cricket: His Writings on the Game, Collins
  Willow, 1984
Another Word from Arlott, Pelham Books, 1985
The Essential John Arlott: Forty Years of Classic Cricket Writing,
  Collins Willow, 1989

Swanton:

Last Over, Richard Cohen Books, 1996

E. W. Swanton: A Celebration of His Life and Work, Richard Cohen Books, 2000. This includes significant biographical material.

In terms of newspapers and magazines that Arlott and Swanton contributed to, our three key sources are the *Daily Telegraph* (Swanton, 1946–75), the *Guardian* (Arlott, 1968–80) and the *Cricketer* (Swanton from the mid-1960s, Arlott intermittently, but including his 'Journal of the Season' in the late 1960s).

In addition, Arlott contributed regularly to *Playfair Cricket Monthly* in the early 1960s and to *Wisden Cricket Monthly* from June 1979.

In order to listen to Arlott's commentaries, the best selection is in the audio tapes presented and produced by Peter Baxter: *John Arlott: The Voice of Cricket* (BBC Radio Collection, 1990).

The full-length biographies of Arlott and Swanton are both by David Rayvern Allen:

Arlott: The Authorised Biography, HarperCollins, 1994

Jim: The Life of E. W. Swanton, Aurum Press, 2004

Both books have been invaluable for our purposes, as has Timothy Arlott, *John Arlott: A Memoir*, Andre Deutsch, 1994.

In terms of what others wrote about the two men, we have generally tried in the text to indicate our sources. In addition: recollections of listening to Arlott by Brian Glanville and Roy Hattersley are from the *Listener*, 30 January 1975 and 11 September 1980; Patrick Symes's recollections of Arlott in the 1970s are from the *Nightwatchman*, autumn 2016; and Patrick Collins's story about Arlott and the hapless commentator is from *Journal of the Cricket Society*, autumn 2016. Alex Bannister's reflections on Swanton in 1932 are from MCC's David Rayvern Allen Audio Archive at Lord's.

The following is a list (reasonably full, but not exhaustive) of books that we found helpful and to whose authors we are indebted:

Bailey, Trevor, *Wickets, Catches and the Odd Run*, Collins, 1986

Baxter, Peter, *Inside the Box: My Life with Test Match Special*, Quiller, 2009

Blofeld, Henry, *A Thirst for Life: With the Accent on Cricket*, Hodder & Stoughton, 2000

Blofeld, Henry, *Squeezing the Orange*, Blue Door, 2013

Botham, Ian, *Head On: The Autobiography*, Ebury, 2007

Brookes, Christopher, *His Own Man: The Life of Neville Cardus*, Methuen, 1985

Chalke, Stephen, *One More Run*, Fairfield Books, 2000

Chalke, Stephen, *At the Heart of English Cricket: The Life and Memories of Geoffrey Howard*, Fairfield Books, 2001

Chisholm, Anne, and Davie, Michael, *Beaverbrook: A Life*, Hutchinson, 1992

Cowdrey, Colin, *M.C.C.: The Autobiography of a Cricketer*, Hodder & Stoughton, 1976

Down, Michael, *Calling the Shots: Correspondence over Fifty Years between Don Bradman and Jim Swanton*, Boundary Books, 2017

Fingleton, Jack, *Four Chukkas to Australia: The 1958–59 M.C.C. Tour of Australia*, Heinemann, 1959

Frith, David, *Frith's Encounters*, Von Crumm Publishing, 2014

Haigh, Gideon, *The Cricket War: The Story of Kerry Packer's World Series Cricket*, Bloomsbury, 2017 edn

Hamilton, Duncan, *Harold Larwood: The Authorised Biography of the World's Fastest Bowler*, Quercus, 2009

Heald, Tim, *Brian Johnston: The Authorised Biography*, Methuen, 1995

Insole, Douglas, *Cricket from the Middle*, Heinemann, 1960

James, C. L. R., *Beyond a Boundary*, Stanley Paul, 1963

Johnston, Barry, *Johnners: The Life of Brian*, Hodder & Stoughton, 2003

Knox, Malcolm, *Bradman's War: How the 1948 Invincibles Turned the Cricket Pitch into a Battlefield*, Robson Press, 2013

Lewis, Tony, *Playing Days*, Stanley Paul, 1985

Lewis, Tony, *Taking Fresh Guard: A Memoir*, Headline, 2003

McGilvray, Alan, *The Game is Not the Same ...*, David & Charles, 1985

Marqusee, Mike, *Anyone But England*, Verso, 1994

Martin-Jenkins, Christopher, *CMJ: A Cricketing Life*, Simon & Schuster, 2012

Oborne, Peter, *Basil D'Oliveira: Cricket and Conspiracy: The Untold Story*, Little, Brown, 2004

Peel, Mark, *England Expects: A Biography of Ken Barrington*, Kingswood, 1992

Richards, Viv, *Sir Vivian: The Definitive Autobiography*, Michael Joseph, 2000

Ryan, Christian, *Feeling is the Thing that Happens in 1000th of a Second: A Season of Cricket Photographer Patrick Eagar*, riverrun, 2017

Waters, Chris, *Fred Trueman: The Authorised Biography*, Aurum, 2011

Williams, Charles, *Gentlemen & Players: The Death of Amateurism in Cricket*, Weidenfeld & Nicolson, 2012

Wright, Graeme, *Betrayal: The Struggle for Cricket's Soul*, Gollancz/Witherby, 1993

Wynne-Thomas, Peter, *Cricket's Historians*, Association of Cricket Statisticians and Historians, 2011

Image credit: Portrait of E. W. Swanton, 1992 (oil on canvas), Festing, Andrew (b. 1941) / Marylebone Cricket Club, London, UK/Bridgeman Images

Acknowledgements

We are very grateful to Tim Arlott for permission to quote from the writings of John Arlott, and to John Woodcock and George Plumptre for permission to quote from the writings of E. W. Swanton.

Those who talked illuminatingly to one or other or both of us about our subjects include Tim Arlott, Stephen Bates, Peter Baxter, Mike Brearley, Michael Down, David Faber and John Woodcock. Responsibility for all facts and interpretations, however, remains ours.

We have other debts: at MCC's Library (the best of its kind in the northern hemisphere, perhaps the world), to Neil Robinson and Robert Curphey for their generous and expert assistance; to Gavin Fuller, the *Daily Telegraph*'s librarian, who provided convenient access to boxes of Swanton's daily journalism; to David Robertson, keeper of Swanton's archive at the Kent county ground in Canterbury; to Paul Bolton of the Professional Cricketers' Association; and to Michael Down of Boundary Books for helping us with the illustrations. Many thanks also to Amanda Howard (Superscript Editorial Services) for transcribing tapes. Others who helped in different ways include Stephen Chalke, Pat Collins, Gideon Haigh and John Littlewood.

The following kindly read and commented on various draft versions: Mike Burns, Prudence Fay, Lucy Kynaston, Harry Ricketts and John Symons. We are especially grateful for the time they took and their constructive criticisms.

We have also been fortunate with those who have assisted with the book's endgame: Richard Collins for his copy-editing; Martin Bryant and Charles Barr for reading the proofs; and Douglas Matthews for his index. Georgia Garrett of Rogers Coleridge & White, assisted by Madeleine Dunnigan, kindly acted on our behalf. While at Bloomsbury, where it has been a pleasure to be published, we are grateful indeed to Michael Fishwick, our editor, and his colleagues Sarah Ruddick and Jasmine Horsey.

London, November 2017

Index

A Note on the Type

The text of this book is set in Linotype Stempel Garamond, a version of Garamond adapted and first used by the Stempel foundry in 1924. It is one of several versions of Garamond based on the designs of Claude Garamond. It is thought that Garamond based his font on Bembo, cut in 1495 by Francesco Griffo in collaboration with the Italian printer Aldus Manutius. Garamond types were first used in books printed in Paris around 1532. Many of the present-day versions of this type are based on the *Typi Academiae* of Jean Jannon cut in Sedan in 1615.

Claude Garamond was born in Paris in 1480. He learned how to cut type from his father and by the age of fifteen he was able to fashion steel punches the size of a pica with great precision. At the age of sixty he was commissioned by King Francis I to design a Greek alphabet, and for this he was given the honourable title of royal type founder. He died in 1561.